GOOD
TIMES
AND
BAD

**From the Coombe
to the Kremlin,
A Memoir**

MERCIER PRESS

Douglas Village, Cork

www. mercierpress. ie

Trade enquiries to:

CMD Distribution

55A Spruce Avenue, Stillorgan Industrial Park,
Blackrock, Co. Dublin.

© Seamus Martin, 2008

ISBN: 978 1 85635 577 3

10 9 8 7 6 5 4 3 2 1

A CIP record for this title is available from the British Library

 Mercier Press receives financial assistance from the
Arts Council/An Chomhairle Ealaíon

Printed and bound by J.H Haynes & Co. Ltd, Sparkford.

Seamus Martin

GOOD TIMES AND BAD

From the Coombe
to the Kremlin,
A Memoir

MERCIER PRESS
WHAT YOU NEED TO READ

To Jimmy and Killian – the next generation

Contents

— Early Days —

My parents were always on the move. The Martins had thirteen addresses after I was born and God knows how many before that. My brother and I inherited this inability to stay in one place and there is some evidence that our need for travel began in the womb.

Eileen Martin, née Mullen, was small. When she was twenty-nine she wrote down her details in a little diary for 1933, which I found after her death. Her height, she wrote, was '4ft 10' and her weight '6st 7lb'. Her size in gloves was six and she wore size three in shoes. Not surprisingly her neighbours knew her as 'the little woman'. In an effort to look taller than she actually was she always wore a hat indoors as well as outdoors, seated at the table as well as standing at the kitchen sink. The size-three shoes were always of the high-heeled variety.

'The little woman' was the driving force in all the moves our family made and so it was no surprise when she took the train from Derry to Dublin early in 1942 heavily pregnant with myself. The Mullens held a certain aversion to the Union Jack that flew over my father's home town of Derry and had played their part in the removal of that flag from Dublin. Uncle Martin Mullen was 'out' in Jacob's factory in 1916. Uncle Matt ended up in Kilmainham Jail as a prisoner of the Free State during the civil war, Aunt Mary was a socialist who knew James Connolly, and Aunt Bridie was active in Cumann na mBan. Mother's aversion to the British flag appears to have had a personal basis, for she frequently spoke of being pinned against the walls of houses in Dublin during the Troubles by British soldiers, who tried to force her to sing 'God Save the King'.

Bridie took it on herself to rid Dublin every November of the large number of people who wore poppies in memory of family members who had fought in the British army. She was the city's leading poppy snatcher, pulling the imitation flowers from the lapels of those who offended her patriotic sympathies. It should be added, by the way, that James Mullen had fought in the British uniform in that bloody feud between the royal families of Europe known as the Great War. He had joined the Royal Dublin Fusiliers, not out of loyalty to the Crown, but because he'd had a blazing row with his tyrannical father who had insisted he should follow the family trade of bricklaying.

Off James went to Gallipoli at the age of twenty-one, and there he was blinded. Later, an operation restored a modicum of his sight and the UK government rewarded him with a civil service job in London, which was moved to Harrogate in Yorkshire for the duration of the Second World War. James had a sad life. His only love, Marie Butler from Bordeaux, died before they were due to be married; and later in life the glimmer of light that passed for his eyesight was compounded by almost total deafness.

Mother had been a singer and had appeared at the Queen's Theatre in Dublin at an early age – billed as 'The Wonderful Child Soprano'. She later took title roles in operettas such as *Maritana*, and her prize possession, which I still have, was a programme signed for her by the great Italian tenor Beniamino Gigli.

Given her family background it was no surprise that the idea of her first child being born a subject of King George VI was enough to put Eileen onto the train to Dublin. What was surprising, though, was that she chose Ena Hughes to be my godmother. Ena came from a northside Dublin family that was completely devoted to the British army. Her brother Toddy returned from Dunkirk dressed as a waiter because his uniform and other clothes had been destroyed. A patriotic restaurant on the south coast of England had togged him out and sent him on his way. Asked if he was going back to the war, his reply was 'someone has to go back', and that was that. He went back and survived.

It would appear that my mother's dislike of the Union Jack and British domination was evident only when in Northern Ireland. There's something in the air up there, and as soon as she arrived in Dublin tolerance quickly set in, only to vanish again when she went back across the border. It even affected Ena Hughes, who was taken into custody for shouting at younger members of the Apprentice Boys during their annual parade to demand why they were not at the front. De Valera's insistence that there should be no conscription on the island of Ireland allowed a small minority of the loyalist community to avoid risking their lives for King and Country.

Eileen booked herself into the old Coombe Hospital, which was just down the road from the family home, and that's where I was born on 24 January 1942. After that it was safe to go back to Derry where, for a brief period, her infant son was known as 'Wee Jimmy'. This was to distinguish me from my father, who was 'Big Jimmy', even though he stood not very much taller than 'the little woman'.

This anomaly was sorted out quickly after my white-blond hair, blue eyes and sallow complexion drew the following comment from a neighbour: 'Wee Jimmy,' she announced, 'is wild Protestant lookin'.' From that day on, in a place where religious identity was worn as a badge of one's nationality, I became known as Séamus. There could now be no case of mistaken identity.

Then one day on Sackville Street in Derry, my mother left me outside in my pram and went into a shop. When she returned, the pram and I were gone. As it turned out a wee girl had simply wheeled me round the block, but who was to know that? Mother went to the RUC station and told them her son was stolen. 'Where did you last see him?' asked the constable. 'On O'Connell Street,' she replied.

At that time O'Connell Street in Dublin was still known as Sackville Street to the diminishing southern unionist community. Mother was not able to bring herself to say those two words even in an attempt to find her only child.

Three years on, mother was on the train to Dublin again, heavily pregnant with my brother, who was christened Diarmuid in case he developed blond hair, blue eyes and a sallow complexion. Mother need not have worried. His hair grew black and his eyes were as brown as hers. There was very little chance of his being taken for a Protestant, and his full title sixty years on is:

'His Grace, Most Reverend Dr Diarmuid Martin, Archbishop of Dublin and Primate of Ireland'.

Almost all my early memories are from Derry. Margaret Jackson, a wee Protestant girl, took me under her wing as wee girls do. I was with her when I saw a man in religious garb on a platform under the Union Jack denounce Dublin as the source of all evil. He got very worked up about it, hot under the dog collar you might say, and I remember telling myself that he was wrong because my mother came from Dublin and she was the best person I knew.

Religion, politics and geography were inextricably mixed together in Derry, but there was never the same vicious sectarianism that existed in Belfast. All the same, it was rumoured that the local rag-and-bone man, Johnny Orr, not the brightest of fellows, refused to cross the border because he believed that the Pope lived in Buncrana.

Then Princess Elizabeth, the future Queen Elizabeth, and her husband Prince Philip came on a visit. There was a garden party for them in Brooke Park opposite where we lived, sharing a house with the McClellands. We lived downstairs and the McClellands upstairs. Mother announced that when King George V arrived in Dublin the Mullens had a flat near Dame Street with a balcony overlooking the processional route to Dublin Castle. Family members were forbidden to venture onto the balcony in case they might 'swell the crowd'. This tradition, she insisted, would be followed in Derry. The blinds were drawn on the night before the royals arrived, to be lifted only after their departure.

My father, a completely apolitical man apart from his strong trade unionism, agreed 'for peace's sake' to allow the blinds stay down. Upstairs things were different. Mrs McClelland, a good Protestant unionist woman, rolled up her sleeves and scrubbed her window sill to let the prince and princess know they were welcome. Mr McClelland, who had politics of a different hue, had other ideas. He put out a flag from the top window. It was not a Union Jack like those that adorned the Protestant houses in the area but a scarlet banner emblazoned in the top corner with a golden hammer and sickle. It was a flag I was to become very familiar with in later life.

The police, the Royal Ulster Constabulary, arrived and asked Mr McClelland to remove the offending flag. He refused. 'Only for this flag,' he told them, 'Hitler would have won the war and there'd be no wee Princess Elizabeth here th'day.' To this day I wonder did Queen Elizabeth and her consort notice a house with the blinds drawn downstairs and the Red Flag of the Soviet Union flying from the top floor over a spanking-clean window sill. I suspect they didn't.

That house was one of three I remember living in in Derry, and there was another one just across the border at Mitchelstown, a straggle of cottages on the hillside above Ture on the Inishowen Peninsula in County Donegal. Father cycled across the border to work as a mechanic in Derry each morning and cycled back each evening while mother moped about not being in Dublin. Once Dad brought me back a rabbit, which escaped as soon as it got to our house. Perhaps it was a loyalist rabbit that yearned to be back under the Union Jack.

The house was given the nickname 'Ture Hall', because the hall was its biggest room. The ceilings were so low that father, all five-foot-five of him, was able to paint them without needing to stand on a chair. There was a fine view of Lough Foyle and there were good neighbours in Seán Gavigan, his wife Alice and their children. Seán was the local schoolteacher and known to all as the 'Master Gavigan'. He was a great man to tell a yarn and if I, in later years, was able to describe important happenings abroad with some clarity, it was at the Gavigans' fireside that I began to learn my trade.

That little house on the western side of Lough Foyle was our home in the terrible winter of 1947. Foxes came scavenging and I saw another neighbour, an elderly widow called Mrs Acheson, attack one in the front of her house with a spade. She did a fine job of it, too.

That spell in Donegal was my only experience of the bucolic life. The hay in nearby Davie Thomson's field was saved by a machine called a 'reaper and binder', for the combine harvester had not yet been invented. We joined our neighbours' children, the Tizards and Gavigans and Gormleys, in the pretence of helping out and, as our reward, we arrived home covered in bites from the field bugs let loose as the hay was cut and gathered.

Although in the 'Free State', as it was known locally, the area was strongly Protestant and the dialect now known as Ulster Scots was prevalent. As a child I learned to distinguish between a 'lock' and a 'wheen' and to know that a young girl was a 'wee cuttie'. But mother couldn't tholl (bear) the thought of staying there. To put it simply, she was totally unsuited to rural life. Like Brendan Behan, whom I was later to know, her definition of a city was 'a place where you were unlikely to be attacked by a wild sheep'.

All the while she was plotting to return to Dublin. A large, wet-cell battery radio was her link with home. The signal from Radio Éireann, as it was then called, was just barely detectable in one corner of the little house. She would listen in each day and imagine herself in O'Connell Street or Grafton Street or

Stephen's Green, far away from dangerous beasts such as badgers and hares, and where strangers knocked or rang the bell before entering your house.

I don't know how she got her way but she did. We were packed off to the station in Derry and onto the train for Dublin. We departed in January 1948. I know this because my father was attempting to come down the narrow staircase encumbered with all sorts of heavy household articles when my mother dashed out of the kitchen.

'Jimmy, Jimmy,' she shouted. 'Gandhi's been assassinated.'

In family tales of the event, Dad, now weighed down and trapped in the return of the staircase, replied with the words, 'To hell with bloody Gandhi.'

It was snowing when we arrived at Amiens Street station and many things were still scarce after the war. There wasn't much petrol to be had and we took a horse-drawn cab to the Mullen house on Lauderdale Terrace just off Dean Street in the Liberties. It was a romantic journey in the snow, like something out of *Doctor Zhivago* – set in a place I was destined to know very well.

We were to stay there with other relatives while mother looked for a house. We were still there in 1948 when a parade went through town to mark the 250th anniversary of the insurrection of 1798, and we watched the march pass from the corner of Francis Street and Thomas Street. A cousin, Brian Mullen, fell from his pram as the procession went by and had to be taken to hospital. For my brother this incident is his earliest memory of Dublin. He does, however, have a vivid recollection of uniformed men arriving to take me to the City and County Infirmary in Derry to have my appendix removed, when I was five and he was just two.

In Dublin I was surrounded by the Mullen side of the family and their advanced republican views. The Martins on the other hand were spread out through the country. Uncle Frank Martin had taken the pro-Treaty side and became a colonel in the Free State army. He lived in Belfast and we rarely saw him. Aunt Josie taught school in Crossconnel in northwest Inishowen and remained a spinster until her death. She was a victim of that rural Irish tradition by which one daughter was kept at home to look after an elderly mother, and it cannot be stressed too strongly that Grandmother Martin was a formidable and selfish woman. She was the only one of my grandparents alive when I was a child and she terrified me and my brother on our visits north. Uncle Leonard, a charming man with a deep baritone voice and a fondness for the jar, ran a wholesale business in Galway. The only one in Dublin from the Martin branch in those days was Auntie Dolly, who lived in Ranelagh. There is no doubt, therefore, that the Mullens had a far greater influence on my early life. The Martins were, by the way, fairly well off and at one time resided in Inishowen House in Buncrana. The boys were sent to Newbridge College in County Kildare as boarders. The exception was my father, Jimmy Martin, who was, wrongly, judged to be interested only in fixing the engines of cars. My Dad was just given the basic primary education required by law and then left to fend for himself. Mother never forgave the Martins for this, and it made her determined that her own sons would get the best education she could afford.

In the meantime, her search for a house in Dublin went on, and help came from an unlikely quarter. Memories of the civil war were still very strong at the time, but a house was a house and even Fine Gael could be approached on the matter. It was Patrick Cahill, the Fine Gael lord mayor of Dublin, and his secretary, known to us children as Miss McCormack, who came up with the idea that solved the problem. Miss McCormack, incidentally, became a lifelong family friend.

There was a new housing estate in a place called Ballyfermot, but at the time Dublin Corporation gave preference to those people who lived in slums. The answer was, therefore, to move out of Lauderdale Terrace and into a single room in a condemned building. The Mullen house was overcrowded at this stage in any event, with Aunt Bridie, childless and twice widowed, as well as Uncle Matt, his wife Annie and their growing family, taking up most of the little house.

It was in that house by the way that I caused deep embarrassment to my mother when stricken with one of those childhood diseases. The family's politics extended even as far as the choice of doctor, and the famous Protestant-republican medic, Dr Kathleen Lynn, was called to my bedside. My ungrateful response was to ask the following question of my mother in the illustrious doctor's presence: 'Why does that lady have a moustache?'

We moved, at some stage in 1948, to the top floor of a rickety tenement on Digges Street and lived in a single room there. This was a typical Dublin slum dwelling. The front door was always open and the smell of urine struck your nostrils as soon as you entered the hall. There were some consolations though. Very close by was the Skibo ice-cream parlour, where my brother and I were treated to ice-creams at weekends, I suspect in compensation for having to live where we did. Children, though, don't give much thought to living conditions as long as they have the security of being with their parents, and that was something we had in abundance.

The treats came thick and fast at our first Christmas in the slum. There were toy cars for me, with a large piece of plywood on which my father had painted roads and fields and gardens. It was the most wonderful present to my child's eyes, and it came, I was told, not from my parents but from someone called Santa Claus, who was known to Dublin children of that era simply as 'Santy'.

The news of the new house came on a spring morning. It was to be on Sarsfield Road and its number was 173, the biggest number for a house that I had ever heard of. The one on Digges Street was number 2, the Mullen house was number 10, and one of the Derry houses was 12 Mount Street. Father, who had gone to work in Huddersfield in Yorkshire, had come back to look for work in Dublin, so the whole family was together once more. Ours was a small family by the standards of the time, just my parents, my brother and myself. Mother and father had married late in life and the biological clock had ensured that we were not like other families in Ballyfermot, in which four or five children was very much the average, with many families considerably larger. We were fortunate in that respect, and we were lucky, too, that our father was a teetotaller.

Many of the fathers in the area were not. There were fist fights frequently outside the pubs in Dublin in those days, with drunken women screaming support for their menfolk. There was violence at home, too, and alcohol-induced poverty as well as simple poverty. Children walking the streets in their bare feet were a common sight.

But Dad arrived home on Fridays, opened his pay packet and handed it over to cover the family's upkeep. If he kept anything for himself I never saw it. His main vice was smoking Craven A cigarettes, which had a little black cat on their red packet, and he struggled against his addiction. But he succeeded in giving them up long before the days of nicotine chewing gum or the nicotine patch. His wages, I remember, were £9 per week and I think he worked in a motor company called Howard McGarvey. He later became a mechanic for Dublin Corporation and his final job was at the CIÉ Works in Inchicore.

In those days, by the way, families were moved out to the new estates as soon as there was a roof on the house they had been allocated. There were no schools, few shops, and in our case, initially, no electricity either. Candles were lit in the dark nights and trips were made into town for groceries.

There were occasional travelling grocers who brightened things up. Potatoes were sold from door to door by a large family of growers. Allotments known as 'the plots' were nearby and the men who tended them would sell vegetables to all comers. On Fridays a man came around with a large wicker basket of fish. His cry of 'Fresh fish' was regarded with great scepticism in our house, because as well as being a fishmonger he, like most Dublin men, was fond of the odd pint of stout and something extremely unhygienic happened each time he went to the local pub.

The pub, the Old Pine Tree, had been there before the corporation estate was built. It served a small concentration of red-brick houses known as the 'Ranch', where the poet Thomas Kinsella lived. Our house was directly across the road from this establishment and from the front window we could see the 'Fresh fish' man lay down his basket of produce outside the pub door and nip in for a quick one.

He was rarely quick enough, however, and the sight we regularly witnessed ensured that he never sold a single herring to number 173. He was hardly in the door of the pub when the dogs of the neighbourhood would arrive, cock their legs over the basket and pee on the produce. Some time later he would emerge from the bar and resume the cry of 'Fresh fish'. That cry became a standing joke in our house if the lavatory was occupied by someone else when you needed to go.

After we had settled in the house, the issue of schooling arose. The Model School in Inchicore was nearest, but there were no places, and mother got us into the Oblate National School, which was quite a distance farther away. It was here that I came into contact with the domineering side of the Church for the first time. This high-handed attitude was personified by a man called Father Devine, who terrorised all and sundry by shouting and roaring at them in an attempt to cow them. But in what was something of a bad-cop/good-cop situation, there was also Father Haslam, a kind and intelligent man who spoke softly.

In Ballyfermot there were no schools and no churches. Mass was celebrated in a sort of concrete shed known as 'The Mass Centre', and those children who could not find a place in schools in Inchicore were bussed into Whitefriar Street each day. As we trudged to the Oblate school, the buses would pass by the Model School, and the Whitefriar Street kids would instantly burst into a chorus of 'Boo the Model'.

Mother found new friends in a convent called Sevenoaks, staffed by nuns from the Little Sisters of the Assumption. The nuns took over the housekeeping duties of poverty-stricken young mothers who were unable to attend to their families due to illnesses or their constant trips to the maternity hospital. Mother and her socialist sister Mary set up a sewing class so that these women could make clothes for their children, and Diarmuid and I became altar boys at the early-morning convent Masses, setting out before dawn and before a day's schooling.

As is pretty obvious now to those who know me, the religion

rubbed off more on my brother than it did on me. He re-enacted the Mass at home, using a lemon as the host. In this playtime, by the way, he was always the priest and I was always the altar boy. Although not a religious person, my experiences at Sevenoaks served to ensure that I did not become an anti-religious person either. Mind you, I could have had good reason to go down the anti-clerical road, for the parish priest, Canon Troy, and his assistant Father Daly, were overbearing and authoritarian men, and I was already developing a healthy disrespect for authority.

Canon Troy's mission in life was to save Ballyfermot from communism. He was a Canon of St John of Jerusalem, a title which, it was rumoured, he bought on a visit to the Holy Land. His first campaign was directed against a co-operative that sold vegetables cheaper than they were available in the shops. The power of the Church was such that the co-op and its 'red' carrots didn't stand a chance, and the good capitalist shopkeepers emerged victorious.

In one particular election, Michael O'Riordan stood as a candidate for the Irish Workers' League, the name under which Irish communists then stood. Canon Troy announced from his pulpit that anyone who voted for 'Red O'Riordan' would go 'straight to hell'. To my ten-year-old mind the admonition was taken literally. If you voted for O'Riordan you would literally go straight to hell and you wouldn't even have to die first.

It was a great cause of worry, therefore, when my father told me he was going to vote for O'Riordan. I knew he was not a de Valera supporter like my mother, for whenever she mentioned the man's name my father would, in his strong northern accent, ask the question: 'Would that be the dee Valeera who said he'd never wear a top hat?' As children we knew to get out from under their feet at this stage and let them at it.

To hear, however, that Dad was going to vote for O'Riordan

and therefore would go straight to hell as soon as he marked his ballot paper gave me some sleepless nights. But when the dreaded descent to the abyss did not take place, my belief in the hereafter took a bit of a shaking.

Father Daly took on a far more difficult task than the canon's fight against the Kremlin. For most men of the cloth, there were Seven Deadly Sins, but for Father Daly there were eight: Lust, Gluttony, Greed, Sloth, Anger, Envy, Pride and, worst of all, *Soccer*.

In Father Daly's eyes, if you played soccer you were not a true Irishman but a West British shoneen who betrayed the cause for which the men of 1916 had laid down their lives. I found this attitude difficult to understand, for Uncle Matt had contracted TB while playing soccer in the yard as a republican prisoner in Kilmainham Jail in the 1920s, and later devoted his life to the fortunes of some slow racehorses and his beloved Shamrock Rovers. Uncle Jack Fitzpatrick, who was married to my mother's sister Lily, was the secretary of the National Graves Association, a republican organisation that erected headstones and plaques to commemorate the struggle for independence. He had been in prison, too, but his devotion to 'the movement' was at times overshadowed by his commitment to Shelbourne FC.

To mention this to Father Daly would have been a waste of time, and a war of attrition continued between him and us kids. Soccer was the game for all of us. We even played it in Croke Park, where we had been enlisted as extras in the Pageant of St Patrick. Mostly, however, we played in the Memorial Park nearby, and Father Daly would frequently emerge from the bushes to give us a lecture on our duty as Irishmen.

In the end, Canon Troy's battle was won and the idea of a

Soviet Republic of Ballyfermot has long since faded. I suspect, indeed, that I may have become the area's first Russian speaker, for the Kremlin's ideals never really caught on in that part of the world thanks to the canon's unstinting efforts. Father Daly, on the other hand, never achieved his aim of eliminating soccer, and I presume he must have gone to his grave a defeated man.

By the time I sat the Primary Certificate in Inchicore, a primary school had been opened in Ballyfermot, and my brother was moved there. There was no secondary school in the area, though, and mother went into action again. I was hawked around the country to do entrance exams in the hope that I would win something called a 'bursary' or an 'exhibition'. These were types of scholarships open to kids whose parents could not afford the fees. I remember there was a letter offering an exhibition from Roscrea College in County Tipperary, but the offer from Gormanston in County Meath must have been better. Having completed first year in Westland Row in Dublin, where relationships between me and the Christian Brothers were strained, to say the least, I was packed off to boarding school to have manners put on me.

I liked Gormanston very much but there were problems. For the first time in my life I met the sons of strong farmers, some, but not all, of whom bore a deep suspicion and strong dislike of Dublin and anything connected with it. 'Go back to the slums of Dublin' was a cry I frequently heard. This, I presume, was meant to annoy the boys who came from Dublin's posher suburbs, and I don't think any of these young rustics suspected for a moment that one of their fellow students had once actually lived in a slum.

Most boys were without prejudice, but there was always a feeling that one did not completely belong. This was compounded on return to Ballyfermot during holidays, where I was branded as the 'college boy'. As a result, I felt I did not completely belong in either place. If anything, being something of an outsider both at school and at home instilled in me an independent spirit, which became both a help and a hindrance in later life.

The most welcome aspect of school at Gormanston was the absence of corporal punishment, but psychological punishment existed. This was administered in abundance by the 'Dean of Discipline', Father Paulinus O'Sullivan, who was psychologically unsuited to the job. To be fair, as soon as this was discovered, he was transferred to watch over the ancient documents stored at the Franciscan house in Killiney.

He was replaced by the gruff Father Otteran Duane from Waterford, who, though he imposed very strict discipline, did so in a very fair way. School was marked by quite an easy-going attitude, especially in the final year when Leaving Cert students had their own rooms and, incredible as it may seem today, were allowed to smoke cigarettes.

There were escapes across the way to drink cider in the Mosney Arms and to ogle the barmaid a little farther away in the Cock Tavern on the road that led to the Gormanston army camp. Some of the escapes were more innocent, especially those made by a Longford fellow called Andy MacEoin, whose addiction to baked beans made him a frequent visitor to the village shop, which was officially out of bounds to all students.

Andy was a nephew of General Seán MacEoin, who stood as Fine Gael candidate for the presidency against Éamon de Valera (whose nephew, also Éamon de Valera, was in that school, too). It was a tribute to Andy's popularity that in a mock election held by the pupils he handily defeated young Dev.

These rare illegal forays to the outside world were dwarfed

by an event known as the Great Escape in 1958. The rules were clear. Only on school holidays were students permitted to leave the substantial grounds of Gormanston College. There were two exceptions: the first an annual, strictly supervised excursion to Clogherhead in County Louth; and the other on St Patrick's day, when Leaving Cert students were allowed to travel to Dublin for the day. The latter was ostensibly to let pupils go to the Railway Cup hurling and football finals in Croke Park. But when my turn came for release on 17 March, the rival attraction of an inter-league match at Dalymount Park proved stronger.

In 1958, however, Gormanston won the Leinster Colleges Senior Football Championship by beating Ballyfin. On the following day, the rumour spread like wildfire that the whole school had permission to go out for the day. I only got as far as Drogheda before being rounded up; others had made it to Dublin, and one enterprising escapee made it as far as Belfast.

Late that evening, there was a roll-call reminiscent of those seen in movies about POW camps in the Second World War. All students were ordered to be at their desks in the study hall. An unattended desk would indicate that its usual occupant was still at large and would be severely punished. We knew that Ronnie McPartland, later to become an airline pilot, had not returned and quick action was needed. We moved his study-hall desk to a classroom so that when the roll-call took place all desks in the study hall were occupied and the threats of expulsion died out.

Also in school and in the same class as myself was Joe Lee, who managed to get full marks in history in both the Intermediate and Leaving Certificate exams. Joe was later to become professor of history at University College, Cork, and author of a number of books on Irish history.

Joe was under the strong impression that Dublin was the least Irish place in Ireland, especially when compared to his native Kerry. With my family background, I was inclined to disagree strongly with his analysis, and we had it out over that issue on more than one occasion. Having only got ninety-six per cent in history in the Inter, I was at a disadvantage in these arguments, especially as the class schedules for the Leaving were set in such a way that French and history clashed and I had to opt for one or the other. I took French, and my interest in languages has lived on to this day.

After the Leaving Cert it was back to Dublin and the search for a job. The idea of going on to university at that time was almost out of the question unless one's parents had enough money to pay the college fees. There were scholarships all right, but there were less than a handful for the entire city of Dublin. As far as I know, my brother and I were the only two boys of our age group on our street to make it to secondary school, let alone university, and my brother would not have made it to university if he had not entered the Church.

As it turned out, he took his primary degree at UCD and was then sent on to study theology at the Angelicum University in Rome, run by the Dominican order. He completed his doctorate in moral theology but never got round to doing the public defence of his thesis that is part of the continental system. He is probably not entitled, therefore, to be described as Dr Martin, but Irish newspapers insist that all bishops are automatically 'doctored'.

I wrote to the newspapers looking for a job in journalism and got a single reply from Irish Press Ltd to go to an interview at their O'Connell Street premises. Leading the interview team was the personnel manager Colm Traynor, son of Oscar Traynor, who had been head of the Dublin Brigade of the IRA and was president of the Football Association of Ireland, the Irish governing body of the game of soccer that Father Daly had sworn to annihilate.

Also there was the formidable Bill Redmond, news editor and chief tyrant of the organisation, and the sports editor, Oliver Weldon, son of Brinsley McNamara, a successful writer and author of *Valley of the Squinting Windows*.

During the interview, Redmond's antagonism to my answers became obvious very quickly, but Weldon seemed slightly more interested in what I had to say. A week or so later a letter arrived at my home bearing the *Irish Press'* stylised blue eagle insignia and twin mottoes of 'The Truth in the News' and '*Do chum Glóire Dé agus Onóra na hÉireann*'. It began with the words 'we regret to inform you' and went on to tell me that there was no place for me in the organisation.

So off I went looking for any work I could get, and my first job didn't last long. I was employed as a 'stock-control clerk' in a wholesale hardware merchants in Smithfield. My task was to enter into a ledger the number of screws or washers or whatever left the stores and subtract them from the number of screws or washers in stock. My sums hardly ever added up, either because my arithmetic was faulty or because screws and washers were 'walking' out of the stores without my knowledge.

A month of excruciating boredom and unrelenting frustration among the screws and washers was brought to an end by a completely unexpected turn of events. I returned home one dark winter's evening to be told a letter had arrived for me. I opened it and there once more was the blue eagle and the twin mottoes. This time the letter began with the words: 'Further to your interview we wish to inform you that a successful candidate has been unable to take up our offer of a position as trainee journalist.'

It went on to inform me that as I was next on the list I would be offered the job at £3 10s 6d per week, slightly less than half my wages for counting screws, washers, nuts and bolts. I wrote back immediately accepting the offer.

— The Tivoli Never Closed —

Having accepted the offer of employment at the *Irish Press*, I was called in to meet Colm Traynor again. He told me to report for duty at 10.00 a.m. at the sports department in the Burgh Quay premises of Irish Press Ltd and to ask for the sports editor, Oliver Weldon. If the latter was not there, he told me with barely concealed disdain, 'a person called Hennessy' might be present.

As it turned out there was no one there when I arrived, a callow seventeen-year-old, on the morning of 2 November 1959. I was directed to a place called the 'Glass House', where three desks for the eleven members of the sports reporting staff were squeezed into a tiny room that opened on to a corridor leading to the newsroom. The door to the editor's office was directly opposite, and a little bit to the right was the office of

Terry O'Sullivan of the *Evening Press*, perhaps the best-known journalist in town.

O'Sullivan's real name was O'Faolain and he was the father of the popular writer Nuala O'Faolain. He wrote the 'Dubliner's Diary' column and was also 'on the take'. He accepted all sorts of gifts from people who wanted him to cover their favourite social events, upon which he lavished extravagant praise commensurate with the bribe he had originally received. He did, however, elicit a famous quote on one occasion from a worker in the foundry at the Guinness brewery.

Under the mistaken impression that they were helping their foundry workers to replace the body liquids lost through working in such hot conditions, the management supplied the workers with free Guinness. Asked by O'Sullivan how much he would drink in the course of a day, a burly foundryman replied in his Dublin drawl: 'Some days I might drink 20 pints and other days I might drink me fill.'

This was one of the memories that kept me going while I twiddled my thumbs waiting for someone to arrive at the Glass House. Then, at about 11.30 a.m., someone turned up. It was the soccer correspondent Vincent Mathers, whose report of a stunning 3–2 win for Ireland against World Cup runners-up Sweden at Dalymount Park was in that morning's edition. In my anxiety to get to work on time, I had not read the paper, but I had seen Vincent's reports previously and I had been at the match myself to see John Giles play his first game for Ireland.

Vincent spoke to me as if I had been working at the paper for years and asked my opinion of his report. I had enough gumption to say it was very good and that I enjoyed it very much. That made me a friend of Vincent's for life.

After a short while I learned that my official title of 'trainee journalist' was recognised by no one. I was a 'copy boy' and that was that. Among my copy-boy colleagues were John Redmond, now in public relations, and Donal McCann, who became one of the most accomplished actors that Ireland has produced. Donal and I remained in contact, mainly by post, until his death from cancer in July 1999.

My job was to make tea and to fetch proofs from the 'random' in the composing room, or the 'case room' as it was known in the trade. I would also make regular visits to the wire room, known as the 'creed room', to check out wire reports with the help of the wire-room chief, Séamus O'Shea, the father of a Dublin journalistic dynasty. From time to time there were visits to the art department, where Bob Dillon was in charge of the photographers, to the block-makers, run by the Kincaid father and son, to the guillotine, where copy-paper was cut, and to the machine room, run by a portly and jovial Welshman called Davies.

Most frequently I was sent to the library, where the boss Aengus Ó Dálaigh, whose brother Cearbhall was to become president of Ireland, was the only saint I met in the course of my journalistic career. He would do a good turn for anyone without demur and, of course, was taken for granted by some of the worst touchers in town, including one man called Liam Creagh, who sold a subversive publication called *Aiseirí*.

A semi-permanent resident of the library was a man known as Dr Croaty. He, rumour had it, was a Nazi sympathiser from the Balkans who had found refuge in Ireland under an assumed name. He would frequently be seen sitting at Aengus Ó Dálaigh's desk reading *Pravda*, presumably to keep up with the thinking of his enemies.

In this manner I learned not only how a newspaper was produced but also how to deal with some of the most contrary characters in Christendom. It was a wonderful training in those days of 'hot metal' production, and I discovered in other Dublin newspapers I later worked for, that I knew much more about the process of newspaper production than most journalists who had not begun their careers in Burgh Quay.

I also learned that most journalists in the *Irish Press* shared a single overriding ambition and that was to get out of the place and find a job somewhere else as soon as possible.

Most sports reporters achieved this ambition. Mick Dunne, the GAA correspondent, moved to RTÉ, where he had a highly successful career. Vincent Mathers became Irish sports correspondent of the *Sunday Express*, Tom Keogh moved to the *Daily Mirror*, Seán Diffley became rugby correspondent of the *Irish Independent*, John Barrett moved to London, Dermot Gilleece went to the *Daily Mail* and then to *The Irish Times* as golf correspondent, and I, eventually, accepted the offer of a job with Independent Newspapers. Only Oliver Weldon, the office manager Mick Hennessy, the racing correspondent Tony Power and the deputy GAA correspondent Peadar O'Brien stayed with the *Irish Press*, either until retirement or until the newspaper group folded in the 1990s.

The same applied in other departments, and at one stage the editors of almost all the national papers in Dublin were graduates of the Burgh Quay school. They included Douglas Gageby, the great editor of *The Irish Times*, Vinny Doyle of the *Irish Independent*, Mick Hand of the *Sunday Independent* and Kevin Marron of the *Sunday World* who was later killed in a plane crash in southern England.

The sports reporters moved to spacious accommodation in a large room over Corn Exchange Buildings a few months after my arrival. The woman's editor, Sheila Walsh, had an office nearby, and another room on the same floor was allocated to the literary editor, Benedict Kiely, the Irish-language editor, Breandán Ó hEithir, and Arthur Hunter, who had the unusual title of day editor, which, logic suggested, was the opposite of night editor. The night editor was in charge of the paper at night when the editor was absent, but it seemed unlikely that the day editor could be in charge during the day when the editor was present.

The need for this particular job was questioned by the powers-that-be in one of the many palace coups that took place unexpectedly. The position of day editor was abolished, and Arthur was appointed gardening correspondent because he was a Protestant, and Protestants, the logic went, knew more about civilised pursuits such as gardening than did the wild Catholics, who spent their time drinking and carousing during much, and in some cases all, of their waking hours.

Ben Kiely was rarely present in the office, for he travelled the country writing the Patrick Lagan column, which was designed to include articles on every remote corner of Ireland in order to boost circulation. Even when he was in Dublin, he was rarely to be seen in the building. Frequently he would be found upstairs in the White Horse pub with Brendan Behan, or in the Scotch House, where Myles na gCopaleen drank, or in the Oyster Bar of the Red Bank restaurant, where he would regale the customers with his sonorous rendition of 'The Flower of Sweet Strabane'. He also had the unique habit of travelling from the White Horse to the Scotch House by taxi, a distance of about seventy-five metres.

Behan at that time was a man to be avoided. His drinking bouts were laced with aggression and he often threw bar furniture around the place. Once, when in a destructive mood upstairs in the White Horse, he proceeded methodically to wreck the joint. This provoked the owner Mick O'Connell from Croom in the County Limerick, to respond in the male-chauvinist manner that was predominant at the time. He went to Brendan's wife Beatrice, whom he always called 'BeeAAAtrice', and in an annoyed voice asked her: 'Have you no control over that man of yours at all?'

At this stage I was a mere apprentice, not only in journalism, but in that very important secondary activity of the trade, the drinking of pints. The Silver Swan, now closed, was the hostelry inhabited by some locals from City Quay and a rare collection of people connected with the newspaper trade. Dominic O'Riordan, the poet, would arrive with his companion Máire Noone and drink himself to a standstill or quite often to a fall-down. Once, on a Saturday afternoon, Mick Hand and his impresario twin brother Jim had the doors closed while the Everly Brothers, a very famous duo in their time, sang for a select company, including myself.

When Breandán Ó hEithir was departing to live for a while in Germany, his uncle Liam O'Flaherty arrived for the farewell party. I had been in awe of the great writer but was extremely disappointed by his personality that night. He would start to sing a song which began with the words 'On the top of Cave Hill we have planted a gun'. He would then fall asleep for a while before waking again to intone the words once more and then fall asleep again. This procedure was repeated throughout the night.

I was beginning to wonder if all the well-known writers in Dublin at that time were nasty people. Behan was aggressive, O'Flaherty boring when in his cups, and Brian O'Nolan (Myles na gCopaleen) was a bitter, little man who rarely had anything good to say about anyone.

But Ben Kiely turned out to be kind and hospitable. He would frequently invite Vincent Mathers, a townie from Omagh, for drinks or for a meal. Vincent would ask me along and we would meet in Wynn's Hotel in Lower Abbey Street, a place which attracted a clientele of provincial clergy on their visits to Dublin. It was known to Ben as the 'Priests' Hole' after the hiding places for Catholic priests during the religious geno- cide carried out on the orders of Elizabeth I.

With a few on board, Ben would launch into song and, when in Wynn's, could not resist a resounding chorus that referred to

> … the priests in a bunch,
> round a big roaring fire drinkin' tumblers of punch,
> singin' 'bainne na mbó is na gamhna,
> and the Juice of the Barley for me.'

The Burgh Quay premises, by the way, were once the home of the Tivoli Theatre, a music hall famous for its comedy acts. It was frequently said by the journalists of the *Irish Press* that 'the Tivoli never closed', such was the unpredictably comic nature of the place.

In charge of all was Vivion de Valera, the editor-in-chief and vicar-on-earth of his father Éamon de Valera, whose stern portrait hung in the boardroom in the commercial headquar- ters of the group in O'Connell Street. A complex type, Vivion mixed his Irish nationalism with his admiration for Lord Beaverbrook and the *Daily Express*, the most imperialist of the Fleet Street newspapers at that time. When planning permis- sion was finally granted for the renovation of the old Tivoli, he had it clad in black like the *Express* building in London.

Vivion de Valera's appointment by his father to run the *Irish Press* was the cause of some sharp comments from the staff. The most memorable of these came one evening when he arrived in the newsroom to see the entire sub-editors' desk rocking with suppressed laughter. Séamus de Faoite, the Kerry writer and poet, had noticed his arrival and, *sotto voce,* parodied the Bible with the words: 'Behold my beloved son, whom I have well placed.'

He also carried the title of major, a temporary commission given to officers who signed up for what was known in Ireland as the Emergency and elsewhere in the world as the Second World War. Officers of equivalent rank in the permanent defence forces carried the title of commandant.

He was one of three majors I encountered in my years in the newspapers. Major Eddie Murphy (Irish Guards Retd) held sway at Independent House, and Major Thomas Bleakley McDowell ran the show at *The Irish Times.*

The Irish Press Group was quite military in everything except its efficiency, and there were some serious problems regarding rank. The big boss, Vivion de Valera, was a major, but the editor of the *Sunday Press*, Matt Feehan, was a colonel. He once insisted that Breandán Ó hEithir should address him as Colonel Feehan in ordinary conversation, to which Breandán responded by asking to be referred to as Lance Corporal Ó hEithir. Feehan was furious, not at Ó hEithir's insolence, but at his use of a rank which existed only in the British army.

Colonel Feehan was a patriot and his term of office at the *Sunday Press* saw the introduction of the 'ambush series' and the 'patriotic article'. The ambush series celebrated the deeds of the IRA flying columns in the War of Independence and was accompanied by murky photographs of barren hillsides. Printers' arrows would point to sections of the pictures with captions such as 'Tans in their big Crossley tenders here' and 'Boys of the column waiting here'.

On Mondays a conference would be held at which the previous day's paper would be dissected and plans laid for the following week's edition. Breandán Ó hEithir was a frequent attender and told me that there were very strange goings-on at these meetings. Feehan's office overlooked the river with a fine view of Eden Quay on the northern side. Michael O'Halloran, the 'ambush editor', had become so immersed in his job that he scanned the passers-by with an imaginary sniper's lens as they walked along Eden Quay. Now and then he would pick one or two of them off with his fantasy rifle and issue his version of the loud report that it would have made when fired. The colonel would not pay a blind bit of notice to the antics of his ambush editor, as he had at this stage generally worked himself into a fury at some mistake that had appeared in the previous day's paper.

Perhaps his biggest fury was reserved for an incident concerning the patriotic article. On this occasion, the readers were to be treated to an exposition of the unstinting patriotism of the 'Manchester Martyrs', Allen, Larkin and O'Brien, executed in 1897 for the murder of a police sergeant while rescuing two leading Fenians from a prison van in Manchester. The 'murder' was an unusual one in that the rescuers fired a shot through the keyhole of the van in an attempt to break the lock, but Sergeant Brett, at the same time, decided to peer through the keyhole to see what was happening outside. Manslaughter would probably have been a more suitable charge, but the three men were found guilty and, on being sentenced, uttered the words 'God Save Ireland' – hence the song 'God Save Ireland Cried the Heroes.'

One member of the staff may not have been aware of this piece of history, but he happened to be in the wrong place at the wrong time. Tom Hennigan suffered from narcolepsy, a condition that led to the possibility that he might fall asleep at any given moment. When the rest of the editing staff were out on their break (known in the trade as the 'cutline'), Hennigan dozed at his desk.

A compositor working on the page in which the 'patriotic article' was to appear, noticed that a woodcut of the three men with their arms upraised at the dramatic moment of their sentence did not have a caption. He emerged from the case room, poked at Hennigan until he awoke and asked him to write a caption. A quick glance at the article gave him the names of the three men and, still half asleep, he wrote the following: 'Manchester Martyrs, Allen, Larkin and O'Brien, beg for mercy.' The compositor, a Hungarian, knew no better and the caption was set in type.

Having returned to the office Colonel Feehan waited in the machine room to pick up the first copies of the paper as they came off the press. As usual he first checked the patriotic article and was almost felled by the offending caption. The presses were stopped and thousands of copies burned in the furnace, normally used for more mundane hot-metal purposes.

The *Sunday Press* may have missed the train connections that ensured its delivery to the provinces but at least the readers were spared the idea of the Manchester Martyrs begging for mercy. That many of them were also spared the entire *Sunday Press* was merely incidental.

Colonel Feehan, in true military manner, had running battles with quite a lot of people. Amongst them were Major de Valera and the future editor of the *Irish Independent*, Vinny Doyle. The clashes with de Valera resulted from the colonel's difficulty in taking orders from a mere major. The clashes with Vinny Doyle were of an editorial nature.

In any event, the colonel found out in dramatic fashion

that the major was his superior officer. Vinny Doyle discovered this in an even more spectacular way. His phone rang and the colonel's voice at the other end of the line issued the peremptory order: 'Come to my office immediately.' On Doyle's arrival, Colonel Feehan shook his hand and said: 'Goodbye Doyle, it has been interesting to know you.'

Assuming he had been fired, Doyle went out to the Silver Swan for a stiff one. A group of journalists was already there and one of them approached Doyle. 'Have you heard the news?' he asked. 'The colonel's been sacked.'

The other two editors in the Irish Press Group, Joe Walsh of the morning newspaper, the *Irish Press,* and Conor O'Brien of the *Evening Press,* were very different types. Walsh was rarely to be seen and his only communications were by memos to heads of department. Conor O'Brien was one of three journalists in Dublin who bore the same name. Nicknames were therefore in order.

Conor Cruise O'Brien retained his personal moniker, while the others became known as Conor Booze O'Brien and Conor News O'Brien. Our man was Conor News O'Brien and he had taken over the *Evening Press* editorship from Douglas Gageby. He was a man of the utmost probity and also made himself known to even the most insignificant members of the staff, of which I was one.

The man who wielded the most power, though, was the news editor Bill Redmond, and he wielded it with a vengeance. The reporting staff under his control worked for all three newspapers in the group and he could allocate or withdraw them from any of the three editors at will. He was a big, dark, gruff man from County Wexford, who showed no mercy and publicly humiliated members of his staff in front of the entire newsroom. He was also very careful with the company's money and once refused Dick Walsh, later political editor of *The Irish Times*, his bus fare to the Four Courts on the grounds that he should have walked.

Once, however, Redmond had the wind taken out of his sails and the man who did it was the morning paper's cartoonist and caricaturist Bobby Pyke. A dapper man, usually dressed in tweeds with his grey hair swept back, Pyke was almost permanently drunk and in that condition was capable of the most outrageous behaviour. He emerged into the newsroom on one occasion when Redmond was bawling out a very senior reporter.

Always one to make a dramatic entrance, Pyke in full voice made the following attention-grabbing statement: 'I am the Lamb of God ...' Not surprisingly the newsroom fell silent. Pyke then pointed an admonishing finger at Redmond, saying, 'and you are the black serpent that I shall crush beneath my heel'. Needless to say, that was the end of Redmond's dominance over his underlings, at least for the rest of that day.

Pyke was also reputed to have once embarrassed Major de Valera in even more dramatic fashion. The major decided to reduce the fees paid to Pyke for his cartoons and caricatures. He did so, in the true *Irish Press* style of management, without informing Pyke in advance. The revised rates were discovered by the artist when he opened his pay packet on a Friday. As it turned out, the major was attending a diplomatic function for a visiting head of state from Africa at what was then the Department of External Affairs at Iveagh House.

Security in those days was much less strict than it is today, and Pyke, always well dressed for such an occasion, vowed to confront the major at this very formal event. Incensed not only by the fall in income but also by the perceived slight on his professional ability, Pyke fortified himself with several Baby Powers and headed off to Stephen's Green. Showing his press card at the door, he was admitted to the grand surroundings of Iveagh House, where the reception was in full swing. Champagne was being consumed with the canapes, and smoked salmon abounded as the important people of Irish society welcomed their visitors. Pyke, his face even more scarlet than usual due to his rage, spotted the major almost immediately and made a beeline for him.

At that precise moment, Major de Valera was deep in conversation with an official from the visiting delegation. Pyke butted in with the words: 'There you are Major Vivion de Valera, TD, entertaining Africans and starving your fucking own.' The end of a long cartooning career beckoned.

Pyke was matched in his heavy drinking by many others in the Tivoli, perhaps the most notable amongst them being Arthur McGahon, an extremely talented writer from Dundalk in County Louth. There was great bitterness amongst the sports reporters in 1960 when two outsiders were chosen to represent the group at the Olympic Games in Rome. McGahon, a news sub-editor, was one, and Fionnbar Callanan, a solicitor in the national transport company Córas Iompair Éireann, the other.

Those who had braved the rain, hail and snow at sporting events to bring their coverage to *Irish Press* readers were ignored and this type of insensitive and often downright arrogant management was partly to blame for almost every journalist wanting to get out of Burgh Quay as soon as possible.

On this occasion, however, the *Irish Press* management got its come-uppance. McGahon and Ireland's Olympic team were welcomed to Rome at a reception held by Aer Lingus at the international airport of Fiumicino. McGahon wrote a glowing report of the airline's hospitality, which was a bit short on news and didn't make the paper. Worse still he did not write another word on the Olympics and spent all his time sampling the wines of the region and a considerable supply of Stock and Vecchia Romagna brandy to boot.

Needless to say, the full-time professional sports reporters spurned by those who had selected the outsiders were delighted at this turn of events and celebrated their good fortune in the Silver Swan – though by no means to the same extent as McGahon was doing in Rome. As the junior, I was delegated to phone Arthur and tell him to come home. It seems that those who sent him there in the first place did not have the courage to call him back.

In those days, making a phone call to continental Europe was quite a major event. The call had to be booked in advance. The Dublin exchange would contact their colleagues in London and the call would then be routed through various centres, and in this case Paris was also involved.

Most of my attempts to reach Arthur McGahon failed, but eventually I managed to find him in his hotel room. He had perhaps gone back there to get some *lire* to buy more drink in a local hostelry. For all his drinking, Arthur had retained a certain amount of native cunning, and he immediately took advantage of the poor phone line and the occasional burst of static that invaded our conversation.

'You are to come home,' I told him.

'Grand weather here,' he replied. 'What's it like back there?'

Our conversation continued in the following manner: 'You're to come HOME.'

'Yes I'm in ROME.'

'Not ROME. HOME. You are to come HOME.'

'I TOLD you, I'm already IN Rome.'

A loud crackle on the line ended our conversation and Arthur remained in Rome until the Olympics ended without putting pen to paper or touching a typewriter key. He kept his job on his return to Ireland and later achieved the universal ambition of getting a job elsewhere, in his case with the *Irish Independent*.

Despite these irregularities, the *Irish Press, Evening Press* and *Sunday Press* not only continued to be published regularly but produced some extremely good journalism and regularly beat the *Independent* and *The Irish Times* to important stories. Some of the credit for this must go to Bill Redmond, for all his bullying arrogance and domineering attitude. A lot of the credit too was due to the highly professional attitude of the majority of the staff, who rose above the management's insensitivity.

Redmond managed to increase his power towards the end of my time in Burgh Quay by placing trusted members of his reporting staff into positions in charge of other editorial departments. Liam Flynn, who had never been a professional photographer, was put in command of the photographic department, and Maurice O'Brien, who had never reported on sport, was made head of the sports-reporting section. I was to learn later that Redmond was instrumental in my appointment as the group's golf correspondent, which put me onto an extremely steep learning curve, as I knew absolutely nothing about the game.

To say that Maurice O'Brien and I did not get on well would be an understatement. He was an indecisive man, given to hypochondria, and spent a lot of time on the phone to his mother. He treated me, the youngest member of his staff, as something of a messenger boy. I was frequently sent on errands to his uncle, who ran a shop on Cathal Brugha Street by the corner of O'Connell Street, with little notes safely enclosed in envelopes. His uncle, Moss Twomey, had had a little sideline apart from running his shop. He happened to have been, in his time, the chief of staff of the IRA.

Contact between the *Irish Press* and former and current members of the IRA was quite frequent at the time. There were regular visits from strange men from the country to the headquarters of the newspaper founded by 'the Chief'. Elderly Americans with backgrounds stretching back to Clan na Gael were frequent callers, too. At this time, many who had fought in the War of Independence and the civil war were still alive; and although Dev had been ruthless with the IRA during the Emergency and during the course of the border campaign in the 1950s and 1960s, there still appeared to be a bond of affinity between the Fianna Fáil-oriented newspaper and Sinn Féin-oriented republican activists.

The eccentric Geoffrey Coulter, who travelled around Dublin on a bicycle to which he attached a sail for wind-assisted journeys, had been a sub-editor in Burgh Quay, having previously been deputy editor of *An Phoblacht*. Terry Ward, whose son Seán was later to be editor of the *Evening Press*, was a former editor of *An Phoblacht*.

Seán Cronin, an *Irish Press* man who became Washington correspondent of *The Irish Times*, had also been the IRA's chief of staff. It was said that many journalists of the generation previous to mine felt very much at home in the oppressive atmosphere of Burgh Quay because it reminded them of their previous experiences in prison.

In my time there, many of the old IRA men from the 1920s were coming to the end of their lives. There was a strict rule for reporting these deaths. It was anathema, for example, to write that an individual 'took the republican side in the civil war'. The approved method of announcing the dead man's loyalties was that 'he *remained* on the republican side in the civil war'.

Another old IRA soldier was Paddy Clare, who was the permanent 'night town' man. His job was to man the news desk when everyone else had gone home, in case there might be a late-breaking story. Paddy had a strong, gravelly Dublin accent and was a keen sailor with a very basic idea of navigation. Once, when he announced that he was going to sail to the Isle of Man for a long weekend, he was asked how we would find his way there. 'That's an easy one,' he replied, 'you just go up to Drogheda and turn right.'

He was not the most enthusiastic of workers and it was widely believed that he owed his job on the *Irish Press* to his revolutionary past rather than his journalistic present. He was renowned for his behaviour on the night of 8 December 1954, when the most serious flooding on record in Dublin took place. He was accompanied on night-town duty that night by a colleague called Mick, to whom he reported the results of every phone call received from those responsible for flood warnings. 'The Tolka is rising, Mick,' he would announce. 'The Tolka is just a foot from the top of the embankment, Mick,' he declared after another phone call, until finally the word was that, 'The Tolka is riz. The whole of the North Strand is under water.'

To this announcement he added the following rider: 'I think you'd better go out there, Mick, for my shoes is lettin' in.'

Paddy made one particularly strong contribution to my life. One winter's night, the word got round that there was a party to be held by Josephine Burke and Dardis Clarke, son of the poet Austin Clarke, in a house on Leinster Road in Rathmines. When I got there, Paddy and the librarian Tommy McCann were deep in conversation with a young woman who struck me as being particularly attractive. I joined them immediately and Paddy introduced me. 'This is Anita Staunton. She lives in the flat upstairs.' Anita and I were married on 3 April 1968, by which time I was a member of the staff of Independent Newspapers in Abbey Street.

It was one of my many blazing rows with Maurice O'Brien combined with an uncanny stroke of fortune that led to my departure from Burgh Quay. Having noticed that Maurice and I had just had another altercation, my friend Michael Keane, later to become editor of the *Sunday Press*, came over to me and suggested we take our meal break together. We went to the restaurant of the Carlton Cinema on O'Connell Street to get away from the *Irish Press* crowd, who frequented the Wimpy Bar on Burgh Quay.

Having eaten and discussed the matter of my difficulties with the boss, Michael suggested we call into the Oval Bar on Middle Abbey Street for a pint on the way back. I was a bit worried that the smell of drink from my breath on my return might make things even worse, but I eventually agreed.

We were in the Oval for less than fifteen minutes when Mitchel Cogley, the celebrated sports editor of the *Irish Independent*, arrived and saw myself and Michael seated in a corner. He beckoned me to come over and speak to him. 'I've been looking for you,' he said. 'How much are the *Press* paying you?' I told him. 'Well, we'd like you to join the *Indo* and we will pay you much better than that.'

The offer could not have come at a better time. I finished my pint, returned to Burgh Quay, typed out my resignation giving a month's notice and handed it to Maurice O'Brien. The word spread quickly. Colleagues thought I had acted hastily and in anger, but when I told them I had been offered a job in Abbey Street I became something of a hero who had achieved the ambition that most of them had held for themselves.

For all the difficulties I had with the *Irish Press* management, I was grateful for the in-house training they had provided, and my resignation letter contained no note of bitterness. The *Press*, along with the *Independent* and the *Times*, had also had the prescience to send their younger journalists on a two-year course of further education at the College of Commerce in Rathmines.

This course, as it turned out, was the forerunner of the current journalism course at the Dublin Institute of Technology. The juniors drawn from all three newspaper groups and from RTÉ attended Rathmines for two full days each week and worked at their staff jobs for the other three. There was a considerable amount of research and reading to be done at home on the prescribed subjects of newspaper law, economics, English and Irish.

As often happens in Ireland, there was a paradoxical twist to the course. Our law lecturer, Joe Christle, known also as Seosamh MacChriostal, was known to both sides of the law. On the one hand he was a qualified barrister, while on the other was under constant surveillance by the Special Branch as a well-known subversive.

Joe arrived very late for his lecture one morning in 1966, apologising for his tardiness with the wry statement, 'I was up till all hours last night.' On the previous night, the Nelson Pillar in O'Connell Street had been destroyed by an explosion designed to mark the fiftieth anniversary of the Easter Rising.

When Douglas Gageby asked me to find out what I could about the explosion twenty years later, I met Joe Christle at a burger joint in Rathmines. The choice of venue was his. He immediately laid down what he called the parameters of the interview. 'I will not talk about any part I may have taken in this action and I will not talk about any part I may not have taken in this action.'

This left us with very little to talk about and I asked Joe was there anything at all he could tell me. He said he would be able to tell me who was not involved in blowing up the pillar. He then went on to name almost everyone who was known to be a subversive republican at the time. The one exception was himself.

— Culture Shock —

Independent House on Middle Abbey Street was totally different from the chaotic scene dominant at Burgh Quay. The building, for a start, was far more impressive; and not only was there a lift to transport you to the building's different floors, but there was also a lift attendant to convey you to your destination.

My destination was room 88, the home base of the *Independent*'s sports reporters. In charge, upon my arrival, was Bill Murphy, the group's chief sports reporter and soccer correspondent. His name appeared in the paper as W.P. Murphy, and these unfortunate initials led to the nickname Waste Paper Murphy. Reporters' bylines at the *Indo*, according to the rule in force at one time, consisted of two initials and a surname.

The older writers kept the old-style bylines: so Mitchel Cogley was M.V. Cogley and John Hickey was J.D. Hickey. The younger sports writers used their names in full, so I remained Séamus Martin and joined others such as Tom Cryan, Noel Dunne, Colm Smith, David Faiers and Con Kenealy.

The writing style of some older colleagues was positively Victorian, and John Hickey in particular became noted for his verbosity. In one celebrated report, he wrote this of the great Kerry footballer Mick O'Connell: 'Such was the majesty of the Valentia Islander that one thought he had dispensed with the official ball and substituted one of his own.' Donie Nealon, the Tipperary hurler, 'wielded the camán as though it were part of his anatomy', and those who made little of a win by Wexford were admonished in a report that began with the words: 'Fie to those who will cavil with Wexford's victory ...'

Hickey was a Tipperary man and his county bias showed from time to time, at least in the eyes of Con Kenealy, who was from the city of Kilkenny. Con, affectionately known as 'Bonkers', had the last laugh, for he discovered that John Dillon Hickey was actually born in County Kilkenny because, as he told the story, his mother at the time of his birth was on her way through that county from one part of Tipp to another.

Tom Cryan and Mitchel Cogley were old Burgh Quay men and retained some of the eccentricity that was endemic in that institution. Cogley, a small man with a large appetite for alcoholic beverages, would spend the afternoon on a circuit from the office to the bookies to the pub and back to the office. He was very good company and had a ready wit and a sharp turn of phrase. When the great commentator Mícheál O'Hehir was replaced by an American called Lefty Devine for a match in the US, the American in his commentary showed an extreme lack of understanding of Gaelic Games. Mícheál O'Hehir, when questioned by the media on the subject, was extremely generous in his remarks and entirely uncritical of Lefty's errors. The headline in the *Independent*, credited to Cogley, read: 'O'Hehir is human to forgive Devine'.

Mitchel developed diabetes in later life and his hangovers became more and more severe. I once met him in the Oval Bar in Abbey Street and he was in a pretty bad state. He spoke to me as follows: 'I had a right few last night and I arrived home in very good form. I felt wonderful. Indeed I could have danced around the flat I was feeling so good. Then I went to bed and woke up this morning and felt like death. Do you know what I'm going to tell you? I'm convinced it's the sleep that does it.'

Cryan was the paper's larger-than-life boxing correspondent and also covered athletics from time to time. He bore a great hatred for a former *Irish Press* sports editor called Seán Piondar. In fact, every reporter I knew who worked at the *Press* in Piondar's time hated his guts, but Cryan managed to convey his dislike in a more spectacular way than most of them.

Tom and I were, at one time, covering the College Races at Trinity College together. We were sitting at a press table in the middle of College Park and right beside us was the trophy table laden down with some of the most magnificent silverware I had ever seen. The old Ascendancy had the taste, and the money, to provide trophies of great style and value.

After a while, Piondar could be seen coming in our direction from the Lincoln Place cricket pavilion. Cryan rose to his feet and walked to the trophy table. He grabbed the most impressive of the Victorian silver cups and waited until Piondar arrived.

Then, in a voice loud enough to be heard by the spectators on the other side of the field, he announced: 'Seán Piondar, I hereby present you with this magnificent trophy for being the greatest bollocks of all time.'

Life at the *Independent* was so different from that at the *Press* that it was something of a culture shock to me. The former military men here were not from the IRA but from the Free State army, the British army and the Blueshirts. When I completed my first week and wished to have my expenses authorised, I discovered that the signature of the head of the sports reporters' department was not sufficient. I had to have the docket countersigned either by the managing director, Bartle Pitcher, the company secretary, Jack Mitchell, or in their absence by Major Eddie Murphy, a member of the Murphy family that owned the paper.

Murphy was a former officer in the British army's 'Irish' Guards, and he greeted me quite warmly to his office. He welcomed me aboard, signed my expenses and left me dumbstruck by inviting me to have a drink. 'Gin and tonic perhaps?' he ventured. I nodded in approval. Major E.M. Murphy went to his cocktail cabinet, fetched the gin, the tonic, some ice and lemon and two glasses. Into one he poured an overgenerous bumper of gin and into the other went a tiny trickle which he handed to me. He took the large one for himself and toasted my arrival at Independent Newspapers.

Down in room 88, overlooking the busy activities of the sports reporters, stood a 'flong', representing Major Murphy's forebear, William Martin Murphy. A flong, I should explain, was a papier-mâché mould into which a newspaper page was impressed in preparation for the making of curved metal plates that were fitted to the rotary presses. This particular flong was framed and bore the effigy of William Martin Murphy and an inscription that informed us that the 'evils of syndicalism' would not be tolerated in Independent House.

I can now admit that while on the late shift one night, I drank one too many during my cutline. As I sat there waiting for nothing to happen, since sports news rarely breaks at night, the face of William Martin Murphy – founder of the *Irish Independent* and arch-enemy of Jim Larkin and the Dublin workers during the 1913 Dublin Lockout – appeared to glower at me from the wall. My atavism took over and I dumped the flong, frame and all, out the window. A few weeks later I happened to meet Conor News O'Brien on the street. He told me that he was returning from the pictures at the Adelphi when an object crashed down in front of him from a window in Independent House. It was none other than William Martin Murphy himself. He decided to keep it as an historical memento.

A proper portrait of Murphy, I am told, still hangs in the boardroom of Independent News and Media in its new head-quarters in Talbot Street, but this was trumped by an etching I was later to see in the dingy little boardroom of *The Irish Times*.

The editor of the *Irish Independent* when I arrived in 1967 was Michael Rooney, but he retired soon afterwards and Louis McRedmond took over. Louis, a kind and erudite man, was perhaps too nice to be editor of a national paper, and he was ousted quickly. Aidan Pender, a patrician former army officer, then took over, to be followed by Vinny Doyle, whom I knew well from Burgh Quay. Brian Quinn was the editor of the *Evening Herald*, and the *Sunday Independent* editor was Hector Legge, a tall, quite arrogant man with aspirations to West Britishness.

All reporters, sports and news, worked for all three of Independent Newspapers publications, and as well as doing general work I also became soccer correspondent of the *Sunday Independent* and the main golf writer for the *Evening Herald*. The soccer job took me to England virtually every weekend in the winter to cover major fixtures, particularly those involving Irish players. Most frequently my trips took me to Old Trafford to watch Manchester United, to Anfield for Liverpool, and to Elland Road, where John Giles was a rising star.

I also made it to continental Europe from time to time and one fixture I particularly remember was the European Cup final between Liverpool and Borussia Mönchengladbach at the Olympic Stadium in Rome in 1977. Liverpool won 3–1 to take the trophy for the first time, with Ireland's Steve Heighway in their side. The match was a great one but it also provided me with one of the most nerve-wracking moments in a journalistic career that has included being caught in the middle of a group of chanting Zulus in Ulundi and being under fire for thirteen hours in Durres in Albania.

What occurred in Rome on that day had little to do with football and was directly linked to a series of strikes by air-traffic controllers in continental Europe. RTÉ was covering the match, but as kick-off time neared, the commentator Jimmy McGee had not arrived. RTÉ's producer Mike Horgan decided that I would have to step into Jimmy's shoes and do the commentary. 'Don't worry. I'll prompt you into the earphones in case you get flustered,' he told me.

My perspiration was beginning to form a small pool on my match programme as kick-off time approached. Then, just as the sides were ready to come out on to the field, there was a commotion at the foot of the stairs leading to the commentary box. Jimmy McGee had made it to the stadium despite the airline chaos and I was spared what might have become the most embarrassing moment of my life.

Reporting on golf, a subject that I had now learned something about, brought me to many of the great tournaments in Ireland, the UK and mainland Europe, and also helped me make the acquaintance of journalists such as Paul MacWeeney, the travelling sports editor of *The Irish Times*. MacWeeney was almost a legendary figure in Irish sport and had been an accomplished sportsman in his day. He was also well able to take care of himself as far as expenses were concerned and liked to travel first class and stay in the best hotels. His reputation as a serious golf writer extended beyond Ireland and, at one stage, he was made a member of the Royal and Ancient Golf Club at St Andrews. This honour, however, involved a hefty fee and, as he told the story, he got around this in his usual manner.

'I approached Douglas Gageby,' he said in his slightly hesitant Anglo accent, 'and told him of my acceptance as a member. It was, I informed him, the golfing equivalent of a peerage. He extended his hand in congratulations. I took it and in doing so I palmed him the bill for the membership fee.'

Many's the young journalist who would have given everything to have my job at the *Independent* at that time, but I was getting tired of writing about the same subject week in, week out. I needed greater variety and I had always nurtured the ambition of becoming a foreign correspondent at some stage in my career. In order to do that I would have to move to the news section of the paper and eventually leave Independent Newspapers who, other than their correspondents in London and Brussels, took their foreign news mainly from British sources.

I had been talking to the news editor Bill Shine about moving out of sport for some time when Vinny Doyle, then editor of the *Herald*, asked me to take over the evening paper's diary column, which was the rival to Terry O'Sullivan's 'Dubliner's Diary' in the *Evening Press*.

I took the job and tried to bring a bit of humour to it, but this venture came to an end in pretty dramatic fashion when one afternoon I got an irate phone call complaining about my column of that evening from a close friend, Michael Keane, in the *Sunday Press*. I was on a day off and had not seen that day's *Herald* but it quickly became obvious that he was complaining about something that I did not write. Having bought the paper, I discovered that the offending piece had been written by someone else and inserted under my name. Naturally, I was furious at this and went in a temper to the hall in order to ring the office.

As I got there, the phone rang. A voice at the other end said: 'My name is John Mulcahy and I am starting a new paper called the *Sunday Tribune*. Would you like to be sports editor?' He caught me at just the right moment. I went to see him and agreed to take up the job.

At the *Tribune* I was part of a journalistic staff that included Jim Farrelly, who had been with me at the *Indo*, and a number of others who became prominent journalists at *The Irish Times*. These included Conor Brady and Geraldine Kennedy, both of whom became editors of the *Times*, Joe Carroll, who was to be Washington correspondent, Kieran Fagan, who became an editorial executive, and Noel McFarlane, who had lived just up the road from me in Ballyfermot as a boy.

John Mulcahy was an unusual character in that he was avowedly nationalist in his views but affected a very British tweedy image and ran the show in a decrepit Georgian house in Beresford Place from his top-floor office in which his roll-top desk, a vestige of the British Raj, was marked 'Made in Calcutta'.

The newspaper struggled for survival right from the start. It was printed at Sandyford Industrial Estate on a second-hand press which had arrived from England in crates. By the time it was up and running and printing the *Tribune*, two cases remained unpacked. Needless to say, there were numerous breakdowns and other incidents that caused difficulties for the paper and its readers.

The pages were put together in the basement of Beresford Place under the strict control of Jim O'Shea. Jim, who prided himself in looking like the character J.R. in the TV series *Dallas*, was not the person I most admired on this earth. He was a complicated character who was extremely kind to children but invariably referred to his wife as 'the Bag'.

The pages were then photographed and sent by motorcycle courier to Sandyford, where they didn't always arrive. On quite a few occasions they fell off the back of the motorbike and the whole process had to begin again.

I had arrived as sports editor, I realised later, at the suggestion of my friend Breandán Ó hEithir, and together with my deputy, Eoghan Corry, we planned a new departure in Irish sports journalism. The declamatory style practised by the likes of John D. Hickey was to have no place in the *Tribune*. Breandán was joined in the GAA section by Eugene McGee from Longford, who, in addition to his superb knowledge of Gaelic games, brought a great deal of entertainment to the GAA coverage and invented an archetypal official whose imaginary activities became a great favourite with the readers.

In racing, the author Anthony Cronin brought a new perspective to coverage of the sport, and rugby columns were graced by the presence of Carwyn James, the great Welsh player and writer.

Our soccer correspondent and columnist was Éamon Dunphy, and I therefore had the 'honour' of giving him his first regular job in journalism. Éamon, even then, was something of a character and found it difficult to cope with the idea that he could not write anything he liked in his column. The laws of libel were, he felt, designed specifically to impede his freedom of speech.

On one occasion he almost resigned because I had excised a section of his column. The offending passage read something like this: 'When the lid is lifted from the stinking dustbin that is the Football Association of Ireland, the first face to peer out will be that of Dr Tony O'Neill.' There was no way I was going to allow this piece of defamation to appear in print, and eventually, after a great deal of persuasion, Éamon withdrew his resignation threat.

If the piece had been let through, not only would Éamon have lost his job but the damages demanded by the libel court might have put the entire *Tribune* staff out of work. It was an appeal to his responsibility towards his colleagues that eventually persuaded Éamon to back down.

In those days, Sunday newspapers sold a great deal of copies in the pubs on Saturday night to those who were keen to get up to date on the sports results of the day. The *Tribune* decided to enter this market in a unique way. A Saturday-evening 'street edition' was produced, but because of technical difficulties was printed so early that the day's sports results were *not* included. It did not, therefore, sell particularly well.

While Mulcahy ran the editorial side, the commercial part of the venture was organised – and I use the word 'organised' in its loosest sense – by Hugh McLaughlin from Donegal, who had some previous publishing successes. McLaughlin dispensed largesse in the form of hard cash which he lugged around in an old shopping bag. The cash went to people outside the journalistic area, and the reporters and sub-editors relied on payment by cheques which, when they arrived, were cashed instantly for fear they might bounce.

Then a white knight arrived in the form of Michael Smurfit and his organisation. Things looked very bright indeed, and the arrival of Conor Brady as editor of the *Sunday Tribune* was greeted with relief and anticipation. Journalists were relieved, because the paper had failed to make significant progress under the editorship of John Mulcahy.

Mulcahy was the only one to make money out of the old *Tribune*. He sold his share to the Smurfit organisation and later set up the gossip magazine *Phoenix*. His editorship had, however, succeeded in bringing the new paper to a reasonable level of quality and circulation but had failed to make any progress beyond that.

Now that the Smurfit money was involved, it was hoped that real advances could be made. But there were worries about Brady. Geraldine Kennedy, the leading former *Irish Times* member of the staff, considered him to be a journalist of quite average talent, not any better qualified than those already on the *Tribune*'s staff. James Downey, the *Irish Times* deputy editor who had been turned down as a candidate, would, according to Kennedy, have been a better choice.

But Brady turned out to be a better journalist than Kennedy had imagined. His inspired editorship was, however, accompanied by poor management skills and a lack of forthrightness in his relations with staff, which later manifested itself at *The Irish Times*. He was also put under considerable pressure by a now dead ruthless and inconsiderate Smurfit manager, who felt no compunction about invading the Brady household to demand better results. These invasions of privacy, often of an extremely bullying nature, took place late at night, despite the presence of Brady's wife and small baby.

There were brief moments of humour. At a lunch in a private dining room in the Shelbourne Hotel, senior journalists were told by Mr Howard Kilroy of Smurfit's incentive scheme: 'If you work hard. If you are devoted to your job and the organisation.

If you get the results demanded of you, then you get to keep your job.' All this was delivered in a mock American twang and as if to emphasise his point and to strike fear into his audience he stabbed his knife into his cauliflower. This was to be his undoing, for a small family of caterpillars emerged to defuse the situation entirely.

For Brady, though, the pressure continued. He had been successful in switching the paper from tabloid to broadsheet and also in increasing the circulation. By the time his editorship was coming to an end, the circulation had reached more than 130,000, a figure the *Tribune* never approached since. But to achieve this, he spent a lot of money, and the Smurfit people were not prepared to take the usual tried-and-tested route for new papers, which was that money – and often a great amount of it – had to be spent in order to get a publication onto its feet before any reasonable return could be made.

So the Smurfits left the *Tribune* and went back to doing what they knew best, the manufacture of cardboard boxes. For Brady, trouble was in store. He faced a management now dominated by the other partners, led by Hugh McLaughlin, founder of the *Sunday World*. McLaughlin was an old-fashioned entrepreneur whose methods lacked the finesse of modern business. McLaughlin and his cohorts opted for a huge gamble. They decided to launch a daily tabloid newspaper called the *Daily News* in the wild hope that it would take off and keep the *Tribune* alive with its surplus revenue.

As staff worried about their jobs, wild rumours spread about the imminent collapse of the company. Two senior journalists, the late Mary Holland and myself, finally cornered Conor Brady in his office and pressurised him into addressing the editorial staff about the situation.

A group of journalists later invaded a board meeting of the

Daily News and demanded further information. This invasion was greeted with undisguised hostility by the *Daily News* staff. The *Tribune* journalists were regarded as troublemakers who were upsetting the prospects of the most exciting development in Irish journalism since the launch of the *Evening Press* in the 1950s.

As it turned out, the hastily produced *Daily News* collapsed after just one week and brought the *Tribune* down with it. McLaughlin had been instrumental in hiring journalists for the *Daily News*. Some had left good jobs in Ireland and others had been head-hunted in the UK. Now, thanks to the totally irresponsible actions of McLaughlin, they were out of work and signing on at their local labour exchanges.

In my case, the weekly visit was to the garda station at Clondalkin, because no labour exchange existed there at the time. There was a very long queue at each visit because the Clondalkin Paper Mills, the largest employer in the district, was in its death throes at the time.

In the meantime, attempts were made to revive the *Sunday Tribune* by those of us who felt some responsibility to keep the jobs of those who would not get work elsewhere. I was very much involved in this, as were Colman Cassidy and Des Crowley of the business section of the paper. Conor Brady was also very keen to get the paper going again, even though he knew he would not be involved. His purpose was entirely altruistic in that he wished to help those he would leave behind. He and I had several meetings with possible purchasers or financiers of a revived product. These included the PMPA motor-insurance company, who had already become involved in other publishing projects; the venture capital section of Allied Irish Banks; and a group of businessmen involved in factoring new projects.

In the end, the *Sunday Tribune* title was sold through the

receiver and the courts to Vincent Browne. He relaunched the paper that still exists today, though on a much-reduced scale and with fewer pretensions towards quality.

My time on the dole was the most distressing and, indeed, the most depressing period of my life, and after a month or two I had convinced myself that I would never get a full-time job again. But in January 1983, *The Irish Times* advertised for a sports sub-editor and I applied. The interview was one of the most bizarre I had experienced. Ken Gray, the managing editor, at one stage asked me if I would take the job if it was offered to me. This naturally gave me a great boost and my confidence was increased when at the end of the interview the sports editor Gerry Noone leaned towards me and said, 'I'll see you across the road in half an hour.'

'Across the road' in Gerry's language meant the local hostelry and it was there that I was told I had a job at the *Times*. The only people happier than me at the news were Anita and my bank manager. At this stage, we had two young daughters, Ruth and Deirdre, a large mortgage and very little money.

The job in Fleet Street was a steady one, though it involved a great deal of night work in preparing the sports pages for publication. I was also involved from time to time in writing the occasional editorial on sporting matters, including the participation of cyclists such as Seán Kelly and Stephen Roche in the Tour de France. Eventually, I was given an opinion column of my own which appeared on the Focus page, a job I enjoyed very much.

After I had spent some time as a sports sub-editor, Conor Brady returned to the paper in an executive position in the features area. He approached me and told me I should apply for the position of Focus editor, in charge of the main features area, which had become vacant in a dramatic manner. John

Cooney had been in the post and was having some problems with Douglas Gageby. The paper's opinion columnists, myself included, were at the centre of the dispute.

Cooney decided to run these columns across the top of the page rather than down the side. Gageby wanted the columns to stay where the readers were used to seeing them. Cooney simply sent a note to the editor with the words of the paper's advertising slogan: 'Keep up with the Changing Times.' That note heralded the end of Cooney's reign as Focus editor.

Having taken over the job, one of my first tasks was to bring Conor Cruise O'Brien to lunch. O'Brien was one of the opinion columnists at the time and devoted almost every one of his columns to attacking the then Taoiseach, Charles J. Haughey. I felt that he should from time to time choose another subject, and I told him this over lunch at the Lord Edward seafood restaurant in Christ Church Place in Dublin.

After a while, it became obvious that O'Brien was not paying a blind bit of notice to what I had to say. His eyes and ears were fixed on what was happening at another table quite close by. Seated there were Pat O'Connor, Haughey's election agent, and a man who looked quite like Declan Costello, who was then a senior counsel. O'Connor had recently been caught voting twice in the general election and earned the soubriquet 'Pat O'Connor Pat O'Connor'. O'Brien began to mutter phrases such as, 'What's a decent man like Declan Costello doing having lunch with that man?'

Eventually, I convinced O'Brien that the man with O'Connor was not Declan Costello but simply someone who looked rather like him. The white wine was now flowing furiously and the Cruiser asked me the following question in a very loud voice: 'What's the difference between Danny Morrison and other people?' I replied that I did not know. O'Brien then answered in an even louder voice than before, with the obvious intention that O'Connor would hear him, 'Danny Morrison advocates the armalite in the one hand and the ballot paper in the other while OTHER PEOPLE advocate TWO armalites in the one hand and TWO ballot papers in the other.'

Back at the afternoon editorial conference, Gageby and his deputy Bruce Williamson told me that I was in remarkable shape for someone who had lunched with the Cruiser. Usually, the lunch victim, they said, would become overwhelmed by the Cruiser's aptitude for ordering more wine. I suppose I was able to hold my drink more than others at the time, but I have to admit to being overwhelmed by the cost of the meal, which came to more than £85, a massive sum back in the early 1980s. Gageby's editorial conferences, by the way, were more dramatic than those held by any other editor I had worked under. He was completely on top of his brief on most occasions, having, it would appear, stayed awake all night previously. 'That story was on the BBC World Service at 2.30 this morning,' he would say. Later he would comment on hearing another story on the BBC at 5.00 a.m. and on RTÉ at 7.30.

'What did we miss today?' he asked the news editor Conor O'Clery at the first conference I attended. Conor mentioned some minor court case or other having been missed by *The Irish Times*. Gageby replied that we did not miss that story and that it was on page twenty-five, halfway down column three. He appeared to know every day's paper off by heart by the time conference time came around, but on one occasion this was obviously not the case.

What was obvious was that he was in a foul humour. He held the paper up between finger and thumb as though it were the source of some highly infectious disease. 'This is the worst *Irish Times* I have ever seen!' he said. 'There isn't a single piece of fresh news in it. It's a disgrace.'

The silence from the paper's editorial executives was almost deafening. It was broken by the then news editor Eugene McEldowney. 'Douglas,' he said, 'that's yesterday's paper.'

Gageby's devotion to the army and his low regard for those who had served in the armed forces of other countries caused a stir at another conference I attended. The then pictures editor, Gordon Standing, ventured a comment about his time in the British Royal Air Force. The context was a remark by Conor Brady that the young garda recruits in Templemore were spending a lot of their time shining their buttons and not learning enough about how to fight crime.

Standing told the conference that he was amazed that the garda recruits had to shine their own buttons, adding that when he was in the RAF, self-shining buttons were supplied to officers and gentlemen like himself.

Gageby's complexion reddened. He peered out over his glasses and said in tones of very obvious irony: 'Gordon Standing, when you were in the RAF you didn't have to shine your buttons. Wasn't it well for you now, you fucking traitor.'

When the Troubles broke out in Northern Ireland Gageby was described in a letter by the British ambassador Andrew Gilchrist to his superior Kelvin White of the Western European Department of the Foreign and Commonwealth Office in London as a 'white nigger' because of his views on Northern Ireland. Marked 'Secret and Personal' on British embassy notepaper and dated 2 October 1969, the letter read:

Dear Kelvin,

Your letter of September 24th – Major McDowell and No. 10
Downing Street

2. I had McDowell to lunch today. It is all about something he
mentioned to me before, but now he is hotter under the collar
about it.

3. McDowell is one of the five (Protestant) owners of the Irish
Times, and he and his associates are increasingly concerned
about the line the paper is taking under its present (Protestant,
Belfast-born) Editor, Gageby, whom he described as a very
fine journalist, an excellent man, but on Northern questions a
renegade or white nigger. And apart from Gageby's editorial
influence, there is a difficulty lower down, whereby sometimes
unauthorised items appear and authorised items are left out.

4. So far (except for the last item) nothing new. But McDowell
went on to say that he now felt that a certain degree of guid-
ance, in respect of which lines were helpful and which unhelp-
ful, might be acceptable to himself and one or two of his friends
on the Board; this was what he had had in mind in telephoning
to No. 10.

5. Oddly enough I had had McDowell in mind in certain
conversations I had in London a fortnight ago. His present
approach requires rather careful handling and I shall discuss
it in London next week. I am writing this letter merely in
case you wish to brief No. 10 and to assure them that we will
do what we can to explore this opening. I am destroying the
correspondence.

A.G. Gilchrist

Major McDowell was extremely upset by this. As he told *The
Irish Times*, 'I have never used the words "white nigger" in my
life about anybody. I have always had the highest respect for
Douglas Gageby, both as a person and as a journalist.' He also
rejected the suggestion that he may have sought to interfere with
editorial policy. 'My only interest at that time was to help solve
the problems in Northern Ireland. I asked No. 10 Downing

Street if the Irish Times Ltd could contribute towards a peaceful and satisfactory outcome.'

About Douglas Gageby he said: 'The success of *The Irish Times* was entirely due to his editorial judgment, with which there was no interference from me or other persons on the board. He set *The Irish Times* on the path of being a newspaper for all of the people of the island of Ireland and this policy was enshrined in the objectives of the Irish Times Trust when it was established in 1974 to protect the editorial independence of the newspaper.' It seems obvious that the term 'white nigger' was Gilchrist's and certainly not McDowell's.

I soon realised that I was unsuited to the job of Focus editor and asked to be relieved of my post. The position was particularly demanding, and one of the problems was summed up to me by my sporting colleague Edmund Van Esbeck just before I took up the job. Every editor of every newspaper, Ned told me, wanted to put his own imprint on the publication. The editor could not demand of the news editor that there should be a major political crisis. The foreign editor could not be instructed to organise a war. The sports editor could not be told to ensure that Ireland wins the World Cup. The features editor could, however, be ordered about in all directions. That is what happened, but it was even more difficult than Ned had anticipated because Conor Brady also insisted in having his input into the features section. The result was that my own say in the features section was diminished even further.

Once, before I went on holidays, a series of short stories by well-known authors was organised. The idea was that during the holiday period *Irish Times* readers would have more time to read, and the short stories would help them pass the time during their vacations. While I was on holidays myself, Conor Brady organised another series in which leading businessmen gave their views on how the country's economy should be run. These articles were put at the top of each page with the short stories appearing below them.

I had just returned to the office after three weeks away when the phone rang. I heard the familiar tones of Ben Kiely at the other end of the line. The paper, in my absence, had informed the readers that Feargal Quinn of the Superquinn supermarket chain would be writing the next business article and that on the same day Benedict Kiely's short story would appear.

Ben had other ideas. In his wonderfully resonant tones he informed me that he was withdrawing his short story. 'My work,' he told me, 'will appear beneath no wee grocer.'

Fortunately there were other short stories in hand, but I must say I admired Ben for standing his ground. He went straight to Gageby and told him exactly what he had told me and that was that.

I went to Gageby, too, and told him I wanted out of the features job. He asked me to stay on for three months and to come back to him if I still felt the same way. Three months and ten seconds later I came back to him and said I still wanted out. His reply gave me an insight into the way he looked at the paper and its journalists. 'You have made the right decision,' he said. 'There are only two jobs in *The Irish Times*. One is writing … and I have the other one.'

— A Life Saved – Two Lives Lost —

Contrary to the general belief outside the newspaper business, reporters from rival papers usually regard each other as colleagues rather than competitors. This is especially evident amongst sports journalists, and on one particular occasion when I worked for the *Independent*, I was involved in saving the life of a reporter from *The Irish Times*.

The story started unexpectedly when a Spanish student, Martin Prieto, who was staying at our house in Clondalkin, was suddenly taken ill. He had developed a severe pain on the right-hand side of his lower abdomen and I brought him to our local GP and friend Rashid Bismillah, who immediately diagnosed acute appendicitis and had him removed to Jervis Street Hospital. Poor Martin's parents, who had just returned to Spain having visited him in Ireland, were back on the next available flight. The appendectomy went perfectly well and at the end of the week I set off for Harlech in north Wales to cover the Women's Home International Golf Championship.

My opposite number from *The Irish Times* was Edmund Van Esbeck, who covered golf from time to time but was later to become known as Ireland's most expert commentator on rugby. That Ned is still alive and enjoying a lengthy retirement is largely due to a remarkable coincidence and my own persistence.

We had arrived at Harlech by car, having taken the ferry from Dún Laoghaire to Holyhead. We booked into the Rum Hole Hotel beside the golf course and settled in for our day's work of checking the order of play, interviewing the Irish captain and writing our preliminary articles. That work done, we settled down to a leisurely dinner at which I enjoyed some red wine, while Ned, a teetotaller, sipped his tea.

From time to time I noticed him grimace. I asked him what was wrong. He was having some sort of stomach cramps, he told me, and hoped he was not suffering from poisoning. Next day the pains were worse and Ned's description of them matched perfectly those suffered by Martin Prieto less than a week earlier. I told him that it appeared he had acute appendicitis but he scoffed at the idea and reminded me that we had a job to do. A day later the pain was so bad that Ned stayed in bed at breakfast time but still refused medical attention. It was then that I decided to take the matter into my own hands. I rang the local doctor and told him there was a case of acute appendicitis at the Rum Hole Hotel.

The doctor, a retired practitioner standing in for the local GP, sounded slightly sceptical that a sports reporter from Ireland could be so sure of such a diagnosis. He would, he said, be the one to decide if it was appendicitis or not. He arrived quite promptly and Ned was in such a bad state that it was obvious not only that he needed his appendix removed but that it needed to be done as soon as possible. An ambulance was called and Ned was stretchered out of the hotel bound for the Caernarvon and Anglesea hospital in Bangor. I can still picture it pulling away, its siren blaring and its blue light flashing. I remember noting a plate on the rear door showing that it was built by PNM O'Hanlon of Longford in Ireland.

When the golf championship was over, I drove to Holyhead via Bangor and called into the hospital to visit Ned. I was shocked to the core by what I saw. Ned's appendix had burst on the way to hospital and he had arrived there in danger of death. He lay there very weak, white as the proverbial sheet and barely able to speak. I was told that he would not be strong enough to return to Ireland for a couple of weeks, so I left the hospital asking him to let me know when he would be well enough for me to visit him in Dublin. I drove on to Holyhead in good spirits that I had helped save Ned's life, but not knowing that the most harrowing period of my own life was about to begin.

Some weeks later, I had a phone call from Ned asking me to visit him in his house in Dundrum. An avid, some would say rabid, supporter of Arsenal Football Club, Ned had named his house Highbury after the club's stadium in north London. We had a good chat about the Harlech incident and other sporting moments we had shared, and then the phone rang. Ned's wife Mary came into the room and told me my mother was on the phone. I knew immediately that something was seriously wrong. My mother would not have known how to contact me at Ned's house unless she had rung Anita to find out where I was and she would not have done that unless something very urgent had arisen.

When I picked up the phone I discovered that my mother was distressed. Dad had been taken ill at work and brought by ambulance to Dr Steevens' Hospital. She didn't know if it was serious or not but felt she should go to the hospital as soon as possible. I left Ned's house in a hurry, drove to Walkinstown to pick up my mother and went on to the hospital, where we found Dad in a terrible state, paralysed and unable to speak. As it turned out my old school friend Seán Cooke, who had worked in CIÉ at Inchicore, where Dad was then employed, had been on ambulance duty that day and was the one who drove Dad to hospital.

It was obvious to me that my father was *in extremis* and could die at any moment; and it was clear that the doctors were very well aware that this was the case. Only immediate family were allowed at the bedside in Ward 11, which was reserved for men who were seriously ill. A sleepless night followed, and then another, before it became apparent that death would not come immediately. There would, instead, be more than three distressing months ahead of us.

The doctors were quick in their diagnosis of a stroke probably due to aneurysms in the brain. They were unable, however, to come up with any kind of prognosis. He could die immediately. He could make a full recovery. He could make a partial recovery. We would just have to wait and see. Back then in 1973, medical science was by no means as far advanced as it is today, and doctors did not have the benefit of the sophisticated technology that is now available to the medical profession. The medical staff did, however, have a great deal of compassion and understanding of the distress we were going through.

My relationship with my dad was, I suppose, typical of that between an elder son and his father. From time to time we had been like two stags battling for supremacy. Even though he did not drink, there were family rows, and I remember at least once intervening physically to take my mother's side. When the time had come for secondary school, he had opposed the idea and wanted me to go to the 'tech' and learn a trade. As a result our relationship had been distant and occasionally hostile, but I was now, to my own surprise, about to realise how much he really meant to me.

There didn't seem to be any point in telling him this for there was no way of knowing if he understood what anyone was saying. Instead, I found myself drawn to him in silence. I would go to his bedside every morning and shave him as he lay there almost motionless with tubes emerging from his nostrils. I would call back to see him after work, sometimes quite late at night.

Anita and I would bring our daughters Ruth and Deirdre to see him at weekends. Ruth, who was four years old at the time, was the apple of her grandad's eye, but Deirdre was just approaching her first birthday and hadn't the faintest idea about what was going on. Dad just lay there, almost without moving and unable to speak. Then one day, when he had been there for more than two months, we arrived and, to our amazement, he spoke. 'Hello Ruth,' he said, and a little vestige of a smile crept across his face. These, as it turned out, were his last words but he was not to die for quite some time and our own suffering had hardly begun.

All the same, as is the way of things in Dublin, there is hardly ever tragedy without some element of comedy. Also in the ward was a little white-haired man who looked like the archetypal Dublin Joxer. Like everyone else in Ward 11, he was in a bad way. He had tubes coming out of various parts of his body and at the end of one of them was a funnel-like device that I presumed was being used for medication or sustenance, as he appeared unable to swallow.

On Friday nights, two of Joxer's pals, men of a certain age, would arrive and keep him up to date about the doings of the regulars at the local pub, the results of the horse races and so on. They would also stage a remarkable, almost military, operation in which the doctors and nurses were very efficiently deceived. One of them would face outwards from the end of the patient's bed and scan the ward to see if Joxer was being observed by the staff. The other would face inwards towards the patient and wait for the signal from his pal. When the coast was clear the observer would exclaim 'Now!' His friend would produce a Baby Powers from his pocket, and pour the whiskey down the funnel. Almost instantaneously, a rosy glow would develop on Joxer's face and he would show his thanks to his friends by the only physical means available to him. He would give them a large and obvious wink.

Throughout Dad's illness, life had to continue for the rest of us. Mam would visit every day and my brother Diarmuid, then a young curate in Cabinteely in County Dublin, would arrive at the hospital whenever he could. I kept up my daily visits but was obliged to do my ordinary journalistic work at the *Indo*, and I also got involved in union matters, something I had obviously inherited from my father. My mother had been waiting to be called for a minor operation to remove a cataract from one of her eyes, and the call to St Michael's Hospital in Dún Laoghaire came during Dad's illness. She told us not to bother visiting her but to continue to go and see Dad in Steevens' as his was by far the more serious case. We did manage to go to Dún Laoghaire before she had her operation and she was delighted to see us.

In the meantime, problems had arisen in the *Sunday*

Independent sports section that required attention from the National Union of Journalists, of which I was an active member. Conor O'Brien, the paper's editor, in an unusual move, had agreed to meet us face to face on condition that we got together at some distance from the office so that he would not be seen talking directly to us. The venue chosen was an upstairs room in a pub on Eden Quay. Conor was a man of absolute integrity and there was little difficulty in making progress. The issue was resolved, but as the meeting ended I was called to the phone. The caller was my colleague Colm Smith, who asked me to ring my cousin Séamus Fitzpatrick at his home.

Séamus told me that there was bad news. Immediately I felt some relief at the prospect of poor Dad having died after such a long and terrible illness, but Séamus' next words were devastating. 'Your mother,' he said 'has died of a massive heart attack in St Michael's in Dún Laoghaire.'

Diarmuid now had to be found. He was not at his house in Cabinteely and I learned that he was having dinner with some other priests at a house in Ballsbridge. I took a taxi there to tell him the terrible news.

The family was now faced with a dreadful problem. Should we tell Dad that his wife had died? The medical staff at Dr Steevens' counselled very strongly that we should not. He was in no condition to be told. The shock would probably kill him. That night I was in shock myself. I had been preparing myself mentally for Dad's death and had been just about ready to accept it when the news of Mam's death struck so suddenly. In bed I began to get severe cramps in my arms and legs and then started to shake all over. Anita phoned Rashid Bismillah to see if a sedative would help, but he said it would be better for me to get through the trauma without medication.

The funeral took place in Greenhills parish church, with Diarmuid as one of the celebrants at the Mass. The entire Martin and Mullen clans turned up, as did many of my colleagues from work. I had always been shy about commiserating with bereaved people, but I now realised how important it was to have family, friends and colleagues around at such times. I remember particularly the kindness of my colleague David Faiers and his offers of financial assistance. David was outwardly something of a rogue, to say the least, but on this occasion I saw another side to him that he had kept hidden from almost everyone.

Back at my parents' house, Diarmuid, Anita and I went through my parents' belongings. Dad had stashed away a bundle of red ten-shilling notes for Ruth and Deirdre to show them, when they were able to understand, what the 'old money' was like. It was then that I found Mother's old mottled diary for 1933. On 16 June, she had written in pencil of her own bereavement:

> Mother taken suddenly ill in street. Two men called to house to tell us. Father went in Taxi. I waited for her to come back. Taken to Mercer's Hospital unconscious.' On 17 June: 'Mother still unconscious. Terribly worried. Wired for James.' On 18 June: 'Mother still unconscious. Doctors told me there was no hope for her. Stayed up all night with her in hospital. No hope.' On 19 June: 'Still no change. Absolutely broken hearted.' On 20 June: 'Went to station to meet James. Went back to hospital. Mother dying all day.' On 21 June she had written between asterisks the words 'Mother Dead' and 'May God have Mercy on her soul. Feeling broken hearted. Lost my dearest and best friend.

It was uncanny to read the words of my dead mother on the death of her own mother nine years before I was born. Even today, more than thirty years after I found that diary in my mother's house, her words bring tears to my eyes.

Back in Steevens', poor Dad had no idea that his wife had died. He lay there as usual and I shaved him once more, knowing that if I shared my grief with him it might bring his life to an end. After that it was back to the monotony of visiting each morning to shave him and each evening to see if there was any change in his condition.

Some weeks after Mam's death the doctors told me that although it might still cause him great shock it might now be better to give Dad the bad news as they felt he was beginning to notice Mam's absence. It was left to me to decide when the time would be opportune to tell him. When that moment came it was harrowing for all of us. In the course of one of my visits with Anita, Dad starting trying to say Mam's name. He was unable to say Eileen but managed to make a noise that sounded like 'aaaaa-eeeeee'. It seemed that he was asking for her so I took it on myself to say that she had died and had been buried in Dean's Grange. The response was awful. Unable to speak he roared and screamed his wordless anguish. I look back on that moment as the most heartbreaking of my own life. Not only did we realise how grief stricken my father was, but it also dawned on us for the first time that he may have been able to understand everything we had said to him during his illness. If we had known this for sure we might have been able to brighten up his time with stories from home, with news of what his two grandchildren were up to.

Christmas passed and one morning in January the hospital called to tell me that the end was near. I went to Ward 11 once more and spent the morning with him. During lunchtime I called to the office to explain the situation and then returned to Dr Steevens'. After an evening meal I was back at his bedside. His breathing was becoming more laboured. Anita was at home minding the children. Diarmuid was tied up with his priestly duties. I was alone with my father when he died. I heard the death rattle in his throat as life passed from him. I left Ward 11 for the last time not knowing if he realised I had been with him to the end.

Dad's obsequies were almost a replay of Mam's. The same priests, the same relatives, the same friends. There was just one eerie difference. A power failure left Greenhills Church in darkness on the evening of his removal. Tall church candles in brass candlesticks were placed along the aisle to guide mourners to their pews. It was a scene almost from a past century. For me, at thirty-one years of age, it was the beginning of a new stage in my life, the beginning of a more mature adulthood.

Those days, naturally, brought the family together. They evoked memories of the past, our childhood and the stories Mam and Dad had recounted about the days long before we were born.

Mam was the more expressive of the two. There were wistful hints about an old boyfriend called Kevin McCann. He was a builder and had given her a house on Sundrive Road, but she had sold it and gone to England to follow my father, who was working there briefly.

She had told of her own father taking her into O'Connell Street at the end of Easter Week in 1916 to view the ruins of central Dublin, which had been shelled by the British to force the rebels to surrender. 'Look at what the Huns did,' he said. That racist term had been very much in vogue in those war years in an attempt to depict the Germans as primitive savages. He had turned the slur on those who had invented it.

When she spoke of her father, however, she did so without the slightest feeling of affection. He had been, by all accounts, a drunk and a bully. He had driven her brother James to the desperation that led to his being severely wounded in the Dardanelles. He also seemed to have spent a great deal of the household funds on drink. Badly afflicted with arthritis in his latter years, he had been confined to a wheelchair and used to pay a local youngster to wheel him to the pub and back.

We talked of all those houses we had lived in and of the day that I, absent-mindedly, got the bus home from work for lunch, only to discover that I had gone to the wrong house as we had moved elsewhere the previous day.

It was providential that Diarmuid had been based in Ireland during those stressful months when our parents had died. After his ordination he had been sent to study at the Angelicum in Rome, and my father's last illness began not long after he had arrived home. After both our parents had died, he was sent back to Rome, on this occasion to look after pilgrims from the archdiocese of Dublin, who were preparing to converge on the city for the Holy Year of 1975. He was not to return, other than on occasional visits, until his installation as coadjutor archbishop of Dublin in 2003.

Diarmuid had not been the 'holy' type of person one associated with those who had a vocation for the priesthood. As a child he might have been far more accurately described as a 'holy terror'. He was noted throughout the extended family for throwing tantrums – in a family in which tantrum-throwing had been brought to a fine art.

Mam had perfected her own style of this art form and did a world-class act in pretending to be taken ill when things were not going her way. Uncle James, on his visits from London, calmed his nerves with Green Chartreuse. When Aunt Bridie was upset she took it out on those who wore poppies in November or those who voted for Fine Gael in general elections. I remember she once worked herself into a temper after she had come home from voting. An elderly and apparently illiterate woman had asked her help in marking her ballot paper and had then voted for Maurice Dockrell, the Fine Gael lord mayor of Dublin. Bridie's animus against Fine Gael was due to her experience during the civil war, when her first husband, Paddy Galway, had died not long after being released from the notorious Free State interrogation centre at Oriel House in Dublin.

On the Martin side, dispositions were somewhat calmer, except for our paternal grandmother, who was definitely in the premier league of tantrum-throwing. When things went badly for her she would issue a dire threat from her little house in Clonmany in County Donegal: 'I'm going out to drown myself on Binnion Strand.' Had she done so, there would have been a great deal of grieving among some members of her family, but others might not have been too upset.

She eventually died when I was eleven and my father had been quite distressed. He went to Donegal for the funeral, which was followed by a traditional country wake. He brought back two clay pipes that had been given out to mourners. Diarmuid used them to blow bubbles from and I, in far more grown-up fashion, filled mine with tea and smoked it.

Diarmuid, both as a child and teenager, could match any of his relations on the tantrum front and would frequently vent his anger on me. Mam was something of a collector of antiques and she once bought a Waterford Glass jug of ancient provenance, which my brother threw at me during one of his fits of temper.

All the same, as his elder brother, I developed a strong, protective sense towards him and ensured that he got home safely from school each day on the long journey from the Oblates in Inchicore to our house opposite the Ranch. Once, his class was let out early and he made his own way home. I remember still the terror that struck my heart when I could not find him. I ran all the way home preparing for the commotion when I announced that he had been kidnapped, but when I knocked at the door he answered it with my mother.

As children, our personalities differed in many ways. I remember my parents telling me that they watched the pair of us when we had been given our pocket money each week. O'Toole's shop in the Ranch was in view of the house and they would see Diarmuid stand at the window, working out what he could buy for his money, while I went in and splurged my few pence on whatever came first to mind. Diarmuid would, they said, always know exactly how much money he had in his pocket while I would never have the faintest idea.

I spent most of my time playing football either in the Memorial Park on the banks of the Liffey or frequently on more adventurous journeys with my friends to the Phoenix Park. There, jackets would be laid down to mark goalposts, and an elaborate procedure would begin in order to get the ball ready for the match. It would have to be pumped to the desired hardness as it would have lost pressure since the last outing. This was no simple matter. A small device, known as a 'friend', was used to link the ball to the bicycle pump that was needed to introduce the necessary amount of air. The 'friend' frequently slipped from the grasp of the person responsible for holding it in place. It would become hidden in the long grass and the sight of a group of small boys on their hands and knees peering at the ground in search of a lost 'friend' was a frequent one in the Dublin of those days.

The tradition of placing coats or jerseys on the ground as

goalposts had a disadvantage in that both teams would have to agree on whether or not a goal had been scored. This procedure could take a long time and prolonged the games well beyond the legal ninety minutes. There were problems, too, when you arrived home and your mother asked where your jersey was. If you had left it behind in the Phoenix Park you faced the long journey back to retrieve it. Nowadays, to send a boy of ten on his own to the fields of the Phoenix Park as darkness fell would be regarded as extremely dangerous, but Ireland was different in those days.

My brother had no interest in football and in any case his playmates were from a different age cohort, so we didn't see much of each other out on the streets. At home, however, there were elaborate motor races in which mother's clothes pegs were used as cars, and in the backyard Diarmuid's fascination with the bus routes of Dublin was indulged. He knew the number and destinations of all the buses in Dublin and drove them round the yard in his imagination and much to the fascination of his elders. One neighbour, Paddy Keller, made quite realistic-looking bus stops that were planted in the ground at suitable intervals to allow him to stop and take on imaginary passengers.

As we sat and spoke about those days after our parents had died, it struck me that his personality had changed dramatically since the days of his tantrums. He had continued to be a menace well into his teens, but after he entered the seminary at Clonliffe in Dublin, his temperament calmed. He became more considerate of other people's feelings and has remained so to this day. My two daughters, neither of whom remember the bad old days, think the world of him.

His return to Rome was designed to be a temporary one to look after the needs of the Dublin pilgrims. He knew the city well and had become quite Italian in his outlook in many ways. This was largely due to the policy of the famous, some would say infamous, Archbishop John Charles McQuaid. While students and priests from the other dioceses of Ireland would live in the Irish College over near St John Lateran's, those from Dublin were sent elsewhere.

Archbishop McQuaid did not want his students or priests to become part of what effectively had become an Irish ghetto in the centre of Rome. It was his intention that a broader outlook be formed, so my brother was lodged at the Teutonic College just through the arch to the left of St Peter's Basilica.

Diarmuid later became the Teutonic College's vice-rector and was in a position to cater for his family members when we visited. I particularly recall the German nuns who ran the college being all of a fluster for an important visitor who was coming to a lunch to which I had been invited. Little 'national' flags were placed on the tables, but they were not the black, red and yellow banner of the German Federal Republic. They were, instead, the blue and white of Bavaria. The special guest was Joseph Cardinal Ratzinger, later to be known as Pope Benedict XVI.

Later, and in keeping with family tradition, Diarmuid began to move house frequently. The first move was a very short one into an apartment in a building just a few yards away from the Teutonic College, where he had lived in quite monkish quarters. In the new building he had enough room to accommodate visitors, and we spent one memorable holiday there. It was memorable for the wrong reasons, mind you. The temperature was in the mid-40s and the washing machine was in almost continuous use to clean sweat-laden clothes.

I was at this stage living in Moscow, working as a foreign correspondent, and one of the items thrown into the washing machine one afternoon happened to contain my passport. It emerged as a sodden mass but was replaced quickly and efficiently by the embassy. What was of greater importance and more difficult to replace was my Russian multi-entry visa, a separate document that had been inserted into the passport for safekeeping. Each day for the rest of that holiday I spent several hours at the consular section of the Russian embassy on the Via Merulana dealing in the sweltering heat with the bureaucracy inherited from the Soviet Union and made more complicated by the Russian Federation of Boris Nikolayevich Yeltsin.

Diarmuid's next move was to a converted water tower in the Piazza San Calisto in Trastevere, and this was made available to us when he was away on diplomatic missions as secretary of the Vatican Commission for Justice and Peace. Trastevere was, and still is, Rome's most vibrant quarter, and we became well acquainted with the area almost as residents, for we spent a great deal of time there minding Diarmuid's flat.

He was living in the water tower when the Pope announced that he would ordain him as titular bishop of Glendalough. The ordination ceremony took place in St Peter's on the feast of the Epiphany and was the occasion of a large family gathering. Interestingly, the Russian ambassador, Gennady Uranov, held a reception to mark my brother's episcopal ordination while the Irish ambassador to the Holy See did not.

Ambassador Uranov and I had known each other from my Moscow days. He had previously been ambassador to Ireland, where he was one of the most popular members of the diplomatic corps. The occasion was covered for *The Irish Times* by Paddy Agnew, who was as surprised as I was when his reference to my presence there as the new bishop's brother was removed from his report by someone in Dublin.

There was a certain antipathy within *The Irish Times* to the Catholic Church, and when Paddy Agnew, himself an Ulster Protestant and friend of my brother's, wrote a profile of Diarmuid on the occasion of his episcopal ordination, I was confronted in the editor's office by two senior journalists. They disdainfully referred to the new bishop in my presence as 'a middle-aged man in a frock'. One of these men has since left the paper, but the other is still a senior editorial executive.

Later, Diarmuid moved out of Italy to Geneva, the 'Protestant Rome', where he was permanent observer to the United Nations organisations there, and to the World Trade Organisation. For a brief period, the two senior churchmen of that city were Irish. My brother ministered to the city's Catholic population, while the Presbyterian dean of Jean Calvin's former church, the Cathedral of St Pierre, was Rev William McComish, an Ulsterman who had been educated at Trinity College, Dublin. They both got on very well together – to the surprise of those who thought that Irish Protestants and Catholics should be sworn enemies.

I visited Diarmuid just once in Geneva, where he was supposed to be in charge but was in fact under the control of a flock of tiny Mexican nuns who ran the nunciature on military lines. They produced a decent lunch, which was also attended by my colleague Lynn Geldof, who worked for UNESCO there at the time, and by Richard and Mary Fallon and their children. The Fallons had been attached to the embassy at Moscow, and Richard at this stage was a diplomat at the embassy to the UN.

Diarmuid's appointment as coadjutor archbishop of Dublin with the right to succeed Cardinal Desmond Connell came as something of a surprise. In many respects it was a sideways move, for he was already an archbishop, but in a situation in which he was in extremely close contact with the 'head office' in Rome.

Despite local opinion here, Dublin as a diocese and Ireland as a country are remote postings and would not be regarded as important as many other dioceses in the eyes of the Vatican.

Diarmuid's arrival to the see of Dublin was favourably received by Irish sources, though strongly criticised by the British *Sunday Times*, which took the attitude that local clergy had been overlooked and a 'foreigner' had been given the job. It also, in apparent ignorance of how diplomacy works, presumed that 'conservative' statements of Vatican policy made by him at conferences abroad also reflected his personal opinion.

Diplomats are required to put forward the views of their masters. These views may coincide with their own personal opinions, but this is not always necessarily the case. My brother and I simply don't discuss these matters, so I don't know precisely where he stands on the nuances of Catholic doctrine. He would, however, be regarded by most as a man of deep compassion whose feet are firmly planted on the planet on which we live.

These qualities were of great assistance to us all in those trying times after the death of our parents. We are still close friends today and while Diarmuid is a regular visitor for the family Christmas dinner, Anita and I, our daughters, their spouses and their children have been to dinner in Archbishop's House in Drumcondra, where, on such occasions, Diarmuid does the cooking himself.

I have to admit that the visits to Drumcondra hardly make up for the occasional use of the converted water tower in Trastevere. They do allow me, however, to respond from time to time to the question 'What did you do on Saturday night?' with the statement: 'I was above in the brother's palace for dinner.'

— 'Viva Nelson Mandela, Viva!' —

On the afternoon of 11 February 1990, Anita and I sat in our living-room to watch the live TV report of the release of Nelson Mandela from the Victor Verster Prison in the Western Cape. There was a long delay before the world's most famous prisoner was to be seen emerging from his twenty-seven-year ordeal, and during that delay the phone rang.

At the other end was the *Irish Times'* news editor Eugene McEldowney. He opened his conversation with a question: 'How soon can you get to South Africa?' As soon as I heard that, I was mentally packing my bags and minutes later I was doing so in reality.

I had been in South Africa nine years earlier and knew my way around Cape Town and Johannesburg. I also knew that journalists were regarded with extreme suspicion by the apartheid regime and that one false move could lead to expulsion.

By that evening, I was on my way to London to apply for a work permit at the South African embassy. Irish citizens did not need visas for South Africa, but in the case of journalists a work permit took the place of a visa. Entry into the country would have been possible without one, but once you started to work, the length of your stay was in the hands of the authorities. In London, the South Africans delayed issuing my permit, presumably because I was on their files as being undesirable. On my previous visit I had broken the terms of my work permit by interviewing the anti-apartheid activist Fatima Meer, who, as a 'banned person' under the apartheid laws, was not permitted to be quoted in the press.

After a couple of days in London, the embassy finally relented and I was on my way. By the time I arrived, Nelson Mandela had given a press conference in Cape Town, but this, like all general press conferences, was widely reported by the international news agencies. What I wanted to do was to get a personal interview with the great man in his home in Soweto as soon as he finished his public engagements down at the Cape.

While the rest of the world rejoiced at Mr Mandela's release there were those in South Africa who took a very different view, and on my arrival at Johannesburg I heard that an anti-Mandela rally was to be held in Pretoria that very evening. The overnight flight had been pretty tiring, with a brief refuelling stop in Nairobi on the way, but fortunately trips to South Africa do not involve jet lag, so I was in reasonable shape to head northward with friends Patrick and Sandra Laurence.

What awaited me in Pretoria was a scene of incredible bigotry, viciousness and fear from twenty thousand right-wing Afrikaners, who had congregated in the city from all over the Transvaal. The turnout had built up from five thousand in the early afternoon and was the first significant manifestation of a white backlash to Nelson Mandela's release. It was also a significant challenge to President F.W. de Klerk and his National Party government. The rally was staged by Dr Andries Treurnicht, whose party held 39 of the 165 seats in the all-white parliament and was intent on gaining the support of a majority of the Afrikaner *volk*.

He gave the crowd the sort of speech they wanted to hear: 'When the storm blows, the mouse lies down, but the eagle soars high.' His message to President de Klerk was: 'We are not a nation of mice.'

Hands shot into the air in what in many cases closely resembled the Nazi salute. At the edge of the crowd, three black youths who had inadvertently strayed into the area were chased away with taunts of: 'Can you run, kaffir?' Dr Treurnicht, a former divinity student of the Dutch Reformed Church, told his listeners that the tiger in the Afrikaner *volk* had been awakened, a strange choice of metaphor in a country in which there were no tigers but where lions abounded.

One young man near where we stood wore an effigy of Nelson Mandela around his neck attached to a hangman's noose. The crowd had now been built into a frenzy of Afrikaner nationalism and naked racism, but earlier there had been a picnic atmosphere in the sunken gardens of Church Square. This was the designated assembly point for the march to the town hall where Dr Treurnicht was to deliver his address.

Buses arrived carrying outsized farmers from the rural areas or *platteland*, a virtual nation of rugby second-row forwards. There were speeches and songs, and every speech and every song raised the tension further.

Then a *dominee*, or minister of the Reformed Church, gave a reading from the Book of Joel: 'Gather together the people, sanctify the church, assemble the ancients, gather the little ones and they that suck at the breasts; let the bridegroom go forth from his bed and bride out of her bride chamber.

'Between the porch and the altar, the priests, the Lord's ministers shall weep and say "Spare O Lord, spare thy people and give not their inheritance to reproach, that the heathen should rule over them. Why should they say among the nations: Where is their God?"'

The message was clear. The Afrikaner *volk* was a people chosen by God who were threatened by the black heathens led by the newly liberated Nelson Rolihlahla Mandela. After that the crowd stood to attention for 'Die Stem van Suid Afrika' played over the public address system and sung hoarsely in Afrikaans.

By now, some members of the crowd had begun to turn on the media. 'Go home to England', they were told. For myself, standing in the middle of the crowd as I was, the thought of explaining my nationality to the gang of tough-looking guys causing the disturbance was not a particularly pleasant one. I simply kept my mouth shut.

Then Ferdi Hartzenberg, once de Klerk's minister for education and who had defected to Dr Treurnicht, began his warm-up speech. The Boers had defeated the British Empire and would, he told us, never give in. 'A veld fire has started and it will spread until the *volk* has reconquered the land. F.W. de Klerk has made a reputation for himself on the international stage but has turned his back on his own people. We challenge you to go to the *volk*,' he said, calling for an all-white general election.

The crowd then prepared for its march to the town-hall

square, where two flags had been placed on the statue of Andries Pretorius, who had led the *volk* to victory over the Zulus at the battle of Blood River in 1838. One was the old *Vierkleur*, the green, red, white and blue flag of Paul Kruger's old Transvaal Republic. The other, ominously, was the red and white banner of the Third Reich with its black swastika in the centre. Those who opposed Nelson Mandela's release had made their sentiments abundantly clear.

Next morning I started working towards getting that interview with Mr Mandela. It was a daunting task and I was not encouraged by Kader Asmal before I left Dublin. Kader, who later held two ministerial posts in the post-apartheid government, was then dean of humanities at Trinity College, Dublin. 'Your chances of getting an interview with Mr Mandela,' he told me, 'are nil.'

Undaunted, I went to the ANC headquarters and was told the same thing. I did, however, get an interview with Walter Sisulu, Mr Mandela's number two, and Sven Oste of the influential Swedish newspaper *Dagens Nyheter* accompanied myself and Patrick Laurence of *The Johannesburg Star* to talk to him. This was a stroke of luck of which I intended to take full advantage. Sven was glad to have an opportunity to interview Walter Sisulu and to some extent he owed *The Irish Times* a favour.

Mr Mandela's African National Congress – the ANC – had been ignored by most Western governments and effectively opposed by some, including Margaret Thatcher's Tory administration in the UK. Successive Swedish governments, on the other hand, not only supported the ANC politically, but had also been giving it an annual grant of several million US dollars for quite a few years.

I was sure, therefore, that if anyone was going to get the call to interview Nelson Mandela it would be the representative of *Dagens Nyheter*. Sven promised me that if he did get the call he would ask that I should be allowed to do an interview as well, and that was the way it turned out. Early on the morning of 22 February, Sven rang to say that he had been given the go-ahead for an interview and that Zwelakhe Sisulu, Walter's son, who was in charge of arrangements, had agreed to fit me into Mr Mandela's very heavy schedule.

We were told to be at Mr Mandela's house at 11 a.m. and to wait there until the interviews took place. We arrived at the house in the Orlando district of Soweto in good time only to find it surrounded by a large crowd of onlookers, as well as a group of international journalists trying desperately to get interviews with the great man. At the gate into the Mandela garden, an official looked up his list. It was a nervous moment. Then he said, '*Dagens Nyheter*,' and Sven was allowed in. My heart beat faster and then he said, '*Irish Times*'. Soon I was sitting in the sunshine of Nelson Mandela's garden.

There were no mobile phones in those days so I could not get in touch with the office. I simply hoped that the interview would be done and dusted in time for me to get back to Johannesburg and ring the office before the afternoon editorial conference. This was not to be, for it was Nelson Mandela's first day at home and, as it turned out, his schedule was arranged so that I would be his final visitor of the day.

Those who got in before me included the British ambassador, Sir Robin Renwick, for official talks on the sanctions that had been imposed on South Africa by the international community and opposed by Mrs Thatcher. There was a delegation from the black-consciousness movement, AZAPO, and one from the South African Clothing and Textiles Union, who had seen to it that *Madiba* had exchanged his prison garb for some very smart business suits. In a similar manner, the automotive workers in Port Elizabeth had gone to the head of the BMW plant to tell him: 'You are going to build a special car for Mr Mandela. It can be any colour you like as long as it's red.'

There were less formal visitors, too. Mr Banda from down the road dropped in to welcome his neighbour back home. A group of elegant elderly ladies, Mr Mandela's contemporaries, arrived, and those in the garden could hear the entire group singing together. Traditional chiefs from different tribal groupings also came to pay their respects. From time to time Mr Mandela emerged for a group photograph. He looked calm and self-possessed, but each time he appeared the crowds outside the garden would erupt into cheers. By now lunchtime had come and gone and my stomach had begun to rumble. There was a small grocery shop nearby but I wasn't going to take the chance of going there in case I wasn't let back into the garden.

To pass the time I spoke to the onlookers on the other side. One of them, bizarrely, a Welshman with a Wexford father, who had been in UCD with the Irish foreign minister, Gerry Collins, offered me a tomato. I accepted it gladly.

The dignitaries continued to arrive. Mr Mandela's voice raised in emotion could be heard from inside: 'Terror, I recognise you after all these years.' He was speaking to Patrick 'Terror' Lekota, who was later to become South Africa's minister for defence. Educated by the Irish Christian Brothers, Lekota had gained his nickname not for any clandestine activities, but for his unrelenting enthusiasm on the football field.

By now it was approaching 5.00 p.m. and my stomach was rumbling like a pre-eruption volcano when finally an official emerged from the little red-brick house and called my name. I was brought into the front room, a small space with bookshelves and a little leatherette couch. Nelson Mandela smiled and asked me to sit down beside him. He was curious about Ireland and thankful for the support given to him there. He knew about having been granted the Freedom of the City of Dublin and was quite specific that he would come to Ireland in person to accept the honour.

In recent times there have been stories and even a film made about his relationship with one of his warders, Warrant Officer Gregory. The story has been told of a friendship springing up between the two men, one of them a political leader who had attempted to end the regime that employed the other. What Nelson Mandela said to me on that day ran absolutely contrary to that account. He spoke straightforwardly of his own opportunism and did not express any sentiment of friendship towards his jailer.

'Well, you know,' he told me, 'the first occupation of a person who goes to prison is the cultivation of good relations with warders, because a warder can be more important than the minister for justice or the commissioner of prisons. You might say to a warder, "I want four blankets," and he will look up the regulations and say, "No, the regulations say you must only receive two blankets," and you come back with empty hands. But if you go to the section warder that you have cultivated and you ask for the same thing, he goes to the stores for the blankets and he takes them out and he gives them to you. Because they can only persecute you through the warders, then if you get the support of a warder, he can give you a bit of advice even before he commits some form of cruelty.'

Most of the rest of the interview was taken up with the intricacies of the political situation at that time, with a strong emphasis on the maintenance of sanctions against South Africa until a political settlement was reached. But he did talk of his vision of the country's future. Education was the key. 'I would like to take the opportunity to clarify a false impression that has got around which suggested that the ANC puts liberation before education. This has never been the case. I have asked the young people in Soweto to return to school and in fact they are taking my advice.

'But the problem is when they follow my advice they go back to school and find there is no space for them and no properly qualified teachers, and the community and the parents have no control over the education system. It is the government, the whites, that determine the education they are to receive.'

But the whites were not to be regarded as enemies: 'I do hope that every white man and woman in South Africa, Afrikaners and English, will give full support to the initiatives that Mr de Klerk has taken. I accept that the Afrikaners, like any other European group in this country, are part and parcel of our population and, secondly, they are in government. They are the only people for apartheid with whom we can negotiate.

'The political situation set-up prevents us from being close to them. But if the political set-up is changed, then our relationship can change. At present, our people are revolted by the fact that Afrikaans is the language of the oppressor and there is great opposition because of that.'

Typing out those words later in the day I thought of my last visit to the country in 1981 when the Irish rugby team, against the wishes of the vast majority of their compatriots, went on a tour of the apartheid state. It brought back memories of their captain, Fergus Slattery, addressing a group of local rugby alickadoos. He began with the words *Dames en Heere*. His use of the language of the oppressor drew the loudest cheer of the evening. The cheer, of course, had come from the oppressors. For me it was a moment when I was far from proud to be Irish.

I was very proud, though, to have interviewed Nelson Mandela, to have sat with him on his little couch and to have talked with him about himself and his country. There is a false impression among many that all journalists are cynical and unemotional people. The feeling is that we are motivated entirely by self-interest. Well, nothing could have been further from the truth that evening. Leaving the house and heading for my hired car, I passed a group of little girls playing the games that little girls play. Added to their skipping rhymes on this occasion was a new chant: 'Viva Nelson Mandela, viva!'

Back in my room in the Johannesburger Hotel I jumped for joy and punched the air. The adrenalin was still surging when I rang the office. The voice at the other end was that of a deputy news editor known to his colleagues as 'Grumpy'. The conversation went something like this:

'Why didn't you ring in time for the conference? Where the fuck have you been?'

'Well,' I replied, 'I have been sitting in the sunshine in a man's garden since early this morning and I just got back to the hotel a few minutes ago.'

'My God, you have some nerve ...'

'You didn't ask me whose garden I was sitting in,' I retorted.

'Whose garden?'

'Nelson Mandela's garden.'

There was a pause, a silence and then the words. 'I'd better put you on to the editor.'

It was now late on Thursday. I spoke to Conor Brady, who made his decision quickly. He would instruct the editor of the weekend section to throw out the front page arranged for Saturday. I should write a very short front-page piece for the following morning's edition to say that Nelson Mandela would be coming to Dublin. After that I should write an entire page on the Mandela interview.

Back in Dublin, I was quizzed by friends and colleagues about my impression of Nelson Mandela. The most interesting conversation was with my friend Breandán Ó hEithir. I told Breandán that the overwhelming impressions I had from the man were his aura of dignity and his total lack of bitterness against his enemies. 'That came over to us back here even from the TV coverage,' Breandán replied. 'You know,' he added, 'if it was one of our fellows who had been released after twenty-seven years in prison the first word on his lips would have been "Vengeance".'

On that trip to South Africa, as well as talking to Nelson Mandela and Walter Sisulu, I managed to meet and talk with other leaders of the anti-apartheid movement. They included Ahmed Kathrada, Mac Maharaj, Murphy Morobe and, most memorably, Archbishop Desmond Tutu at his official residence, Bishop's Court in Cape Town.

Desmond Tutu is a small and extremely passionate and articulate man, who is self-conscious about his height. He spoke expansively, gesticulating frequently. He made a very good point about the ANC, which, according to extreme-right politicians – notably Dick Cheney – was a terrorist organisation. Cheney had already expressed his opinion on Nelson Mandela. Like the racists I had seen in Pretoria, he wanted the ANC leader to remain in jail and had voted against a proposal for his release in the House of Representatives. On that basis I have since regarded Cheney as having a distinctly evil streak in his character.

Archbishop Tutu pointed to the facts. The ANC's record on

the 'armed struggle' had been purely rhetorical for quite some time. In other words, the 'armed struggle' continued to be a policy platform of the ANC even though no 'armed struggle' was now taking place. Its removal from ANC policy before talks with the apartheid regime would result in the removal of an important bargaining chip in forthcoming talks.

It remained questionable, in any event, as to which side was terrorist. The government could hardly be described as legitimate since it insisted that its electorate consisted of less than ten per cent of the population while oppressing the majority by force of arms. It could be argued with increasing justification that the legitimate army of South Africa was Umkhonto we Sizwe (known locally as MK), the armed wing of the ANC, which represented the large majority of South Africa's people. That army had, however, been inactive for quite some time, and comparisons between MK and the IRA, which was then still extremely active, were hardly legitimate.

Claims of similarity had been made by many in Europe, not only by supporters of the IRA, but also by right-wingers who wished to discredit the ANC. Archbishop Tutu made a very clear distinction between the two. He put it this way: '… what we are saying and have said in other statements before, is we understand why people can resort to violence and that our situation is different from the Northern Ireland situation in that our guys did not have the possibility of parliamentary procedures and channels which the IRA do have. I mean they could participate in the political process.'

The IRA and its supporters in Sinn Féin had the vote. The political options of the vast majority of South Africans, whether of African, mixed race or Indian origin, did not include voting. The choices open to them were limited to direct action against a minority government that up to the arrival of F.W. de Klerk as president had hoped to remain in power at the point of a gun. De Klerk at least realised that the future of his country depended on the lifting of sanctions, which could only be achieved through progress towards democracy.

The interview with Archbishop Tutu over, it was time for a very British afternoon tea in Bishops Court's main reception room. There, portraits of the stern white Anglican prelates who preceded the current archbishop looked down on the remarkable scene of their black successor entertaining a congregation composed mainly of patrician English South African ladies. He did so, it should be said, with unreserved panache.

Representatives of the government were much less forthcoming about being interviewed by *The Irish Times* than were Nelson Mandela, Walter Sisulu and Desmond Tutu. Attempts to achieve balance by talking to National Party leaders met resistance from almost all sides. There were some who were helpful. David Graaf, son of Sir de Villiers Graaf, did his best. His background had been in the old United Party of Jan Smuts and he had latterly joined de Klerk's National Party. He was, however, regarded with some suspicion by the 'bitter-enders' of Afrikaner nationalism and his influence was, therefore, somewhat restricted. He and another National Party MP, an Afrikaner with the unusual name of P.J. Farrell, a potato farmer from Bethlehem in the Orange Free State, made some unsuccessful overtures.

In the end it was the suave, English-speaking white South African member of parliament, Glen Babb, who finally pulled the right strings. Babb was a very strong supporter of de Klerk's new policies and wanted the world to know more about them.

It took a long time to convince the National Party that they should talk to someone from Ireland. This was somewhat surprising, for the party and the influential Afrikaner Broederbond – the secret society that ran it – had sent delegations to Dublin some years earlier in order to sound out the Irish government's views on progress towards democracy.

On one occasion, my colleague Paddy Smyth and myself were invited to dinner in the Conrad Hotel by two men who wanted to ascertain our views of the South African situation. The men purported to be academics from leading universities, but the dinner took a totally different course when I recognised one of them as Pieter de Lange, the Broederbond's leader.

Babb promised to deliver a top National Party minister, and he was as good as his word. The problem was that I had already returned to Ireland by the time he was able to organise anything. Back in Dublin, I received a fax from Babb to say that the National Party's ebullient foreign minister, Pik Botha, would meet me a week later in Cape Town. I set out once again on the long air journey, this time with stops at Nairobi and Johannesburg, before arriving at what is known to Afrikaners as the 'Mother City'.

Botha received me in his office on the seventeenth floor of the Hendrik Verwoerd building, in which the main lobby was dominated by a huge granite bust of the eponymous father of apartheid. I had to wait some time before Pik Botha arrived. When he did, he spoke in the hoarse voice of someone who had perhaps not had much sleep the night before.

His answers to my questions were long, convoluted and punctuated by periods of condescension towards the ANC and the black population in general. 'The man who washes your car sooner or later wants to own a car. The man who polishes the rugby ball wants to play rugby sooner or later. These,' he told me, 'are the elementary facts that we brought ourselves to accept, and it is our responsibility to persuade our people that we are not handing over, we are improving, in our opinion, the white man's security position.'

Botha, for all his condescension, had been on the liberal, *verligte*, wing of the National Party, as opposed to those such as his namesake P.W. Botha, who was decidedly conservative, or *verkrampte*. He had been foreign minister for thirteen years when I interviewed him, and in 1978 had stood for the party leadership and failed. In doing so, however, he successfully blocked the candidature of Mr Connie Mulder, who was not only more *verkrampte* than P.W. Botha but also a corrupt politician who brought the party into further disrepute in a financial scandal that became known as 'Muldergate'. This led to the resignation in disgrace of Prime Minister B.J. Vorster.

Despite his condescension, Pik Botha displayed a kernel of racial tolerance that marked him out from many of his fellow party members. He spoke to me at a time when the ANC and the National Party were in serious negotiations on the country's future at Groote Schuur, the former mansion of Cecil Rhodes, who had been Britain's leading imperialist in Africa.

Botha told me he had spoken the previous evening to a leading ANC representative and had said to him: "'Look. We're all in the one boat, one ship, and the sharks on the left and the sharks on the right are not going to distinguish between us when we fall overboard." And he completely agreed with me. He said: "You are so right and we realise it, too."'

Like many white South Africans, Botha was worried that the ANC in power would nationalise everything in sight. There was, mind you, a certain irony in this, for the National Party had been a prime nationaliser in its day in an attempt to balance the economic power of the Afrikaner population with that of the English speakers who controlled the wealth of the country. 'Maybe,' he said, 'the market-oriented system has become associated with apartheid. Then it is essential for the government to take a look, to get rid of apartheid once and for all ...' These were words that would have previously been anathema to all Afrikaners. 'That dream,' he said, 'has failed.'

These were striking admissions from the foreign minister of a country that had brazened it out against world opinion for almost half a century. He was signalling the beginning of the end of the most evil political system that had emerged since the end of the Second World War.

My return to Johannesburg coincided with the end of the Groote Schuur talks and to my great surprise I found myself on the same flight as a large part of the ANC negotiating team. They included the leader of the South African Communist Party, Joe Slovo, and Alfred Nzo, who was to take over Pik Botha's position as foreign minister when democracy finally arrived in 1994.

I introduced myself to Slovo on the plane and his first words to me when I told him I was from Ireland were, 'How's Kader?' I had got to know Kader Asmal quite well when he was dean of humanities and had lunched with him several times in Trinity. I did not realise, however, the high esteem in which he was held in the ANC and that he would, in fact, be placed number four in the party's electoral list in 1994 behind the party's number one, Nelson Mandela.

Kader himself was well aware of his own importance, and I remember over one particular lunch some years earlier he told me that he was certain apartheid was coming to an end. When it ended he did not want to become foreign minister but would prefer to be director general of the Department of Foreign Affairs, a post that carried a greater security of tenure.

I did not realise, either, that my interviewee, Pik Botha, had embarked on a journey that would lead, in 2000, to his application for membership of the ANC and a declaration of support for Nelson Mandela's successor, President Thabo Mbeki.

I returned to Dublin very satisfied with my work in South Africa and looked forward to working there again, preferably as the resident correspondent of *The Irish Times*. This was to happen in 1994, but under tragic circumstances that no one could possibly have foreseen at the time.

I am convinced, however, that my work in South Africa in 1990 played a major part in my selection as Moscow correspondent a year later, at a time when the communist system in Russia was about to meet the same fate as that of apartheid in South Africa.

— Good Times —

After a period editing the Saturday column of *The Irish Times*, I became tourism and aviation correspondent, and was elected father of the chapel of the National Union of Journalists at a crucial time in the newspaper's development. As such, I led the union's side in negotiations for a house agreement that would finally bring the latest technology into the journalistic area of the paper.

The talks with management were long and detailed and at one stage involved getting the help of Patrick McEntee, the senior counsel, to sort out a major difficulty between ourselves and editorial management. Finally, the deal was struck and passed by a very large majority of the membership. After that it was back to work as a journalist; and then a series of events took place that allowed me to achieve my ambition and become a foreign correspondent.

Conor O'Clery, who had been based in Moscow for a few years, was moving to Washington, and the job of Moscow correspondent became vacant. The post was advertised internally at grade E, which had a salary equivalent to that of assistant editor. I was told later that after the interviews the field was narrowed down to myself and Paddy Smyth, who is now the paper's foreign editor.

In any event, I got the job and Paddy was very gracious about it. But the reaction of another unsuccessful candidate was to walk up to me in the newsroom and spit in my face.

The paper then sent me on a course in Russian language and culture at the Trade Management Institute at Blackrock in Dublin. This was an educational establishment financed by the US philanthropist Chuck Feeney to help promote business ties with certain parts of the Soviet Union, especially the Baltic states of Estonia, Latvia and Lithuania.

I was given one-to-one tuition by Dmitri Tsiskirashvili, who is now a lecturer in the Russian department at Trinity College Dublin. Dmitri was a typical Soviet citizen in that his father was Georgian, his mother was a Byelorussian from Poland, and he himself had been raised in Estonia. His exceptional teaching skills had me on course to speak understandable Russian very quickly.

He also gave me some valuable advice on how to deal with certain situations that might arise with the local bureaucracy and with policemen looking for bribes. The course, which lasted a month, gave me a good basic grounding to prepare me for what turned out to be a much more difficult task than anyone had anticipated.

Before I took up the job, Lord Killanin, the former president of the International Olympic Committee, invited me for drinks at his house in Ranelagh. He had moved to this modest terraced house after selling his large residence in Lansdowne Road. In the course of the afternoon he told a remarkable story. He began by saying, with some amusement in his voice: 'I wish I could help you with some contacts in Moscow but all my old Cambridge chums there have died.'

The 'Cambridge chums' in question had belonged to the most successful Soviet spy ring in the UK. They included Anthony Blunt, Queen Elizabeth's art adviser, and the diplomats Kim Philby, Donald MacLean and Guy Burgess.

Killanin went on to tell a bizarre tale set in Dublin. He had been walking in St Stephen's Green when he spotted none other than Guy Burgess, who was making a drunken nuisance of himself by accosting young men and making sexual advances to them. Killanin had been at Eton and Cambridge with Burgess and therefore knew him reasonably well.

'I did what my father had advised me to do with drunken nuisances,' Killanin told me, 'and decided to put much more drink into him so that he would become incapable of continuing to be a pest. I took him to the Shelbourne Hotel, where he was staying with his mother.'

Killanin, who was noted for being able to hold his drink, took Burgess to the Horseshoe Bar, where he got him so drunk that he had to be carried to his room by members of the hotel staff. Some days later, Killanin noticed a very short report in the now defunct *Evening Mail* to the effect that a British diplomat had been questioned by gardaí for being drunk in charge of a car. Killanin made enquiries and discovered that the British embassy in Dublin had pulled strings to get Burgess off the charge and that Burgess had gone straight back to London before skipping to Moscow with MacLean.

I may have inadvertently met many spies from many countries during my time in Moscow, for the Western embassies and newspaper bureaux were full of spooks in those days. The only one I met who was open about his espionage days was George Blake, who lived near my apartment close to Bezbozhny Pereulok (Godless Lane), which reverted to its old title of Protopopovsky Pereulok (Archpriest Lane) when the communists lost power.

Blake, despite being frequently described as British, was in fact a Dutchman, but had become distinctly Russified and had taken to calling himself Georgy Ivanovich. He had a special liking for Irish people, having been sprung from prison in England by the Limerick criminal Seán Bourke; and he made himself available to the RTÉ journalist Kevin O'Connor, who was writing a play about the jailbreak.

Anita and I arrived in Moscow in June 1991 with Conor Brady and his wife Anne. Conor O'Clery and his wife Zhanna were departing for the US, and a reception was held in the Praga restaurant to say goodbye to them and to welcome us as their successors.

It was a typically warm Moscow summer evening and the open doors led to the balconies of the restaurant's Winter Garden Room, the *Zimni Sad*. In the lavish *fin-de-siècle* decor, the vodka and wine flowed freely, and caviar and sturgeon dominated the food selection. The journalistic community and the Irish community were strongly represented, with Ambassador Patrick McCabe to the fore. A good time was being had by all, but the proceedings ended abruptly after short speeches by the two Conors and myself, when the news broke that there had been an incident on the Lithuanian border.

Conor O'Clery was still the *Irish Times* correspondent at the time, so it was back to work for him, while the Bradys and ourselves returned to our separate hotels. Conor and Anne were at the Savoy, then the Russian capital's best hotel, and we were at the newly reopened Metropol, which would shortly oust the Savoy from the number-one spot. *The Irish Times* had money in those days and while the hotel bills must have cost a great deal of money, the reception at the Praga cost a pittance.

The reason for this was that there were two economies in operation in Russia simultaneously. The Praga operated in the rouble economy, in which items, when available, were extraordinarily inexpensive. But the Metropol and the Savoy functioned in the dollar economy, in which everything was overpriced.

In any event, the Savoy had it over the Metropol at that time, simply because it had hot water, which the Metropol did not have. They were just about fifty yards from each other, close to Red Square, Gorky Street and the central department store TsUM. GUM, also nearby, has frequently been described as a department store but in fact it was, and still is, a shopping arcade. TsUM on the other hand was not only a department store but a treasure trove of memories for anyone brought up in the Ireland of the 1950s.

Memories of the Clery's of those days came surging back. There were watches piled loosely on the counters. Women queued for gadgets that mended ladders in their nylons. Brassieres to fit the angels on Daniel O'Connell's statue in Dublin were dumped in piles. Almost an entire floor was devoted to fur hats. There were exquisite handmade rugs from Central Asia that cost next to nothing, for TsUM was part of the rouble economy.

So too was the club at the Foreign Ministry media centre on Zubovsky Boulevard, where a decent meal for four with vodka – there was no wine available that night – came to the very acceptable equivalent of €3.50. Getting around was cheap, too, although the locals were very annoyed that a single journey on the Metro had gone up to fifteen kopeks at a time when the dollar bought nearly sixty roubles.

Taxis were hard to get, but if you stood at the kerb and stuck your hand out, an ordinary citizen would pull in and negotiate a fee to drive you to your destination. Occasionally, a black Volga limousine would stop, and this indicated that the driver worked for the state. He might have driven an official to one of the interminable meetings that took place in those days and, having most of the rest of the day off, would take advantage of the boss' absence and use the car as an unofficial taxi. This procedure still exists in Moscow as one of the very rare throwbacks to the Soviet era.

There was talk of some other very strange economic practices, and the commercial counsellor at the embassy, Alan Buckley, told of coming across a street market where dead light bulbs were on sale. He was puzzled as to why there should be a market for such wasted objects, but a Russian friend wised him up. The Russian word *defisit*, which meant 'shortage', came into play. Live light bulbs were in *defisit*. If you had dead light bulbs you could go to work, remove the bulbs from the office lighting system and replace them with the dead ones so that no one would realise what had been done until darkness fell – and in the Russian summer dusk arrived late, long after workers had returned home.

There was also a street market in front of our apartment building but Anita, having initially regarded this as a distinct asset, soon learned that the standard of hygiene left a lot to be desired. She had been particularly impressed by a man who sold fish and had a little trick that gave him an advantage over his rivals. He had a bottle of water stashed under his stall and from time to time poured some over his fish to make them glisten. This guy appeared to have quickly got the hang of the market economy, but one day Anita passed his stall when the water in the bottle had run out. To make the fish glisten on this occasion our man spat on them. Memories of our 'fresh fish' man in Ballyfermot came flooding back.

I was soon to learn that food queues were a good sign. A shop or supermarket with no queues was to be avoided. No queues meant no food for sale. Long queues meant that something particularly good had arrived. Long queues of men signified that there was vodka. Long queues of women indicated that a consignment had arrived from that great Moscow institution, the Red October Chocolate Factory. It still exists, by the way, under its old Soviet name and produces some of the best dark chocolate to be found anywhere.

Then there was champagne, the Soviet version called *Sovetskoye shampanskoye vino*, at a price so low that I kept it secret from colleagues in Dublin. Moscow's reputation as a 'hardship posting' would have suffered badly if they had known. Internal and international travel was also impossibly cheap, and on one occasion I managed to get a rail ticket from Moscow to Rome for a visiting colleague for the equivalent of five dollars.

But most items were hard to get, and foreigners with foreign currency had the option of going to the state-run Beriozka stores or to the little grocery shop run by the big Helsinki department store, Stockmann's. Here, you could buy luxury items such as Lapin Kulta beer, Valia Maito milk and, from time to time, reindeer steaks. When the latter arrived, the word quickly got out to the city's large Finnish community and the place would be packed to capacity.

Stockmann's was only a short trip across the Krasnokholmsky Bridge in the little *Irish Times'* Volvo 440; but the journey presented some unexpected difficulties. Western cars were still quite a rarity in 1991, and it was not uncommon to park the car and return to find a group of people standing around inspecting it. It was also inspected by less desirable eyes.

As a foreign correspondent I was given a special number plate. First of all it had black letters on a yellow background to distinguish it from Russian-owned vehicles, which had white backgrounds. The numbering was special, too. My number plate read K 037 8 01. The K stood for *Korrespondent*, the 037 for Ireland, the figure 8 was on all foreign-owned cars, and the 01 stood for myself, as the only Irish correspondent in town. At a glance, a traffic policeman, a dreaded *Gaïshnik*, could tell that the car was that of the number 01 correspondent from Ireland.

The *Gaïshniki* were notoriously on the take from foreigners. There were fines for speeding, when the *Gaïshnik* decided what speed you were travelling at without the help of any electronic devices. There were fines for making a u-turn and there were fines when the *Gaïshnik* decided your number plate was not up to his standard of cleanliness. The amount of the fine varied. If you demanded a receipt you paid the full amount. If you said no receipt was necessary the amount became negotiable and the sum went directly into the *Gaïshnik*'s pocket.

There was danger, too, from the spare-parts mafia. When you parked your car you removed the windscreen wipers and locked them in the boot. I only forgot to do so once and therefore had my wipers stolen only once. I did not bargain, however, for the removal of my radiator screen and had to wait nearly a year until one was brought in by a friend from Dublin.

Within a few weeks of my arrival I had moved into the *Irish Times*' apartment on the seventeenth floor of an appalling building at number 1 Marksistskaya Ulitsa. This stood just across the square from the famous Taganka Theatre and it was there that the true hardship began.

Since both our daughters, Ruth and Deirdre, were still students at the National College of Art and Design in Dublin, where Anita was a staff member, family arrangements needed to be sorted out. I had been given a budget for travel home based on the price of four return trips with British Airways. As Aeroflot flew into Shannon, and later to Dublin, at far cheaper prices I was able to use my budget to bring the family out to Russia as well as travelling home to Ireland myself.

I ended up taking my summer holidays in winter when Anita and the girls were in college, while they could spend their college holidays in Moscow while I was at work. It was by no means a perfect arrangement but it worked reasonably well and the hardship posting was softened by their presence.

The hardship began, in effect, with the lift. This contraption, of local manufacture, appeared to have a mind of its own. Frequently it would refuse to open. This was bad enough when you arrived from Stockmann's with a puck of shopping for the week and were forced to lug it all the way up to the top floor. It was considerably worse, however, when the doors remained closed while you were inside. It could take hours before someone came along to rescue you.

There was a beady-eyed concierge at the ground-floor entrance who was supposed to deal with emergencies like this, but did not. Instead, she noted the comings and goings of everyone who lived in that section of the vast building that was reserved for foreigners. I am convinced that she was the only person aware of my absence on a weekend break during one of the more dramatic incidents of my stay in the Russian capital.

I had inherited a small staff from the O'Clerys. Lena Firsova was the secretary, translator and office manager. She had a keen interest in Russian politics, history and especially in literature.

Her good Russian perspective on events was invaluable and so, too, on one major occasion, was her direct link to the Kremlin. Olga Borushek came twice a week to clean the office and knew the price of everything in Moscow and where everything could be found.

Valeriy Chervyakov was the 'driver', whom we shared with the New York newspaper *Newsday*. His job was to run the errands that, under the Soviet system, took up so much time. If there was an airline ticket to be bought or money to be withdrawn from the bank, Valeriy would drive off into the sunrise and spend most of the day in queues in order to get his hands on whatever I, or the *Newsday* correspondent, Alison Mitchell, needed.

Valeriy was a simple soul, in contrast to Lena whose biting humour became a great antidote to the often dour lifestyle of my early Soviet days. In my first week in Moscow Valeriy drove me around town to show me how to get to important places and avoid traffic problems. As we proceeded down Gorky Street a tiny man crossed the road. Valeriy became excited. 'Look at the little man. He's tiny. He must be just one-metre tall,' he shouted.

Then from the back seat came Lena's voice, mocking the boastfulness of Communist Party leaders with the words: 'Our Soviet midgets are the tallest in the world.'

It was Valeriy who met me at the airport and broke the bad news to me when I returned from that fateful weekend break. The apartment had been broken into and was still unsafe, as the main window had been shattered. The embassy had been informed and Richard Fallon, the second secretary, had inspected the damage. I was advised that I would be safer moving out for the night since criminals had the habit of returning to the scene of the crime. Conor Brady, immediately on hearing of the burglary, told me not to spare the expense and to book myself into the Metropol, which was now the city's top hotel.

Next morning I arrived back at Marksistskaya to be told that the thieves *had* returned. In the course of their two visits they had stolen one of the two old Amstrad computers, the fax machine, the TV set and the sheets from the bed, which they used to wrap up their booty. These were tough times in Russia so they also took every scrap of food from the fridge.

It was this incident that gave me my best insight into the ordinary Moscow police, the People's Militia, who turned out to be distinctly more honest than the *Gaïshniki*. I was soon to have my own personal militiaman in residence in my hallway.

Kolya, short for Nikolai, my new, temporary roommate, was a small man in his middle forties. By nationality a Tatar, by religious persuasion a Muslim, he smiled a lot and talked about his family. He came in at about 9 p.m. each night and left in the morning. He also had an insatiable thirst for strong tea.

But Kolya had a more important attribute. Tucked into his belt as he sat in the hallway of my apartment at night was a 9-millimetre Makarov automatic pistol. He had used it in the past and was prepared to use it again.

The story of my acquaintance with Kolya began on the Friday after my apartment had been broken into for the second time. In return, the chief of my local section of the People's Militia, whom we shall call Captain Courteous, gave me Kolya. 'You foreigners are helping us with food aid, so now we will help you. I will give you Kolya. He is my best senior sergeant. You can rely on him totally. If they come back he will deal with them.'

Captain Courteous was one of twenty police officers who arrived at the apartment within an hour of the second break-in having been reported. He apologised for the behaviour of his fellow countrymen and for the inconvenience caused by the presence of so many of his fellow officers.

Some of them were busy taking photographs, others dusted the place for fingerprints, others stood around and watched, while the busiest man of all sat at his portable typewriter making out reports.

The sergeant-typist had four forms to fill in and needed to question me. On each report form, the first question, which bore no relevance to the case, was: 'How high is your education?' This was followed by questions demanding a detailed list of the items stolen. Then a plain-clothes officer, whom we shall call Detective Inspector Gruff, took over. Rugged-looking with a moustache and a face marked here and there with purple capillary veins, he got down to business quickly.

'You left the lights on in the apartment and they still came in. That means they weren't just juveniles. They could be dangerous,' he grunted.

The thieves, he explained, had entered the huge block through one of the entrances where Russians live, made their way across the roof and down through a trapdoor to the section of the building reserved for foreigners. They had then jumped the three-foot gap to my balcony, unafraid of the seventeen-floor fall to the ground that awaited a false move. From there they broke the kitchen window to gain entry.

He asked me who knew I would be out, the exact space of time in which the apartment was unoccupied and told me to see him in his office at 3 p.m.

Back at the station after lunch, Detective Inspector Gruff had four more forms to fill in, each beginning with the question: 'How high is your education?'

I informed him that I had already filled these forms in at my apartment in the morning. He told me that I had not. The morning forms were reports of the break-ins, the afternoon ones, which contained precisely the same questions, were requests to the *nachalnik*, the boss, to pursue the investigation with all due vigour; and in any event, he (Inspector Gruff) came from a different section of the security forces than the man who had taken the earlier reports.

Then he asked me to wait in the corridor. On the wall in front of me hung the portraits of the police station's thirty-one Heroes of the Soviet Union. Two of the honours were awarded posthumously to policemen killed, the citations said, by 'groups of hooligans and bandits'. It was when I returned to Inspector Gruff's office that I began to take a mental note of its contents. Piled on top of a filing cabinet was a heap of car stereos, probably stolen and recovered.

In a corner under a potted plant was a statue of Vladimir Ilyich Lenin seated at a desk. On the wall opposite hung a fading portrait of Felix Edmundovich Dzerzhinsky, founder of the Cheka, later to be renamed GPU, later again to be called OGPU, and later still to be renamed the Committee for State Security, whose initials in Russian are known to us all as KGB. Inspector Gruff was, as he had said, working for a 'different department'.

Inspector Gruff told me the case would be pursued with great determination and that he had no doubt that the culprits would be found and would have to face the full force of the law. I looked at the picture of Iron Felix and felt that perhaps Inspector Gruff was speaking the truth.

A few days later, Senior Sergeant Kutsenko called in. He was the best dominoes player in the Thirty-sixth Precinct, and in a country in which the level of play at chess, draughts and dominoes was positively Himalayan, this was no mean achievement. But another factor made his prowess even more remarkable.

For almost a year and a half now Sergeant Kutsenko had been carrying a 9-millimetre bullet in his head. There were no outward signs of the bullet's entry, but the X-ray pictures he carried around with him clearly showed the slug nestling inside his skull, just above his left ear.

The sergeant was brought to me by my friend Captain Courteous, who saw it as his mission to convince the world media that the Moscow cops were a much less corrupt bunch than they had been portrayed. All the guys down at the Thirty-sixth on Vedernikov Lane were proud of Kutsenko and they wanted him to get into *The Guinness Book of Records*, a publication which was held in the highest regard among Russians.

Kutsenko, who was twenty-nine and married with two children, got plugged by the mafia one night in October 1990 as he was driving a squad car on his own. He was unconscious for a short while and when he woke, his first thoughts were to report the loss of his Makarov automatic to the nearest station, as losing a firearm was regarded with the utmost seriousness by the authorities.

After the necessary procedures had been completed, it was decided that having a bullet in the head was a pretty good excuse for losing the weapon, so its loss was recorded and no action was taken against him. Kutsenko then moved from hospital to hospital for tests, and in the end the doctors decided that to remove the bullet would be more dangerous than leaving it in. The boys down at the station wanted the people at *The Guinness Book of Records* to hear about the case.

The sergeant was just one of seven officers from the Thirty-sixth that I got to know since my office and apartment had been burgled on two successive nights. Captain Courteous was all apologies for the inconvenience of the burglaries and questions about the height of my education; and Detective Inspector Gruff, obviously from the KGB, was determined to get the culprits and have them dealt with in the most serious manner.

Gruff, who came from the town of Chop, smack on the border between Ukraine and Hungary, was paid four thousand roubles a month, more than four times the average salary, but could barely get by. His main interest, other than his job, was discovering how much policemen were paid in other countries, what their standard of living was like, and whether they had to pay for their health services or the education of their children. He was particularly badly hit financially by the fact that he had to pay one thousand roubles a month to the primary school his daughter attended. If someone was ill, the doctors in the hospital had to get a backhander, too.

In the same office as Gruff worked a man we will call the captain from Odessa. He was a handsome guy approaching forty, still unmarried, but not for the want of trying. One night during the week, we went out to the only real pub in town, the Shamrock Bar, which had been set up by Aer Rianta. After five minutes of acquaintance, he had proposed to Orla Guerin from RTÉ, now a senior correspondent with the BBC. He also invited a large group of imbibers to visit his father and mother down Odessa way for the holidays in June.

In contrast to the captain, Kolya, my bodyguard, was much quieter. He was so devoted to his job that when given a lift in the office car he took notes in the course of the journey in case I needed to be charged for breaches of the highway code.

Others I got to know were Rashid, another Tatar from the Volga region, who hardly said a word but hung around the periphery of the company; and young Sasha, who was quiet, too, with an abiding interest in TV game shows. All my new friends had two things in common. The first was a bulge just under their left shoulders, where their Makarovs were stashed in their holsters; the second was that not one of them on any occasion even hinted at payment in cash or kind for the protection they had lavished on me.

Yes, the boys from the Thirty-sixth were an exemplary bunch in a town where corruption was rampant in all spheres of life. The correspondent of *The European* newspaper had had a different story to tell at that time. He was pulled in by the traffic cops and automatically got out his documents for inspection, plus a crisp banknote as a bribe. The policeman first of all walked by and looked at the front wheels. Crestfallen, he told the driver: 'I see you have size-16 tyres. That's a shame. I have a brand new set of size 18s – maybe one of your friends would like to buy them.'

And in that week, too, when hailing a taxi in the centre of Moscow, I was more than surprised when a squad car pulled in and asked me what my destination was. After a few minutes of discussion, the two policemen, not of course from the Thirty-sixth, said they'd drive me home for a hundred roubles.

Eventually, an alarm system was set up with direct connection, not to the boys in the Thirty-sixth, but to a special force known as OMON. These guys took no prisoners, and their counterparts in the Latvian city of Riga had a reputation for excessive use of violence.

As it turned out I had befriended a young African couple who were studying in Moscow at the time. Thabo was a Xhosa from the township of Guguletu outside Cape Town. His girlfriend Tsede was from the little independent landlocked kingdom of Lesotho.

It was from them that I learned of the endemic racism in this land where the workers of the world were daily being urged to unite. Things were not too bad for Thabo, who was a member of the ANC studying to be an army officer when the apartheid system came to an end. He was accommodated in the Frunze Military Academy, which was Spartan but at least cleaned to military standards.

Tsede on the other hand lived in a tiny room in an appalling student hostel out in the Moscow suburbs near the Patrice Lumumba University, but not part of that complex. When I visited her and Thabo there, the rats were running down the corridors on almost every floor. On her first morning in Moscow, Tsede, an extremely elegant and dignified young woman, saw a notice pinned to the door of her room. It read in Russian: 'A black monkey lives here.'

Taking pity on the couple, I invited them to mind my apartment during my first long holiday at home. They deserved, I felt, a little bit of comfort in their lives. Their stay, however, was eventful rather than comfortable. Our friends, the burglars, decided to strike again. This time, however, the alarm went off and OMON arrived on the scene. My two African friends were far more terrified of the forces of law and order than they were of the burglars, so they packed their bags and went back to the squalor and the lack of comfort of their respective abodes.

On my return I was officially informed that two intruders had been arrested and would be charged. One, I was told, was an Azeri street trader, and the other was a good Russian boy, who, naturally, had been led astray by the evil Azeri.

On Saturday nights I was a regular visitor to the Shamrock and regularly took a taxi ride home from a driver called Sasha, who was an exceptionally honest man. Once, shortly after I had arrived home, the doorbell rang. It was Sasha holding my American Express card in his hand. It had slipped out of my wallet when I was paying him his fare. I offered to pay him for his honesty but he refused to take anything.

Some weeks later Sasha found himself in the wrong place at the wrong time. His passenger had got on the wrong side of the mafia and was to be eliminated. Russian hitmen take no chances and don't take the time to discriminate between the innocent and the guilty. On this occasion they simply sprayed the car with bullets. Sasha was shot dead.

There were places, however, that were immune from mafia gang fights, and one of them was the Moscow Commercial Club, situated near my flat, ironically on Bolshaya Kommunisti-cheskaya Ulitsa (Great Communist Street). Here, rival mafia leaders would meet to carve out territory, discuss and iron out problems and, while they were at it, enjoy some of the fruits of their ill-gotten gains in the form of vintage French champagne and foie gras from Strasbourg geese.

They would be accompanied by astonishingly beautiful and expensively dressed young women, who were half their age and twice their number. One man, who wore a white, sharkskin suit even in the most sweltering days of summer, was usually accompanied by four blondes. But when business was being discussed, the young women were told not to bother their pretty little heads about it and sent off to buy mink coats for the winter.

In the same courtyard as the club and its casino, and occupying accommodation rented from the club, was a small restaurant and bar run by a smart group of Slovenians, who shipped produce from their native land weekly in a refrigerated van to Moscow. There they served it in a style not found elsewhere in town.

Once a month or so, Robert Haupt from the *Sydney Morning Herald*, Peter Pringle of the London *Independent* and myself would meet there for lunch to discuss the events that had been taking place. The menu was quite varied for the Moscow of its time, but it included some items that were out of our reach financially. Amongst these was lobster at $150 a plate. Curious as to who might order such an expensive delicacy, we decided one afternoon to enquire of Marko, the head waiter. His response was revealing: 'The lobster is always ordered by Russian businessmen when Western businessmen are paying.' Russians were catching on quickly to the ways of capitalism.

— A Very Russian Coup —

Having taken over the Moscow bureau from the O'Clerys, I began to learn a bit about the life of foreign correspondents in the Russian capital. The first thing to note was that apartments could be bugged; the second important point was that my freedom of movement was subject to certain restrictions.

Theoretically I could travel wherever I wanted, but in order to do so I had to give my minder in the Foreign Ministry forty-eight hours notice. The official title of the minder was *kurator*, which made me feel I was some sort of museum piece. I had heard stories from diplomats about how their private conversations at home had produced startling results.

One told of talking to his wife about the state of the windows on his apartment, only to find the window cleaner at work the following morning. The same diplomat told of attending a performance at the Bolshoi Ballet and returning to his apartment to find a policeman's hat hanging on the hall stand.

I had two such experiences myself. Once, when I asked Lena to speak to the Foreign Ministry minder to advise him that I would travel out of Moscow in forty-eight hours' time, she replied that she was typing a letter and would do so when she finished. Before she had completed the letter, the phone rang. It was the minder. He was finishing work early, he said, and I had better advise him immediately about my travel plans.

The second occasion was more sinister. At that time a type of telephone giving 'caller ID' had come on the market and I, like many other journalists, had bought one. Lena had one at home, too, and one morning she arrived for work and asked why I had been ringing her home three times on the previous night. My number had come up on the screen and each time she answered there appeared to be no one at the other end.

I had been out for the night and was not at home when the calls were made from my apartment. I can only surmise that this, like the policeman's hat on the diplomat's hall stand, was designed to make me feel uneasy and to undermine my confidence.

Having settled down to Moscow life, August and the summer holidays loomed. They were to be the shortest holidays I ever had.

Things had been fairly busy in my early Moscow days, with a visit by Irish foreign minister Gerry Collins and a full summit at the Kremlin by President George Bush the first. Bush had annoyed the Russians by telling them that they and the US had a lot in common, having lost 'thousands' during the Second World War. The Soviets, who had lost twenty-six million, took his comment as a slight.

Then there was a plenum of the Communist Party to draw up a new programme. There were a number of drafts, but one of them appeared to move the party in a social-democratic direction and this was given prominence in the Western media. I took issue with this in the knowledge that the Leningrad party boss, Leonid Gidaspov, an extreme hardliner, had stated he supported a draft that was likely to be successful.

My article drew the ire of the Irish commentator Eoghan Harris, who launched a virulent attack on my journalism on radio. The Communist Party was now social democratic, he said, and that was that. Harris had been in social-democratic mode at that time, but he soon got over that. He also sent a long rambling missive to Conor Brady, suggesting that I change my name to Séamus Martian, as I was not living on this planet. I asked Conor to run the missive unchanged and to allow me to reply by saying that Harris should now change his name to Eoghan Harass.

In the end, Conor felt it better not to run the letter and in any event I felt completely justified very soon afterwards when Harris' 'social democrats' launched a botched *coup d'état* in an attempt to bring the USSR back to its old Stalinist ways. The build-up to the coup was non-existent. It came, in the words of President Gorbachev, 'like lightning from a clear blue sky'.

Early in August, Anita and I got an insight into Soviet efficiency and Red Army discipline during a visit to the wonderful Novodevichy Monastery, one of a ring of fortified medieval church complexes that surround the old city. The moat that still exists on one side of the monastery's walls is populated by black Australian swans and is a favourite place for Muscovites to stroll at their ease on summer weekends.

On the day of our visit we caught our first view of a Red

Army soldier, and it ran completely contrary to what we had expected from Western TV and movies. There he was, the armed representative of the 'Evil Empire', his forage cap slung to the back of his head, his tunic half buttoned, ambling by the pond, linking arms with his mother.

Inside the walls, there was another surprise awaiting us. There, in all his majesty, was His Holiness Alexiy II, Patriarch of Moscow and All the Russias, known in an earlier life as Agent Drozhdov (the Thrush) of the KGB. His Holiness proceeded through the complex, followed by a throng of little old ladies, or *babushki*, all of them eager to touch the hem of his garment.

The patriarch moved from building to building within the complex and each time he emerged into the open air he insisted that the bells be rung from the great bell tower beside the Cathedral of Our Lady of Smolensk. Some of his exits from the buildings were out of the view of the bell ringer, so members of the patriarch's entourage would run round to the bell tower and shout, 'Sasha, ring the bells now.'

After a while, the time came when Sasha did not reply. No bells were rung and the patriarch refused to leave the building he was visiting until the required campanology was exercised. Sasha was shouted at with greater ferocity. The *babushki* blessed themselves with increasing frequency. Finally, a man was sent up to the top of the bell tower, the requisite bells were rung and His Holiness emerged to join his flock. A minute or so later the man returned from the top of the tower bearing an empty vodka bottle as evidence of Sasha's inability to ring the bells. All this was to be reflected and magnified later in the month when the attempted coup took place.

On 16 August 1991, Anita and I and our younger daughter Deirdre went for a boat trip along the Moscow River in the sunshine.

There was Soviet champagne and red-caviar sandwiches. The *Raketa* hydrofoil flew the red flag of the Soviet Union with the blue band of the Russian Soviet Federative Socialist Republic.

Back at number 1 Marksistskaya, a general clear out of foreign correspondents had begun. Peter Pringle of the London *Independent* and Eleanor Randolph of the *Washington Post* had left for their vacation in New England, assuring Anita and myself that 'nothing happens in Russia in August'. Alison Mitchell of *Newsday* had left for New York. Our Greek and Swedish colleagues in the same building had returned home for the month. The only journalists working in the building were a skeleton crew at the ITV Moscow bureau, and Helen Womack, the *Independent's* second string, who was married to a Russian and whose home was in Moscow.

On 17 August I drove to Sheremetyevo airport and put Anita and Deirdre on their flight home. Next day I set out for Dublin, too, and arrived home at 1 a.m. Five hours later the phone rang. It was Paddy Clancy from RTÉ. There had been a *coup d'état* in Moscow. The tanks were on the streets. Mikhail Gorbachev, president of the Soviet Union, had also been on holidays and was being held prisoner at the presidential villa in Foros in the Crimea.

Fortunately I had not unpacked my bags, so I didn't have to pack. It was fortunate, too, that my multi-entry visa for the Soviet Union had been issued just before I left Moscow for Dublin. What I needed now was a fast air connection to Russia and in this case the Aeroflot hub at Shannon provided the biggest stroke of fortune of all.

I was able to get on an Aer Lingus flight for Boston that stopped to take on passengers at Shannon. Just a few minutes after the Boston flight touched down, an Aeroflot flight from

Miami landed at Shannon to refuel for its flight to Moscow. News of the coup had broken, and passengers for Moscow had cancelled en masse. As well as the crew, there were just six passengers on board: four Siberian businessman, who had been visiting the Irish Sugar Company's installation at Mallow in County Cork; a Limerick-based quantity surveyor with a contract for Aer Rianta in Russia; and myself.

The Aer Rianta people who ran the duty-free shop at Moscow's Sheremetyevo airport had been alerted by *The Irish Times* that I was on my way and were asked to help get me through customs and passport control and onto a taxi for Moscow as quickly as possible.

I had two big worries on my mind. One was that I was heading into a danger zone and leaving my wife and daughters behind. The other was that the airport, as in most *coups d'état*, would be ringed by tanks and I would be refused entry and sent home on the next flight. But I need not have worried. This was a very Russian coup and I got my first indication of this when speaking to the crew of the Ilyushin as we prepared for take-off. They had asked me what I knew about the situation and I told them that the people involved included the prime minister, Valentin Pavlov, and the interior minister, Boris Pugo. 'That's very serious,' came the response. I told them that Vladimir Kryuchkov, the head of the KGB, was involved and was informed that this was more serious still.

Then, in Russian, I said, '*Yanaev Novi president.*' ('Yanaev is the new president.') This was greeted with an outburst of laughter. This coup will fail I was told. Gennady Yanaev, the man chosen to take over as the Soviet Union's president, had been regarded by almost all Russians as an incompetent time-serving alcoholic. If he was president then this coup must be a joke.

I didn't share the crew's view of things until some time later.

In the meantime, the crew had turned the Ilyushin into a luxury liner. There was food and drink for more than 200 passengers aboard, and in the Russian tradition of waste not, want not, it was decided that the six passengers and the crew would share the goodies. We were all moved up to the first-class seats in the front of the plane. Then the Siberian businessmen started to crack open the bottles of vodka. The crew started to open bottles of champagne. For my benefit, the captain, who was in touch with Moscow, began to send back messages about what was happening there. Boris Yeltsin, president of the Russian component of the USSR, had defied the coup plotters and had made a speech standing on a tank outside the Moscow White House.

The significance of this was explained to me. Lenin had made an important speech standing on a tank, or more accurately an armoured car, during the October Revolution in Petrograd in 1917. All Russians would therefore know that Yeltsin had begun a new revolution in Russia.

By the time the airliner began its descent towards Sheremetyevo, I had, miraculously, managed to maintain my sobriety in the midst of what had turned out to be an airborne party to celebrate Yeltsin's defiance and the fact that the *coup d'état* was being led by an idiot.

Touchdown was as smooth as ever and I prepared myself for the long queue at passport control, which could take up to two hours, and the possibility that I might be turned back. I need not have worried. The six of us were the only clients for passport control and we were allowed through without the slightest delay. Aer Rianta had organised a taxi to get me to the *Irish Times*' office, and just twenty minutes after touchdown I was on my way down the broad Leningradskoye Chaussee towards the centre of the city.

There wasn't a tank to be seen, but when we reached the inner ring road, the Garden Ring, we were told that no traffic was allowed to progress any farther towards the city centre. Fortunately the *Irish Times'* office and apartment was just off the Garden Ring and not in the proscribed direction towards Red Square. So we turned right at Mayakvoskaya Square and headed towards my Moscow home.

Passing the Foreign Ministry press centre, I saw my first tank. Just a little farther on there was another tank, but this one didn't smack of a hardline communist coup. It was festooned with small boys playing soldiers. I was beginning to wonder whether I was really in a city under siege or had stumbled into a frame of a movie by Federico Fellini. Finally, we pulled up at number 1 Marksistskaya and, having paid the taxi driver, I discovered that the lift to the seventeenth floor was actually working.

The first thing I did on reaching the office was to pick up the phone: it was working, too. I rang the embassy and spoke to Tom Russell, the first secretary. Ambassador McCabe was on holidays, like most other foreigners. Russell was suffering from a very heavy cold but he had some important information. I knew that all traffic into the centre was banned, but I wanted to go there to see what was going on. 'You won't believe this,' Russell said, 'the Metro is working absolutely normally.'

The good old Moscow Metro, with a train every ninety seconds, was in full operation. Tom Russell was right. I found it difficult to believe that a coup was under way without a tank anywhere near the main international airport. Now I was hearing that the plotters had blocked road traffic towards the city centre but had failed to stop people arriving there by Metro.

Then the phone rang. It was Lena, the office manager and translator. She and Valeriy had been given holidays for August but she was bright enough to know that she would be needed in such an emergency. There was no sign of Valeriy and he did not appear until the coup had ended. Lena, who had a very mordant sense of humour, told me afterwards: 'I am sure he was missing because he was driving a tank.'

I soon learned that I was the first journalist back at Marksistskaya. Downtown, there was a bizarre scene on Red Square. A line of tanks had their guns pointed at the Kremlin. Tank commanders faced finger-wagging *babushki*, the formidable grandmothers of Moscow. These ladies took no prisoners. They gave orders to everyone. The orders they were giving to the tank commanders were that they were not to shoot their own Russian people. One commander replied that he had no intention of doing so and even if he wanted he would not be able to since he had no ammunition.

Replete with the first-class Aeroflot meal, I managed to write articles for the front and inside pages of *The Irish Times* and transmit them to Dublin by telex. I had earlier rung home to assure my family I was safe and then at midnight I crashed out into a fitful sleep.

I rose at dawn the next morning. There would be no need to get Lena to translate the main stories from the Russian newspapers since they had all been banned; and the independent newspaper *Nezavisimaya Gazeta* had, according to reports, been under extraordinary pressure from the new authorities. Once again there was a surprise in store. When I walked into the office from the adjoining two-roomed apartment the fax machine was spewing out a special fax edition of *Nezavisimaya*. The wire services, including TASS and Reuters, were also running from the battery of teleprinters. The faint signal from CNN in those pre-satellite days was providing intermittent coverage, but our office was on the wrong side of the building to receive reliable pictures.

Food was now important, so I set out with Lena to the recently opened Aer Rianta supermarket, the Arbat Irish House, on Prospekt Kalinina. Arriving there from the Metro, I met Johnny Murphy from Tralee, the manager of the Shamrock Bar, and asked if the place was still open. 'Of course we're open,' he told me, 'but we had to close the pub at 8 p.m. last night.'

I had a chance to examine barricades put up by those who defied the coup. They were puny in the extreme and far less imaginative than their Belfast counterparts in those same troublesome days in Northern Ireland.

There was a lesson, too, in how TV journalism operated. A screen full of people could be made to convey a vast horde, and this was the way things were presented. The cliché of the day was 'people power', and it had to be applied to the current situation. In fact, those who showed up at the White House were far fewer in number than the TV suggested. Most Russians waited to see who would come out on top before they were prepared to express their views. With seventy years of totalitarianism behind them, their attitude was hard to criticise.

On the second day, a tough-looking army general appeared on TV to tell the populace that a curfew would be imposed that night and those breaking it would be summarily arrested. This was not the way things turned out. Three young men were killed in an incident in an underpass at the junction of the then Prospekt Kalinina and the Garden Ring Road. Dmitri Komar, Ilya Krichevsky and Vladimir Usov lost their lives when a young tank commander panicked and drove over them.

I was fortunate in that Lena's father, Yuri Firsov, was at the heart of things working as foreign-affairs adviser to the prime minister, Valentin Pavlov, in the Kremlin. I asked her to meet her dad and find out as much as she could about the situation. On the morning of the second day of the putsch, she was able to tell me that the self-styled emergency committee had lost control. It had been obvious from the TV appearance of Yanayev that he had been suffering from a massive hangover, as his hands were shaking uncontrollably.

Now I learned that the Russian weakness for alcohol was in evidence elsewhere. Pavlov, I was told, had drunk himself into 'a state of collapse' and had to be carried from his office by a team of bodyguards, who were heard complaining about the prime minister's not insubstantial weight.

Meanwhile at the White House, where Yeltsin had bravely stood on the tank to defy the coup, the BBC correspondent John Simpson was trying to get an interview with Yeltsin, who was nowhere to be seen. He was told by Eduard Shevardnadze that Yeltsin was unavailable. He was in the heart of the building directing operations and could not be disturbed. Some time later, when all the hubbub had died down, Shevardnadze told Simpson that he had been forced to tell a lie. Yeltsin was in the heart of the building all right but he was not directing operations. He was drunk.

On the second night, when the curfew had been declared, I, like most Westerners, was unaware of Russian attitudes to this sort of thing. I had been brought up to think that this was a police state and that people lived in terror. I was therefore worried, as I was sending my reports in the early hours, to see from my eyrie on the seventeenth floor, car after car pull up beside the building. I was convinced that they belonged to the KGB who were rounding up foreigners. I waited for the knock on the door but it never came. I looked out my window again and cars were still arriving. I studied them more carefully than previously and saw that their drivers were going into a side entrance and emerging with small parcels. It suddenly dawned on me. They were going to the *Nochnoi Magazin*, the shop that opened all night, to buy vodka.

Next morning, armed with the information from the Kremlin, I was able to go on the morning news bulletin on RTÉ immediately after the BBC correspondent Bridget Kendall. Bridget was giving dire warnings of troops on their way from Central Asia to bolster the anti-Gorbachev forces in Moscow. I gave a different view, saying that the game was up and that in their main evening news on that day RTÉ would be reporting that the coup was over. There was a stunned silence at the other end of the line – for just a moment. The Kremlin information was added to by statements from senior members of the Communist Party of the Soviet Union that opposed the coup and its plotters. The most significant of these was the party leader in Kazakhstan, Nursultan Nazarbayev, who had been tipped as a possible successor to Gorbachev as Soviet leader.

All the same, things were not one hundred per cent clear and I was biting my nails for a good part of that day. Then, in mid-afternoon, the TASS teleprinter came to life. The Communist Party of the Soviet Union would hold a press conference at the Oktyabrskaya Hotel to condemn the coup. For the plotters the game was now finally up.

By now most of my neighbours had returned. Alison Mitchell of *Newsday* had disembarked at JFK airport in New York and cleared passport control and customs. She was walking through the arrivals area when she noticed a group of people standing round a person with a transistor radio. It was there she had heard the news that the coup had taken place. She went directly to departures and checked her bags for the next flight to Moscow.

Peter Pringle had been up at dawn, fishing on a river in New England some distance from the nearest village. As he settled down to fish, a faint voice could be heard in the distance. Gradually it grew nearer and he heard the words, 'Pringle. Telegram.' It was the local postmistress with the news that he had to return to Russia.

Peter drove me to the Communist Party press conference that afternoon and as we went through the streets of Moscow we could see the truckloads of soldiers withdrawing from the city. We got stuck in a traffic jam behind one and waved at the young Red Army conscripts. They smiled and waved back.

At the press conference we were joined by our friend and colleague Robert Haupt from the *Sydney Morning Herald*. Like Pringle and most other correspondents, he had been deserted by his driver and secretary-translator, who continued on their holidays during the coup. I was fortunate in that only my driver had gone missing.

The press conference was hosted by junior members of the party, who were vicious in their condemnation of the coup. They were insignificant in themselves, but the press conference and its theme served as confirmation that the coup had failed. As I had predicted, the main story on RTÉ's evening news bulletin was the news that the *coup d'état* was over.

There was, however, more drama to come, and for several months afterwards the top-twenty stories in Reuters' world-news headlines every day were datelined Moscow. One of the most dramatic was the return of Gorbachev to Moscow. His press conference at the Foreign Ministry press centre produced two starkly different reactions from the international media.

Space at the press conference was limited. Most journalists had to be content with the transcript of what Gorbachev had to say, and almost all of them dealt with it extremely negatively. It should be said here that there had been a group of reporters which had become little more than a claque of cheerleaders for Boris Yeltsin. Some of them had even fallen for the idea that stories of Yeltsin's fondness for alcohol were an invention of the KGB. This group would have put any of Gorbachev's words in an unfavourable light, but the real reason, in my view, for the negative reporting of the conference was that those present to see Gorbachev in the flesh were astounded by him in a way that those who simply read the transcript could not be.

Pringle and I were amongst those who managed to get seats for the live performance. We arrived at the press centre more than an hour early and pressurised a Foreign Ministry official into giving each of us one of the prized tickets that admitted us to the chamber where the conference was being held.

Gorbachev's performance was stunning. At previous meetings of this nature, he gave long, boring replies that bore little relation to the questions he had been asked. This time, however, he told an adventure story of being held by security forces. He talked of his wife Raisa's nervousness. He spoke of listening clandestinely to the BBC Russian Service, just like the dissidents of the Stalinist era, to find out what was really going on in Moscow. And finally he told us of his rescue.

But Gorbachev had returned to a very different Moscow from the one he had left. The power base had shifted from him and the liberals within the Communist Party to Yeltsin and his supporters. This was dramatically demonstrated some days later when Yeltsin publicly humiliated Gorbachev in front of the parliament and the entire Soviet Union via the TV networks.

This was a different Yeltsin from the one we had seen up to now. His body language as well as his words were those of a bully. His swagger on the tank on the first day of the coup had become the swagger of a browbeater.

My gut feeling about Yeltsin at that time was confirmed some years later when I spoke about him to a man who knew him well. Yegor Yakovlev, the editor of *Moscow News*, was a prime mover of the policy of glasnost. His newspaper epitomised the openness that had become evident in the USSR of the 1980s. Large crowds would gather outside the paper's offices near Pushkin Square to wait for editions of *Moscow News* to come off the presses, such was the impact of the journalism provided by Yakovlev and his colleagues.

Yakovlev later became head of Russian television and a member of the presidential council and, as such, had an inside track to the country's political leaders. His verdict on Yeltsin was damning. Not only did he confirm the president's addiction to alcohol, but he was very forthright about his overweening desire for power.

The picture Yakovlev portrayed of Yeltsin was a disturbing one: 'I think there were two things that were catastrophic for him, and for the first one the whole crowd of us, the democrats, myself included, are to blame. We made a deal with our consciences and decided not to notice it for the sake of democracy.

'You know his moral behaviour and his mentality do not correspond with the role he has to play. His mentality level is that of a [Communist Party] regional secretary. I never blame any official who is doing his best but is unable to achieve much, because when I curse him, it's not going to make him any more clever.

'The second thing is his animal, his beastly, desire for power and from this stems his savage hatred of Gorbachev, who was the main obstacle to his coming to power in the first place.'

During Gorbachev's last days, Yakovlev used to meet Yeltsin frequently in the Kremlin. 'I remember at one stage I noticed that Yeltsin was very sharp in his attitude towards me. I came to him and said, "I have a feeling you have stopped trusting me."

'Yeltsin answered, "Yes." I began to think about what was wrong and I realised it was my relationship with Gorbachev. I mentioned this and he said, "Yes".

'"But," I said, "remember when you were in the politburo, I was the first to talk to you after you were thrown out. You know my self-respect is more important to me than the attitude of the president towards me and I have to tell you that a few days ago myself and my wife had dinner at Gorbachev's *dacha*."

'He said, "Do you think I don't know about that?"

'I replied, "I didn't realise I was being followed so closely."'

Then Yeltsin's attitude took a strange turn. 'Why did he invite you to this dinner but not me,' he asked Yakovlev.

'Are you crazy?' Yakovlev said. 'You are president and he is nothing. He cannot invite you to dinner.'

Yeltsin's response, according to Yakovlev, was the pathetic sentence: 'He never calls me, he never rings me, never phones.'

'This animosity towards Gorbachev,' Yakovlev also said, 'is so deep. It is hidden deeply in Yeltsin's soul. You know it is very unpleasant to see a drunken president conducting an orchestra but for me the important question is: Is he drinking or not? It would not be any easier for me if the public did not know that he was drinking, quietly or not.

'I drink every day myself. I drink with my wife when I come from work but if I was president of Russia and there was a question of whether I should drink or not, I would compel myself to abandon it because any weak point in the leading person will allow him to fall victim to his team. For example, his love of drinking or his admiration of women would also be a weak point in a president.

'I was a witness of one of his meetings with CIS leaders – he was very well dressed, he looked very well, he talked well. The meeting was in Bishkek. Then at lunch Grachev [the defence minister] poured a glass of cognac for him and all this ended: he became a completely different person.'

The major example of what Yeltsin was prepared to do in order to gain further power and get rid of Gorbachev came one Sunday in early December 1991. As usual at weekends I was alone in the office and the TASS wire was quiet. It appeared that the TASS journalists, unlike those in any other wire service that I know, were usually given the weekend off.

On this Sunday, however, the TASS teleprinter came to life and the message it bore was an astounding one. TASS' Russian initials were an acronym for Telegraphic Agency of the Soviet Union, but what it had to say on that afternoon was that the Soviet Union had ceased to exist as a geopolitical entity.

The leaders of three of the fifteen Soviet republics – Stanislav Shushkevich of Belarus, Leonid Kravchuk of Ukraine and Boris Yeltsin – had met at a party *dacha*, or country house, in the forest of Belovezhskaya Pushcha and decided that the USSR had had its day.

This was big news for every newspaper, broadcaster and wire service in the world, with one exception: *The Irish Times*. The death of one of the world's two superpowers might have been big on any other day but on this occasion it clashed with the European Union summit in Maastricht. The *Irish Times'* obsession with the European Union made it blind to one of the biggest news stories of the century, and at an early stage it was decided that the story should be run on an inside page.

I was furious, but was not without support. Patrick Smyth, now the paper's foreign editor, was a sub-editor on the foreign desk that day and moved heaven and earth to ensure that the 'paper of record' carried the death of the Soviet Union on page one. Maastricht was still the lead story and the demise of the USSR appeared under a minor single-column headline.

Ironically, years later, journalists who had been at Maastricht on that day told me that the USSR's demise had been the main talking point there amongst the European leaders.

The first man to spill the beans on what happened at Belovezhskaya Pushcha was Shushkevich. He admitted straight out that the USSR had been dissolved in order to get rid of Gorbachev. Since Gorbachev was the president of the Soviet Union, if there wasn't any Soviet Union he would be president of Nowhere. Yeltsin would now be in charge of the Russian component of the former USSR and that suited him fine.

Incidentally, in later years, the term 'collapse of the Soviet Union' has been widely used by lazier journalists. The system by which the USSR was governed did indeed collapse, but the territorial entity did not. It was deliberately dismantled by three of its fifteen republics, all of them Slavic. The Central Asians were furious and Nazarbayev of Kazakhstan more so than any of the others, as his chances of becoming Soviet president had now vanished.

As for the coup plotters, most of them became victims of a sudden illness known as 'coup flu': Boris Pugo committed suicide, as did the army's chief of staff, General Sergei Akhromeyev, who had offered the plotters his support. Others, including Vladimir Kryuchkov, were freed in an amnesty in 1994.

There were other casualties not directly involved in the coup. One morning Lena came to work and said that she suspected that the foreign minister, Alexander Bessmertnykh, had been fired. I asked her why she thought this and her reply revealed a quintessential insight into Soviet thinking. Her mother, she said, had seen Mrs Bessmertnykh bring her own garbage to a large communal rubbish bin. The wives of Soviet foreign ministers did not do that sort of thing. Sure enough it emerged that Bessmertnykh had been sacked.

There was also the strange case of the Soviet ambassador to Ireland, Guerman Gventsadze. One night in Moscow I received a phone call from Orla Guerin of RTÉ to say that news had broken on a local radio station that he had lost his job for backing the coup. She had been told this by the *Daily Express* correspondent Peter Hitchens, or 'Bonkers' Hitchens, as he was known to his British colleagues. I decided to check it out. I rang Hitchens at home and his wife told me that he had not heard the radio broadcast himself but had been told about it by someone else and was convinced that Gventsadze had been sacked.

I then checked with Reuters, who had local staff monitoring all radio broadcasts. They faxed me an English translation of the transcript of the programme and there was no mention of Gventsadze's dismissal. My story denying the dismissal of Gventsadze made the front page the next day and this was confirmed early in the following year when Gventsadze turned up as Russian ambassador at an art exhibition at the Irish Museum of Modern Art in Kilmainham.

At this stage, like almost all the foreign correspondents in Moscow, I was suffering from near total exhaustion, both mentally and physically. This problem was illustrated dramatically to me when Peter Pringle and Eleanor Randolph plucked up the courage to hold a dinner party for the visiting London *Independent* columnist Neal Ascherson.

At one stage Pringle left the dining room to fetch more wine but did not reappear. We found him crashed out asleep on his bed ... the perfect host.

Now that the Soviet Union had been declared defunct, Pringle and I, occasionally with Robert Haupt, made nightly trips to Red Square to see if the red flag was still flying over the Kremlin. We checked this out until finally it was announced that the flag would remain there until midnight on 31 December.

I returned home for Christmas on a flight from Moscow to Shannon. It was a big, wide-bodied Ilyushin 86, and almost all of Moscow's Irish community was on board. Many of those who worked for Aer Rianta were young people from Clare, with a strong background in traditional music. It may have been the first time in the airline's history that a series of set dances were performed in mid-flight.

When I got home to Dublin and stood on the bathroom scales, I realised I had lost twenty-nine pounds.

— New Times, New Songs —

The red flag came down and the old Tsarist tricolour was raised over the Kremlin at midnight on New Year's Eve, and 1992 appeared to offer hope of dramatic change for the better. It was, however, to be one of the most difficult years Russia was to undergo since the end of the Second World War.

The entity that replaced the Soviet Union was known as the Commonwealth of Independent States (CIS, or in its Russian initials, SNG). Russians were not happy with the title, or more especially with the final initial which in common speech was used as shorthand for 'shit'.

But they had much more to put up with than that. The year began under the direction of Prime Minister Yegor Gaidar, who promised an instant free market that would sweep away the old system and usher in a period of prosperity for all. It didn't work out that way.

The first move was to free prices. Under the old system, prices were fixed by the state to such an extent that most items had a fixed price printed on their labels, and that price might not have changed for decades. Under the new system there was a snag. Prices were now free, but on the supply side almost all products were manufactured by monopolies. There was no competition: so instead of the state fixing the price of, say, wellington boots, the factory that made the boots fixed the price itself. Not only that, but the factory was allowed to decide whatever price it wanted and naturally it opted for the highest possible price.

The result was increased prices all round, and by the end of the year inflation had hit 2,500 per cent. It was quite an experience living under such conditions, but of course as a foreign resident life was much easier than it was for ordinary Russians. I use the word 'ordinary' here, for there were other Russians who did not feel the pinch when inflation bit into the wages and pensions of the masses. Those immune from inflation's worst effects included Prime Minister Gaidar and most of the other 'reformers', led by Anatoly Chubais. With Bolshevik ruthlessness, Gaidar and Chubais pursued economic reform with little or no regard for the suffering of others and in the clear knowledge that they would not suffer themselves.

In many cases this was no surprise, because the young reformers were, in the main, the children of members of what was known as the *nomenklatura* – comprised of leading Communist Party or state officials. These were the privileged people under the communist regime whose health was taken care of at special clinics, and who shopped at stores that were not open to the general public and where shortages were rare.

Gaidar himself was the son of an admiral in the Soviet navy

and the grandson of Arkady Petrovich Golikov, a writer who took the surname of one of his characters and became Arkady Gaidar. The character, Timur Gaidar, was a small boy devoted to the struggle against the *burzhuini*, the bourgeois classes that were out to destroy communism. Arkady's grandson Yegor Timurevich was to become the closest thing to a bourgeois in the new Russia that was just dawning.

Almost instantly the elderly women of Moscow and other cities took to the streets. They didn't organise protest marches or anything as radical as that. Instead, they lined up in the pedestrian underpasses to sell their belongings to passers-by. The space outside the children's department store Detsky Mir suddenly turned into something resembling an oriental bazaar, where thousands gathered daily to buy and sell.

Money was scarce and dwindling in value. In order to survive, the great mass of the people was forced to sell its belongings on the street. Historians have described similar scenes from the early days of the Soviet Union, when 'bag men' travelled from place to place by train to sell goods that were reasonably plentiful in one city to the inhabitants of another town where the goods were scarce.

New words began to enter the vocabulary. The new-age bag man became a *chelnok*, a shuttle. *Krysha*, the Russian word for 'roof', took on a new meaning to become the name for your local mafia boss, who might get things done for you at a price. Many words were copied almost directly from English. A businessman became a *biznesmyen* and a businesswoman a *biznesmyenka*, and in some cases the words *biznesmyen* and *krysha* were interchangeable.

Living with hyperinflation led to disaster for many Russians, but only to adjustments in lifestyle for us foreigners. Prices in all stores were now in roubles but based on the rouble's value against the US dollar – and the rouble was falling precipitately against the dollar. The result was that as soon as you changed your dollar into roubles you instantly began to lose money.

The trick was to change just enough to buy the items you wanted. The concept of the ATM or the credit card had not taken off in Russia, so you went to the shop, priced the items you wanted and then went to a bureau de change to change enough dollars to buy the goods.

In some cases this process became quite dramatic. Anita, for example, spotted a winter sheepskin coat in the Vesna store on the Novy Arbat. She stood guard over the item while Valeriy and I went to get enough roubles to buy it. We arrived back with a parcel of twenty-five-rouble notes that weighed more than 2.5 kilos.

As the pensioners were becoming poorer, the smart young reformers remained comfortably off, with some of their friends becoming immeasurably richer; and another new word entered the language: *vaucher*, pronounced 'voucher', as in English, though its official name was *privatitsionny chek*, or privatisation cheque. President Yeltsin hated the word *vaucher* and did all in his power to discourage its use, but he was unsuccessful.

The *vaucher* plan entailed the printing of 148 million documents entitling the bearer to 10,000 roubles' worth of shares in the state industries that were to be privatised. The idea was that a nation of small shareholders would emerge from the ashes of communism. It did not work out that way. Unscrupulous operators conned the better-off citizens into parting with their vouchers by promising them unbelievably high returns.

Poorer citizens simply sold their vouchers off in order to survive. Early on in the scheme, one saw people standing in

Metro stations with little squares of cardboard bearing the message: 'I buy vouchers' or 'I sell vouchers'. As time went by, the buyers dwindled in numbers and were overwhelmed by the burgeoning number of sellers. To this day I have yet to meet an ordinary private citizen who made any significant gain from the voucher scheme.

Some citizens, however, were very much out of the ordinary. These men included Boris Abramovich Berezovsky, Mikhail Borisovich Khodorkovsky and Roman Arkadyevich Abramovich. Each man made his billions in a different way and fate was kind to some and cruel to others. Berezovsky now lives in a mansion in Surrey, Abramovich owns Chelsea Football Club and Khodorkovsky inhabits a small cold cell in prison.

Berezovsky started out on the road to immense wealth by opening a chain of car dealerships. Acquisition followed acquisition and included the Avtovaz automobile plant, which produced three-quarters of a million cars a year; Channel 1 television; the Aeroflot airline; the newspaper *Nezavisimaya Gazeta*; and some other valuable bits and pieces. His wealth brought him into the company of those in political power and he became a strong influence on Yeltsin's administration, largely through his links with Yeltsin's daughter, Tatyana Dyachenko.

Roman Abramovich, in a joint venture with Berezovsky, gained control of the major oil company Sibneft under a bizarre scheme called 'loans for shares' introduced by Chubais. He also gained control of other areas of Russia's natural resources, notably the giant aluminium corporation Rusal, which now owns the Aughinish Alumina plant in County Limerick.

Abramovich's company Millhouse LLC began to sell off some of its assets as the twenty-first century dawned. It sold its stake in Sibneft for thirteen billion dollars to Russia's vast natural-gas organisation, Gazprom, with Rusal going to another young entrepreneur, Oleg Deripaska, for a mere two billion dollars. In 2004, Abramovich was investigated by the Swiss authorities in connection with an alleged fraud involving an IMF loan to Russia, but no evidence against him was forthcoming.

Mikhail Khodorkovsky's road to great wealth began in the Communist Party of the Soviet Union, or more particularly its youth branch, the Komsomol. As the USSR struggled to avoid economic disaster, an attempt was made at a limited market reform and young entrepreneurs were needed. Khodorkovsky was one of those chosen by the party and, according to insiders, by the KGB to get the limited market off the ground.

He devised a clever method of converting internal Soviet credits into real money, including hard currency, and founded a bank called Menatep that was later alleged to be involved in shifting Communist Party money out of the Soviet Union and into offshore havens in the West.

In order to raise money for the state, Chubais came up with the 'loans for shares' scheme. By this, the government raised money from the banks by auctioning off the state's assets – especially the country's vast natural resources in oil, gas and metals – as collateral for loans.

The result of the scheme was that a small number of financial operators who were well connected with the government of Boris Yeltsin got their hands on the state's most important resources at ludicrously low prices. In effect Russia gave away its natural wealth and made a group of men who were already rich and powerful, immensely wealthy and powerful beyond their wildest dreams.

Wikipedia, the web-based free encyclopedia, under the heading, 'History of Post-Soviet Russia', put it this way:

A tiny clique who used their connections built up during the last days of the Soviet years to appropriate Russia's vast resources during the rampant privatizations of the Yeltsin years, the oligarchs emerged as the most hated men in the nation. The Western world generally advocated a quick dismantling of the Soviet planned economy to make way for 'free-market reforms', but later expressed disappointment over the new-found power and corruption of the 'oligarchs'.

Khodorkovsky was an important beneficiary of the great give-away and got his hands on the vast Yukos oil company. In the end, however, his determination to move the company's assets out of Russia by a series of subterfuges got him into hot water and he was imprisoned on charges of tax evasion.

While technically the 'oligarchs' gained their vast wealth legally, there were others who resorted to simple illegal pyramid schemes to make Russians part with their life savings. The most daring of these was a man called Sergei Mavrodi, who founded a financial organisation called MMM. It first came to my attention one day when I entered my local Metro station to go to central Moscow. I discovered that for that particular day all travel throughout the vast underground network was free. The sponsors of what appeared to be an extremely philanthropic move was Mavrodi's group, and within twenty-four hours MMM was on its way to becoming a household name in the capital.

Then, an unassuming character called Lyonya Golubkov appeared on the nation's TV screens. He became the star of an advertising campaign that used the technique of the soap opera to incredible effect. Russians had already shown their susceptibility for the most appallingly amateurish Mexican soap called *The Rich Also Cry*, which had been crudely dubbed into Russian. Indeed, one morning when Olga came in to clean the office I noticed she was in a foul humour. I asked her what was wrong and she told me she was very upset about the way the dreadful Luis Alberto was treating Marianna in the latest episode.

Lyonya became the star character in the MMM advertising campaign, which included a good measure of humour. In a short period of time the series of ads featuring Lyonya and his extremely acquisitive wife became must-see viewing for Russians.

Lyonya at one stage in the adverts was doing exceptionally well from the imaginary profits generated by his investment in MMM. He had shown his domineering wife Rita a graph on the wall of his apartment rising from a new pair of boots, through a fur coat, to a car and a house. Rita wanted the house to be in Paris, while a disembodied voice said: 'Why not, Lyonya?'

Lyonya's popularity was such that he became a virtual superstar. His ratings rose in almost direct proportion to the disillusionment with Yeltsin's leadership. *Izvestia*, arguably the most liberal, and certainly the most sober, of Russia's daily newspapers at the time, appeared to award him the highest accolade.

A cartoon in one of its issues showed Lyonya and his graph. The boots, the car and the house appeared in order of rising importance, but now there was a new and higher point marked with a gilded throne and the words: '1996, President of Russia'. The disembodied voice, represented by the traditional cartoonist's bubble, said: 'Why not, Lyonya?'

Lyonya, of course, was doing better than any of MMM's real investors. The house in Paris had not materialised and, instead, our hero had turned up with his brother-in-law at a beach near

San Francisco. As Moscow sweltered, he held a cool beer in his hand and revelled in the sea breeze. 'The beer here is good, but our vodka is better,' he opined. The clear implication was that not only had MMM made him rich but it allowed him, at least temporarily, to escape from the stifling weather of the Moscow summer.

It was difficult for Westerners to imagine, but the investment fever in Moscow intensified daily. At my local Metro station, once named after the writer Mikhail Lermontov but now inexplicably renamed Krasniye Vorota (Red Gates), travellers daily ran the gauntlet of bright-eyed young hustlers.

'Go to Hermes,' they would advise. Hermes was a rival to MMM. Just across the road from the Metro, its offices were mobbed by people demanding that their money be taken away from them. Farther down Kalanchovskaya Street, at the cinema named after the civil-war victory by the Reds over the Whites at Perekop in the Crimea, MMM had opened a new office. From it, a long queue snaked its way backwards in the direction of the grotesque Stalinist skyscraper, which housed the Leningradskaya Hotel, the Casino Moskva and Jacko's Bar, run by an enterprising Glaswegian who had deserted the boring confines of Sarajevo for the excitement of the Russian capital.

All those queuing were intent on boots, fur coats, cars, houses and perhaps even a cool beer by the shores of the Pacific. Not all would succeed, according to *Izvestia*, which warned that 'any form of collapse' would not only damage the Moscow securities market but could undoubtedly cause social unrest.

There were those who counted on both. Some spoke highly of Adolf Hitler, others were hard-line communists and nationalists, and others still were simply disillusioned with the way things were going.

The disgruntled met at a building on Tsvetnoy Boulevard in the centre of town to form a new political bloc in opposition to the Yeltsin administration. Most of the old familiar faces were there: Anatoli Lukyanov, the former speaker of the Supreme Soviet, grey and haggard-looking after his term in prison following his involvement in the coup of August 1991; nationalist leader Sergei Baburin; and former vice-president Alexander Rutskoy.

Asked who would lead the country in future, Mr Rutskoy was confident. His new political movement would produce an explicit statement on the matter as early as October. He didn't say what year, and all of Russia still waits, though not with bated breath.

In the past, the popular charisma of Mr Yeltsin had triumphed over these very same opponents. But that charisma was waning now, and a collapse in the securities market, in which so many naive Russians had invested so much, would pave the way for further disillusionment. In that eventuality it was confidently predicted that Lyonya would arrive at Copacabana Beach in Rio de Janeiro, accompanied, in all probability, by a woman other than Rita.

The humour of the advertising campaign that had charmed many Westerners, let alone its Russian victims, came to an abrupt end. MMM was believed to be earning $11 million a day at the height of its operations, but, like all pyramid schemes, it ran out of steam and at the same time some of its chief operators ran out of the country. Amongst them, it was believed, was Sergei Mavrodi. Others believed that he remained in Russia, moving from apartment to apartment to avoid arrest.

Finally, the police closed the offices of MMM for tax evasion. The company tried unsuccessfully to continue operations but soon gave up. It turned out that the fictitious folk-hero Lyonya Golubkov and Sergei Mavrodi and his associates were the only ones to make money from MMM. One of its associate companies owed more than $20 million in taxes and MMM had reneged on its investors to the tune of perhaps $1.5 billion. It was believed that up to fifty investors committed suicide, having lost every kopeck they owned.

All the same there were those, mainly elderly women, who still idolised Mavrodi and Lyonya Golubkov in the way that they still admired Stalin. They demonstrated daily in their favour. Mavrodi was finally tracked down and jailed in 2003.

On a lower level, there were still hit-men, thieves and pick-pockets, many of them connected directly to the higher level *biznesmyeni*. One poor American called Paul Tatum, for example, developed the naive idea that just because he had provided forty per cent of the funding for a hotel in Moscow he therefore owned forty per cent of the hotel. His dream ended dramatically when he was gunned down at the Kievskaya Metro station.

Another American, Paul Klebnikov, the editor of the Russian edition of *Forbes* magazine, wrote extremely unfavourable things about Boris Berezovsky and was gunned to death outside his office. Mr Berezovsky, needless to say, had no hand or part in the killing but took no action to clear his name against such untrue allegations.

Less scrupulous people became involved in a new tradition called the *razborka*, or settlement. This euphemism involved the killing of business rivals just to ensure that the competition was put in its place. One of the most dramatic of these *razborki* took place at a Moscow cemetery, where one group gathered at the grave of a colleague to mark the first anniversary of his death. In the Russian tradition, they made something of a picnic of the occasion. There was vodka and shashlik, or shish kebab, and a general atmosphere of celebration of the dead man's life and career. Whole families of those connected with the deceased had turned up and everything was going well until the gravestone exploded violently. TV cameras later showed the crows of Moscow feasting on human flesh in the branches of the cemetery's cypress trees.

Not surprisingly under such dramatic economic circumstances, robberies were frequent. After my apartment on Taganskaya Square had been attacked three times in four months I convinced Dublin that it was time to change abode.

Foreign residents, especially journalists and diplomats, who were regarded as potential spies lived in accommodation provided by an organisation called UPDK. Pronounced 'oo-pay-day-ka', this institution not only looked after the place where you lived, but also organised your hotel accommodation when you went to a different city and your air or rail travel to that city. It worked well enough under the circumstances of the day and it had the added advantage that its prices, particularly for accommodation, were well below the market average.

This allowed Anita and I to make trips out of Moscow for pleasure as well as for journalistic business. Our favourite destination in this respect was Tallinn, the beautiful capital city of Estonia which had been part of the Soviet Union when we arrived in Russia and an independent republic thereafter.

In earlier times, getting out of the grim confines of Moscow on a recreational break known as an 'out' had been a major feature of the scene. Helsinki had been the favoured destination and one Irishman who lived in Russian in the 1970s told me that while air passengers in some countries applauded when their aircraft touched down, those travelling from Moscow to Helsinki applauded when their plane took off.

Things were not as bad as that in our day but the trips to Tallinn, involving a long overnight train journey, were always something to look forward to. Even in Soviet times consumer items were more readily available in Tallinn than they were in Moscow.

The Baltic States had become known as the 'Soviet West'. Here, the notices and signposts were written in the familiar Latin script, most of the churches had spires rather than Russian onion domes, the Kaubamaja department store had items one rarely found in Moscow and, wonder of wonders, a basement on the town-hall square housed an Indian restaurant.

There were some disadvantages to UPDK, and the main one was that every request usually had to be accompanied with a bribe. Now that the new market economy had arrived and kiosks had begun to open on the streets selling sub-standard goods, a solution to the bribery problem was found.

In one particular kiosk on the New Arbat – as Prospekt Kalinina was now known – a remarkable item was to be found. The label described it as 'Silent Glen Scotch Whisky' and it contained a picture of a kilted piper against a mountainous background. It was exceptionally cheap at a couple of dollars, and its low price was explained by a message at the bottom of the label in the tiniest print. When a magnifying glass was brought into operation the words 'Produce of Indonesia' became legible.

Large quantities of this hooch were bought by myself and other correspondents to bribe the officials at UPDK in order to obtain quicker service. Naturally my application for a new flat was accompanied by a large quantity of Silent Glen and, after a minor delay of a month or so, I was told to go to Bolshaya Spasskaya Street and talk to the *kommandant*, an Armenian man known to all as Boris Spartakovich.

He told me that a three-room apartment was available and had been allocated to me by UPDK. The Russian system of counting rooms excluded kitchen, bathroom and toilet, so I discovered that I would have a living room, dining room and bedroom, which was considerably more than I had at Conor O'Clery's old apartment on Taganskaya Square.

The building was also in far better condition and its design was based on that of an apartment block in Sweden that had been allocated to the staff of the Soviet embassy in Stockholm. It was also in a part of town close to the embassy and to two central Metro stations and right beside the Garden Ring Road. The only snag was that I would have to work from the dining room as no office space was available.

Peter Pringle and the *Independent* office had already moved out of Taganskaya to a location far away from the centre of town. I was against moving so far out because of the necessity to travel in to the endless meetings and press conferences, all of which took place in the centre.

At the same time as I received my offer, Ken Fireman and his wife Susan Benkelmann, who were the *Newsday* correspondents, were also allocated a much larger apartment and an office in the same building – on the basis that they had lived in an apartment block that had been burgled several times. The fact that the burglaries had taken place in my apartment did not give me or *The Irish Times* an advantage.

Russians in general, and the authorities in particular, focused their attention on big countries to the exclusion of the smaller nations. This was particularly illustrated to me on one occasion at a Foreign Ministry reception for some visiting dignitary. I went there with Robert Haupt of the *Sydney Morning Herald* and in the queue at the reception line, each person was asked by a Ministry official to state the country he or she came from.

When I said I was from Ireland I got the response I expected. 'Ah yes, Shannon,' replied the official. Most Russian officials on their way to Canada, the US, Cuba or the countries of South and Central America had stopped over at Shannon, as Russian jetliners of that time did not have the fuel capacity to make it all the way from Moscow without a refuelling stop. While the planes refuelled the passengers took advantage of the duty-free shop.

Robert was up next and told the official in Russian that he was from *Avstraliya*. The official's response was such that it could only have come from a Russian, the inhabitant of a country that was by far the largest on Earth. '*Da. Avstraliya! Eto malenkaya strana.*' ('Yes. Australia! That's a small country.')

In any event, the authorities had decided that the size of one's apartment and office accommodation was to be allocated not according to need or because one's previous apartment had been the subject of numerous burglaries. Instead, size depended on the size of your country.

The next step was to approach a leading international removals outfit with an office in Moscow to get a price for moving the office and apartment furniture. I was dumbstruck when I was told that this would come to several thousand dollars, and I knew the *Irish Times*' budget would never stretch to this sum.

I was at a loss as to what to do about this, for I had no option but to move as the Taganskaya apartment had already been allocated to someone else. The problem was solved in unexpected fashion. The following Saturday I went to the Shamrock Bar as usual and, in the course of conversation with a member of the Irish community, mentioned the vast price demanded by the removal firm.

'Mick,' my compatriot shouted down the bar to another Irishman, 'do you still have that truck available next weekend?' Mick replied that he did and that I could have it for the day if I paid his two Russian workers $50 each, a lot of money in Moscow at the time.

The deal was done and the following weekend *The Irish Times* moved premises. Thabo and Tsede helped with the installation of the furniture, and the office was set up in the little dining room while I waited for proper office accommodation to be allocated in the same building. Two women workers from UPDK did the painting and wallpapering as a nixer, and an electrician checked the wiring, provided he was paid in vodka.

The office was on the fourth floor, a big improvement on the seventeenth floor on Taganskaya, especially on the occasions when the lift was out of order. A month later, once again out of the blue, the new office was allocated. It was in the same building but in a different entrance, and it meant a great deal, psychologically, to be able to leave the apartment, go out into the courtyard and in through another entrance to go to work. Home and office were separated and that was a good thing.

My new neighbours at Bolshaya Spasskaya included most of the staff from the Irish embassy, which was nearby. These included Richard Fallon, his wife Mary and their daughter Niamh. The Fallons were to become good friends both in Russia and back home in Ireland. Brian Earls, the embassy's number two, was also based there.

Amongst the media representatives at the new address were Pierre Bocev of *Le Figaro,* his partner Regula Schmid, who worked for *Les Dernières Nouvelles d'Alsace,* Adi Ignatius of the *Wall Street Journal,* and Mark Frankland of the *Observer.*

Boris Spartakovich ran a much more organised show at Bolshaya Spasskaya than his counterpart at Marksistskaya. His most impressive achievement was to inform us slightly in advance of forthcoming problems. These warnings were subtly made and usually in the form of notices placed beside the lift that began with the words *Uvazhaimiye Arendatory* (Respected Tenants) and also included the words *po tekhnichiskem prichinam* (for technical reasons).

We 'Respected Tenants' would be told on one day that for 'technical reasons' there would be no hot water. On another day there would be no electricity. The notices became totally redundant when they told us that the lifts were not working, for we would already have found this out by waiting interminably for the lift to come and bring us down to where the notice was posted.

Once when the water supply failed, Boris Spartakovich and his two associates Sasha and Misha embarked on a remarkable feat of exploration. They decided to dig in the courtyard to find out precisely where the water supply to the building was coming from. It was the heart of winter and their efforts were greeted with a truly amazing success. Sasha, a Muslim Tatar who later refused to allow his daughter marry a Russian of Orthodox Christian beliefs, and was sacked for his trouble, managed to find the source of the problem.

He did so by puncturing a water pipe with a pickaxe. It happened to be the main hot-water pipe and the result was the formation of a hot geyser, similar to those found in Iceland or

New Zealand, at the entrance to the courtyard. For nearly a month, residents arriving at the building and heading for the yard, where all the entrances to the apartments were situated, had to run through a near-boiling mist in order to get home.

Then, without even a 'Respected Tenants' warning, the phones went on the blink. Fortunately a new means of communication had arrived in the form of a private e-mail system through the American company Sprint, so articles could be sent directly into the *Irish Times*' mainframe computer.

Making a phone call to consult with the office, however, became almost impossible. One of the articles sent via Sprint recalled how I had given up trying to contact the *Irish Times*' news desk by telephone after 187 futile attempts. The following day, after a mere fifty or so efforts, I managed to get through and was told by a harassed assistant news editor: 'I'm busy – can you ring me back in five minutes?'

Although infuriating, this response was not particularly surprising, for some news editors, and eventually there were eleven of them, did not really work for *The Irish Times*. In fact, and this incident confirmed my suspicions, they often didn't even read the paper.

They really worked for a 'publication' called the Newslist, a detailed listing of proposed news items for the following day's paper. It had two deadlines each day, and failure to meet these deadlines was considered by some to be a far worse offence than missing the deadline for the paper itself. Dedication to production of the Newslist often meant failing to read *The Irish Times* in detail.

Obviously my frustration at 187 failed attempts to reach Dublin by phone may have been noticed by some of the people who paid to read the paper but had gone completely unnoticed by those who helped produce it. I was tempted to ring the editor to complain, but desisted for two reasons. Firstly, I didn't want to get a colleague into trouble and, secondly, my chances of getting through were negligible.

The domes of the Orthodox Monastery at Sergiev Posad north of Moscow. Inside the monastery is a painting of 'The Roman Catholics' undergoing eternal punishment in Hell.

Anita and I outside the Church of the Assumption in the Potteries (Tserkov Uspenie v Goncharakh) near our first apartment in Moscow. Here I witnessed the first post-Communist Easter Service.

A Lenin impersonator and myself on Revolution Square in Moscow. At a time of general impoverishment this man's resemblance to Lenin allowed him to make a living by charging for his presence in photographs.

Genrikh, Mairead, Irina, Barry McLoughlin and myself in my apartment in Moscow.

Photo of my mother in her opera days.

Bertie Ahern and myself in the Irish-owned Silvers Bar in Moscow. The Taoiseach visited Moscow at a time of extreme crisis in Russia, marked by the bombing of a number of apartment blocks in Moscow and the provinces.

Andile Apleni once known as Thabo Ntsome, a major at the Red Army's Frunze Military Academy in Moscow, with myself at the foot of Table Mountain. By this time democracy had finally arrived in South Africa and Andile had become a business student at the University of Cape Town.

Andile Apleni with his parents and myself in Gugulethu Township near Cape Town on polling day in South Africa's first democratic election in April 1994.

Relaxing at the Cape of Good Hope with Irish election observers after the first democratic vote in South Africa had taken place.

Saint Patrick's Day, Cape Town 1994. Left to Right: Professor Kader Asmal, later to be Minister for Water Affairs and Minister for Education in the first post-Apartheid Governments, Anita, myself, Louise Asmal, Andile Apleni (alias Thabo) my friend from the Moscow days, and Fr Basil van Rensburg, Parish Priest in the black township of Gugulethu.

Diarmuid's ordination day at St Patrick's College, Drumcondra. Left to right: Anita, Dad, Diarmuid, Mam and myself.

With Mikhail Gorbachev for lunch with President McAleese at Áras an Uachtaráin. Also in the picture are: David Donoghue, former Irish Ambassador in Moscow, Professor Ron Hill, TCD, Brian Farrell, RTE, the architect Maria Kiernan and Ian McGonigle of the Irish Museum of Modern Art.
Courtesy of Maxwell Photos, Dublin.

The Martin family: myself, Deirdre, Ruth, Anita and Diarmuid with Pope John Paul II in Castel Gandolfo. Deirdre has just asked the Pope for permission to play with the Mummies in the Egyptian Room of the Vatican Museum in Rome.
Courtesy of Arturo Mari l'Ossservatore Romano.

Conor O'Clery hands over the keys of the *Irish Times* Moscow office in 1991.

The Brian Friel dedication from A Month in the Country.

A visit to Ruritania. A visa from the unrecognised Republic of Abkhazia in 1994. Perhaps the first such visa to be stamped on an Irish passport.

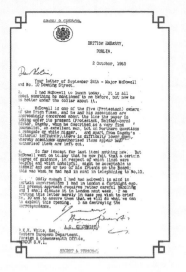

The 'white nigger' letter from the British Ambassador to the Foreign Office in London.

Postcard from my old friend and Irish Press colleague the great actor Donal McCann during the Gate Theatre's American tour with Juno and the Paycock. Donal loved 'the Empire State of Chassis' as he called it.

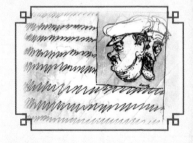

The other side of the same postcard.

— Enter Genrikh —

One morning in the office Lena was reading through the Russian papers as usual when she brought my attention to an article in *Komsomolskaya Pravda*. Because of the dreadful events of the Stalin purges and the displacement of millions during the Second World War, there had been a steady demand from people who wanted to find lost friends and relatives. *Komsomolka*, as it is affectionately known, had taken advantage of this over the years and found many a sought-after relative and friend.

On this occasion, however, the article revealed that the person found by *Komsomolka* was of particular interest to Irish readers. He was the son of an Irishman who had come to Russia as a communist and had been sought by his half-sister in Dublin.

It was in this way that Genrikh Patrikeyevich Kreitser entered my life and the lives of those who worked in the Irish embassy on Grokholsky Pereulok, just a couple of hundred yards from the *Irish Times'* new office and apartment on Bolshaya Spasskaya Street.

I phoned him at his apartment in the little town of Pushchino, a little more than a hundred kilometres south of Moscow, and he took the bus into town to meet me. It conveniently stopped near the great Komsomolskaya Square, which was just a short walk from the office.

Genrikh was a little man with a beard, thoroughly Russian-looking apart from his eyes, which were bright blue with a certain Irish twinkle. His father, Patrick Breslin, was one of the small group of Irish citizens who came to live in Russia in the 1920s.

Breslin had come to Moscow in 1928 to study at the international Lenin School, but soon realised that the USSR in reality had little in common with the USSR of his dreams. The school was a forcing ground designed to turn young revolutionaries into party apparatchiks. Everything was designed to produce officials who would do exactly as they were told by Moscow when they returned home and worked in communist organisations abroad.

There were further problems. Breslin had a strong interest in the supernatural. He believed he could tell the future through astrology. He was attracted to the theosophy of the famed Madame Blavatsky and leaned towards spiritualism and Indian mysticism.

None of this went down well in a country devoted to total materialism, and young Breslin was expelled from the school. He had already married Katya Kreitser, a member of the NKVD (one of the KGB's forerunners), and applied to stay in the Soviet Union.

Foreigners were under severe pressure in those days, but

Breslin got a job as a journalist and translator of children's stories. In order to convince the authorities that he was not an agent of a foreign country, he applied for, and was granted, Soviet citizenship in 1936.

This was a major mistake, for after he had divorced Katya and fallen in love with Margaret (Daisy) McMackin, a brilliant Belfast-born linguist who lived in Moscow as a teacher, his thoughts turned to the possibility of going back to Ireland. The yearning for home became stronger after Daisy went back to Ireland to have her child. Their daughter Máiréad Breslin-Kelly still lives in Dublin.

To get home he would need to regain his Irish citizenship and passport and in order to do this he would have to make frequent visits to the British embassy in Moscow, which acted for the Department of External Affairs in Dublin at that time. The visits became numerous, because officials in Dublin in those days were, to say the least, reluctant to allow communists of any nationality into the country.

The visits to the embassy and an unfortunate, if drunken, rendition of 'God Save the King' at a Moscow club was enough to convince the secret police that Breslin was a British spy. He was arrested and by Christmas 1940 found himself under interrogation in the dreaded Lubyanka prison in Moscow. He was declared a 'socially dangerous element' and died in the summer of 1942 in a transit camp near Kazan from 'heart failure caused by TB'. Breslin's story, and that of two other Irishmen who died in the Soviet Union, is told at length in Barry McLoughlin's book *Left to the Wolves*, published by Irish Academic Press.

Breslin was the father of two of Katya Kreitser's children. Irina, their daughter, became a distinguished ecologist and environmentalist, and Genrikh became a scientist. Their mother was also sent to the camps, apparently because her ability to speak Japanese made her a possible Japanese spy.

The children were sent to an orphanage in the Urals, and Irina, who remembered her mother being taken away, would say with the stoicism so prevalent in the Russian nature that 'we were better off than the children who were not sent there'.

Irina was a gentle soul who lived in the countryside near the Estonian border between Saint Petersburg and Pskov. She and Genrikh both paid frequent visits to Ireland to visit their sister Máiréad, who, with her daughters, paid frequent visits to Russia. That article in *Komsomolskaya Pravda* reunited a family that had been divided not only by thousands of miles and dozens of years but by a sharp interval of terror and death.

Irina, by the way, was given her father's surname and was known as Irina Patrikovna Breslina, while Genrikh was given his mother's surname Kreitser, which indicated the Jewish heritage on the maternal side. It was his patronymic Patrikeyevich that hinted at his Irish descent.

If Patrick Breslin could be described as a 'socially dangerous element', his son Genrikh qualified as a 'dangerously social element'. He was a warm, charming man, liked by everyone who met him, and having spoken to his Irish sister for the first time over the phone from the *Irish Times*' office he became a frequent visitor to my Moscow apartment.

As time went by, Genrikh's desire to become Irish grew. He began to learn some phrases and frequently when he arrived at my door he would point to the neck of a vodka bottle peeping from his coat pocket and intone the words '*ar eagla na h-eagla*' ('to be on the safe side').

Later, when the bottle had been opened, instead of raising the pedestrian Russian toast of *Za Nas*, he would utter the lengthy Irish one: *Sláinte agus saol agat, Bean ar do mhian agat, Talamh gan cíos agat, Gob fliuch, Agus bás in Éirinn*. Genrikh did enjoy good health for a while, but his life was not long, and he died at sixty-five. He had, as the toast said, the woman of his choice and to some extent *talamh gan cíos*, or 'land without rent'. The last two wishes were prophetic. *Gob fliuch* (a wet mouth) was something that Genrikh made sure he would have in the form of vodka, and it was this that ensured the final wish of *bás in Éirinn* (may you die in Ireland) was not fulfilled.

One summer's afternoon, Genrikh told his wife Tamara he was going out to buy a bottle of vodka. He did not return. He was found dead in the street, the newly bought bottle unopened. Genrikh had suffered a stroke and by all accounts died quickly and without pain.

While Genrikh was a frequent visitor to my place in Moscow, he never left empty handed. The contents of my food store diminished after every one of his visits. It was the same with Julian Clare, second secretary of the embassy, who lived in the same apartment block. Genrikh was the sort of man who could not only charm the birds in the trees, he could also charm the food from your fridge.

I never left Genrikh's apartment in Pushchino empty handed either. The place was by no means palatial, and there was barely enough room for Genrikh, Tamara and their totally undomesticated dog, Gerry. Genrikh called him 'Gerry Gav Gav' to distinguish him from any visiting scientist from the West who might bear the same first name. In Russia, dogs don't go 'woof-woof', but *gav–gav*, just as horses don't neigh but say *iggogo*! Cats, those most cunning of creatures, say *miao* in both English and Russian.

Pushchino is quite a modern town, known in Russia as an

Akademgorodok, a place devoted almost entirely to science; it was notable for its prize invention: an artificial skin for burns victims. At one time it must have been one of the most highly educated places on earth. More than 1,000 of its population of 22,000 held scientific doctorates in one discipline or another. As time went by, however, the brain drain, mainly to the United States, eroded Pushchino's significance on the international academic scale. The younger scientists were the ones tempted to go away, leaving the older ones behind as the town began to stagnate.

Visits to Pushchino were made on special occasions. The drive out of Moscow was a long one, as the city is vast and clogged with traffic. Once away from the city, the typical Russian countryside takes over, flat and monotonous. When I made long train journeys through the snow-covered landscape, it seemed that the only element of variety was the possibility that the forest might change from *les* to *bor*, from birch to pine.

But the approach to Pushchino was different. Firstly one crossed the mighty Oka River that joins the Volga at Russia's third largest city Nizhny Novgorod, which, under its previous name Gorky, was the Nobel Laureate Andrei Sakharov's place of internal exile.

Then having left the main highway that led, more than a thousand miles away, to Simferopol in the Crimea, a rare and wonderful sight came into view. A hill emerged from the great Russian plain. It was a mere bump in the ground compared to hills in most countries, but a hill all the same – and a very rare element in the topography of central Russia.

On my first visit, I had planned to stay in Pushchino's modern and comfortable hotel, but this was not to be. I had left my passport behind in the Moscow apartment and the stern lady at reception was under strict instructions that there was no room at the inn for those who arrived without the necessary documents.

This meant that I had to stay in Genrikh and Tamara's tiny spare room, which was also inhabited by the dreaded hound, Gerry Gav Gav, who made frequently unwelcome and intimate incursions under the bedclothes. Later visits to Pushchino would consist of day trips from Moscow, but on that first occasion my abiding memory is of a walk in the snow at night with Genrikh.

This snow was different from that which we knew in Moscow. It was pristine in its cleanliness, untouched by the pollution of the huge city. It was a moonlit night and the snow sparkled like a field of diamonds.

I learned a great deal about Russia's traditions and superstitions in the course of my visits to Genrikh and Tamara in Pushchino. Tamara would make the special dishes that marked particular times of the year. *Kulich*, a high cylindrical cake, and *paskha*, a traditional dessert, would appear at Easter, along with eggs dyed dark red by boiling them with onion skins. *Kholodets*, a meat dish in aspic, would appear along with traditional *blini* (pancakes) at *Maslenitsa*, the Russian Shrovetide. Roast goose with apples was a frequent dish as were wild mushrooms and freshwater fish.

Once, when I asked Genrikh how he got by on his tiny wage, he replied, 'There are fish in the Oka and mushrooms in the forest.'

There would be strict instructions not to shake hands across the threshold with anyone who arrived at the door. One was permitted to shake hands only when the visitor had come into the house. Failure to observe this custom, it was said, would eventually lead to trouble and enmity between you the other person. This tradition caused me some problems when I was posted as the *Irish Times* correspondent in South Africa. In the little cottage I lived in in the suburb of Melville in Johannesburg, black visitors would immediately extend their hands across the threshold and I would instinctively recoil. I am sure many of them regarded this as a racist reaction, but fortunately there were a few who had been educated in Moscow and immediately recognised my reaction as a peculiarly Russian trait.

Another especially Russian superstition was that you should not tell anyone if you were going on a business trip, or *komandirovka* as it was called. If your destination was known, then evil spirits could follow you there. They couldn't get into your house, by the way, if a pin was stuck into the lintel of your doorway. I paid little attention to this superstition until one day I noticed a safety pin implanted in the doorway of my apartment and another one in a similar position at the entrance to the office. They had, I discovered, been put there by Olga, the cleaning lady. It showed, I suppose, that she had my interests at heart.

There were superstitions regarding flowers as my younger daughter Deirdre discovered. In the market outside the Marksistskaya apartment she once saw some roses on sale and decided to buy some for her mother. She asked for half a dozen and managed to convey that they were for her mother. Her request was received with consternation. The woman selling the roses called over some of her friends. A discussion broke out. The sign of the cross was frequently made by those involved in the conversation. Finally, a man who spoke English was found. He explained that in Russia even numbers of flowers were for the dead and if you bought an even number for a living person it meant that you wished they were dead. Deirdre arrived at the flat with seven roses and an education in Russian ways.

While I was learning about Russian traditions, Genrikh was

determined not only to find out about everything Irish but also to become an Irish citizen; but before that there was a great celebration when news came through that his father had been officially rehabilitated. He was no longer in the eyes of the law regarded as a foreign spy or a traitor to the country of which he had become a naturalised citizen. This meant a great deal to Genrikh and his celebration was a tearful as well as a genuinely happy one.

Genrikh's work on obtaining his Irish citizenship continued for some time, for though his father, Patrick Breslin, was genuinely Irish and had been raised and educated in Ireland, he had been born in London. It was then necessary to go back a further generation to prove Genrikh's credentials.

It was when documents concerning his grandfather arrived that Genrikh and I realised we had far more in common than we could have imagined. They showed Genrikh to be the grandson of Francis Breslin, who had been born in Ardara in the County Donegal in 1864. My own grandfather, Francis Martin, had been born around the same time in Sandfield, just outside the town of Ardara. In those days in a part of the world where neighbours knew each other's breed, seed and generation, there can be little doubt that our respective grandfathers knew each other.

Here we were, more than a hundred years later and two thousand miles away from the Ardara of our grandfathers, a Russian scientist and a Dublin journalist, meeting as good friends.

Genrikh got his Irish citizenship and began to make a poignant pilgrimage to the Irish embassy on Grokholsky Pereulok each St Patrick's Day. As part of the research done by Genrikh and his Irish family, he had come into possession of the photographs of his father taken by the secret police. They showed a young man of thirty in right profile and in full face. Pasted underneath was his prison identification number, 5667; the name 'Breslin P.F.' in Cyrillic script; and his birth year of 1907. On 17 March each year Genrikh Patrikeyevich Kreitser-Breslin would arrive at the embassy reception in his best attire and place the prison photographs on the baby grand piano that stood in the main reception room. He was fulfilling his father's wish, the wish that had led to the latter's death in exile, the wish to be back in Irish territory one more.

Genrikh, by the way, must have had a genetic detection mechanism as far as police were concerned. Once, during one of his visits to Dublin, we were sitting in Doyle's Bar in College Street in Dublin, which was frequented occasionally by members of the Special Branch. One of them seated himself near us at the bar and Genrikh, to my astonishment, turned to him and said in his strong Russian accent: 'You are Irish KGB, yes?'

He also had a very mischievous and very Irish disrespect for authority, something completely missing in most Russians. Once, when his pension had not arrived for months, he decided to take action. Most people employed by the state or on state pensions had not been paid for months and with typical Russian fatalism just sat back and tried to survive with no income.

Genrikh had different ideas. After the New Year's celebrations had ended he opened another bottle of vodka, poured himself a large one, knocked it back and went to his post office.

'I want to send a telegram,' he told the formidable *babushka* in charge.

'Yes. To whom do you want to send it to and what is the address?'

'Yeltsin, The Kremlin, Moscow,' Genrikh replied.

'You can't be disrespectful like that to our president. You must send it to Yeltsin, Boris Nikolayevich, The Kremlin, Moscow,' she told him.

'All right give him his full title,' said our Genrikh.

'What is the text?'

'The text is: "Where's my pension? signed Genrikh Patrikeyevich Kreitser."'

Amazingly the postmistress agreed to send the telegram, and more amazingly still, on 1 February, Genrikh's pension arrived. It came on 1 March as well, but after that the payments stopped once more, and I don't think he was paid again before his untimely death.

Patrick Breslin was not the only son of an Irish citizen I met while in Moscow. Pyotr Nilovich Guverov's father was Neil Goold Verschoyle, an Anglo-Irishman from County Donegal who had lived and worked in Russia before returning to Ireland. Pyotr's name was a concoction that attempted to represent his father's names in phonetic Russian. Neil became Nil, thus the patronymic Nilovich, the first two syllables of Goold and Verschoyle were joined together as Gu and Ver, and the Russian suffix Ov was added to make up the surname Guverov.

Pyotr Nilovich's personality was virtually the opposite of Genrikh Patrikeyevich's. He was a gentle soul but totally devoted to Communist Party work, which took up a great deal of his time. No one was more surprised than I when he jumped from the Communist Party to a party run by the famous eye surgeon Vyacheslav Fyodorov. This political grouping espoused strong neo-liberal economic views and was similar to the Progressive Democrats in Ireland. It was the sort of political leap that even Eoghan Harris might find daunting.

It was through Pyotr Nilovich that I came to know Professor Lev Krylov, an expert on the old Tsarist political archives. Lev, through Pyotr, was also interested in things Irish and from time to time came up with some very interesting items that made it into *The Irish Times*.

One of these concerned the Fenian leader John Devoy and his plans to set up an Irish brigade in the Russian army to fight against the British and hasten Irish independence. Another seemed to prove that the rebel leader 'Countess' Constance Markievicz was not a countess at all.

In November 1876, a letter reached the Imperial Russian embassy in Washington suggesting the formation of an Irish brigade in the Russian army by a secret organisation with Irish links. Russia was at the time preparing to defend Bulgaria from an attack by Turkey, which – and this explains the motives behind the letter – was supported by Britain.

The letter was signed 'on behalf of the foregoing and self' by three men: John Devoy, who gave his address as the 'Editorial Rooms, New York Herald'; F. Millen, 'Ex-General, 532 Second Avenue New York'; and Wm. Carroll MD (late Battalion Lt. Col., US Volunteers) of 617 South 16th St., Philadelphia.

The secret organisation mentioned by John Devoy was undoubtedly Clan na Gael, as Devoy, General Millen and Dr Carroll were the three key men in that organisation at the time. The 'foregoing' on whose behalf the three men signed was in fact a list of twelve men headed by S.B. Conover, US senator for Florida, and including Jeremiah O'Donovan Rossa of Chatham Square, New York, and Thomas Clarke Luby of East 41st Street in the same city. General Millen, in that unfortunate tradition of Irish revolutionary organisations, has now been uncovered as a British spy.

Among the other names attached to the letter were those of Thomas Francis Bourke, an American Fenian officer who took part in the 1867 rising in Ireland; Rickard O'Sullivan Burke, another Fenian officer; and John F. Scanlan of Chicago, a well-known Irish nationalist in that city.

The proposition was a remarkable one, couched in remarkable terms. 'The Irish People at home and abroad,' the letter stated, 'would be pleased to see both Turkey and India pass into the possession of Russia, believing that the change would be for the best interests of those countries, of humanity and of Ireland.'

But perhaps the most striking proposition in the letter – written, incidentally, in the clearest of copperplate hands – was the 'respectful' suggestion that the 'nucleus of an Irish Brigade' be established in 'the Russian Service', officered by Irishmen who were 'through force of circumstances in the British Army and who would prefer to fight against England'.

The 'undersigned' were 'prepared to enter into negotiations with the Government of His Imperial Majesty the Czar for carrying into effect the above propositions, on any terms, consistent with Irish National Independence, that will be satisfactory to his Majesty's Government.'

Unfortunately for the 'undersigned', there were no terms of any nature which were satisfactory to the imperial rulers in St Petersburg. It is not known if the autocrat of all the Russias, Alexander II, ever got to hear of the plot that was hatched in the editorial rooms of the *New York Herald*, but there exists in the archives a draft note from Ambassador Shishkin in Washington to the foreign minister, Prince Gorchakov, in St Petersburg. It advises him to have absolutely nothing to do with these men because they were republican revolutionaries devoted to overthrowing the crowned heads of Europe.

The documents concerning 'Countess' Markievicz were even more remarkable, for not only did they cast doubt on the legitimacy of her title but they also showed that the diplomatic services of Europe in the nineteenth and early twentieth centuries were concerned not only with high matters of state but also acted as a sort of marriage bureau for the aristocratic classes.

The first letter in the batch delivered to me by Professor Krylov was from the British ambassador in St Petersburg, Sir Charles Scott, to the Imperial Russian foreign minister, Count Muravieff, dated 'March 11/24 1900'. The date 'March 11/24' indicated the thirteen days' difference between the Gregorian calendar, used in most countries, and the old Julian calendar, which was still in operation in Russia. The differing dates, by the way, explain why the Great October Socialist Revolution was celebrated in the Soviet Union on 7 November.

The letter, marked 'Private and Confidential', read as follows:

Dear Count Muravieff

I find that the Russian address of the Polish Gentleman, M. de Markiewicz, [the name is spelled with a *w* throughout this entire correspondence] of whom I spoke to you on Thursday is: Zyvotovko, Staro Zyvotow, Grot Kiew, and that his Paris address is 83 Boulevard Montparnasse.

This may perhaps be of assistance in any endeavour to ascertain whether he is the sort of person whom the young lady's friends would like her to marry. Forgive me again for [bothering?] to trouble you on such a delicate matter, but I do not know to what source here to apply to satisfy my correspondent.

Yours very sincerely,
Charles Scott

The entire nexus of the Tsarist secret service moved into action, and the head of the secret-police force known as the Okhranka, State Counsellor Pyotr Rachkovsky – in Paris where Constance

Gore Booth and Casimir Markievicz were living at the time – was ordered to find out if Markievicz was a count or a cad.

Perhaps in order to expedite matters the good Count Muravieff put the delicate matter in the following terms: '… the above mentioned Dunin Markiewicz has won the trust of a relative of the Marquess of Salisbury, who resides in Paris as an art student and, calling himself a nobleman and the son of a Count, is trying to persuade her to marry him.'

Rachkovsky, by the way, was one of the most efficient secret policemen in the business at that time, with something of an unsavoury reputation. According to some historians he may have been involved in the concoction of that notorious and fraudulent anti-semitic document known as 'The Protocols of the Elders of Zion'.

In any event, Rachkovsky had noted every move of Constance Gore Booth, or 'Miss Gorbut' as he described her in his reports to St Petersburg. In his final message to the Russian capital he wrote:

I have the honour to inform you that Mr Markiewicz, Casimir Joseph, is said to have been born on March 15th 1871 (at Denefow Russian Poland) son of Paul and Marie Chrzaszczewska. Without right, he takes the title of Count Dunin-Markiewicz, in that Poland has never had a Count of that name.

He claims that he has the right to add Dunin to his name, in 1678 the King of Poland having conceded this emblazonment to a Markiewicz family which has never been known to be a noble one, none of its members having become historic. On the other hand he may have been able to buy this title at the Vatican, or to obtain it in Austria.

Mr Markiewicz was married to one of his compatriots, a Demoiselle Edwige Neymand, who died in Poland a few months ago, at the age of 21 years, by whom he has a son: Stanislas, born in Paris around the month of July 1897, who is to be found in Poland with his paternal grandmother.

He arrived in Paris from Russia in the course of 1896 accompanied by his wife, and having lodged for a short time in a hotel, he installed himself in his rooms at Rue Sainte Placide 18, where he occupied an apartment and a painter's studio from the month of October 1896 to July 1897.

At that time, he said when leaving that he was returning for some time to Russia. One found him lodging alone in January 1898 in a painter's studio, Rue Vaugirard 114, where his wife came to join him some months later.

Having become pregnant, his wife left Paris around March 1899 to return alone to Poland, but she went into labour on the journey, and having arrived at her relatives she became ill and died of peritonitis.

Mr Markiewicz is an artist painter, student of Mr Bouguereau, member of the Institute, artist painter, professor at the Academie Julien, Rue du Dragon, 31. He has completed two large paintings, one titled Legendary Russian Love and the second the portrait of an Irish woman which he will exhibit, having been admitted to the Salon ...

The portrait which he is going to exhibit is of an Irishwoman who passes as his future wife whom he is due to marry around next September. The couple have known each other for a long time already, she having been known in all the houses in which Mr Markiewicz has passed, and there can be no mistakes here as this woman (demoiselle) is very tall and her fiance measures about two metres.

One has known that she belongs to a great and rich English family, that she was Miss Gorbut [sic], artist painter, who owns a studio at Rue Campagne Premiere 17, and has her domicile on the right bank. One does not know the fortune of Mr Markiewicz, but one knows that he spends a lot of money.

He has always received at his place a very large number of young people of both sexes of eccentric appearance and disposition, but who are nothing more than students at the Beaux Arts and some models. He is known as somewhat original, but he is known as a Bon Vivant, liking the noisy life (le chahut), to receive at his place his comrades to drink a great deal of champagne, to dance at his friends places, or in his own studio where he pays to bring musicians or if there are none, where they amuse themselves at the piano.

He also adores billiards and cards, and in that regard it is told that he is so passionately given to gambling that he allowed himself to lose his prized bicycle ...

In a word, he likes his pleasures. At the last Bal des Quat' Lords, he was chosen to be the Drum Major and led the parade in a costume which sat well with his size. At the last Mardi Gras he rented a costume to disguise himself as the Huzzar of Death and one of his friends and compatriots had the inspiration to paint him in this costume and one can view this painting which has been received at the Salon.

He claims not to have been very happy during his marriage and also since the death of his wife he indulges in all pleasures which take up every instant of his time. Apart from this stormy life, there is nothing with which to reproach him. One would say that if he is not serious at present it is because of his youth and that reason will dominate him through age or another happy marriage.

When I had read the Markievicz documents, my mind turned to the historical revisionists back home, who, I imagined, would have a field day. In fact, the report was presented in *The Irish Times* in such a way that hardly anyone in the historical professions noticed it.

My comments on revisionism, however, drew from Lena one of her more mordant and very Russian remarks: 'In your country historical revisionism is in its infancy. Here in Russia we have a saying: "How can we know what our future is today when we do not know what our history will be tomorrow."'

— Not the End of the World —

In the Ireland of the 1950s and 1960s the Catholic faithful were asked to pray for the 'conversion of Russia'. No one was told exactly what that meant, but it was connected with the visions of the Virgin Mary at the Portuguese town of Fatima in 1917, just before the October Revolution took place in St Petersburg.

We were not asked what we were praying for Russia to be converted to. It was simply assumed that the Orthodox Church there was as near to the Catholic Church as made no difference. I was not long in Russia before I realised that the Russian Orthodox's view of this matter was very different indeed. One senior Irish diplomat discovered this in a very unusual way.

He and other members of the diplomatic corps were taken on a tour of the great monastery at Sergiev Posad, the former Zagorsk, by one of the more important monks. Sergiev Posad is a wonderful place of golden domes and ancient churches. The first glimpse of it on the horizon on the short journey north from Moscow was one of many magical moments during my early days in Russia.

The diplomat, while walking along a corridor in the monastery, noticed a strange painting. It represented a vision of hell in which those suffering eternal damnation were dressed in religious garb. He asked the monk who these unusual members of the damned were and was told: 'Oh, those are the Roman Catholics.'

My first experience of Russian Orthodoxy came in 1992, when the first Easter celebrations after the dissolution of the Soviet Union took place. Moscow had not seen an Easter like it since before the revolution. At midnight on Saturday, the Russian Orthodox Church's greatest festival began when, for the first time in seventy-four years, the bell in the Ivan the Great Tower in the Kremlin was rung. It was then joined by the bells of all of Moscow's churches, which traditionally numbered *sorok-sorokov* (forty times forty) but are now, thanks to Stalin, considerably fewer.

For the political and religious leaders, the main ceremony was Midnight Mass at the Cathedral of the Epiphany, celebrated by Alexiy II, Patriarch of Moscow and All the Russias, and attended by Vice-president Alexander Rutskoy, Moscow's mayor, Gavriil Popov, and a number of diplomats from foreign embassies in Moscow, who were, by the way, charged two thousand roubles a head for the privilege of attending.

In his message to all the Orthodox faithful, the patriarch stressed that this Easter came at '... a difficult time, full of hardship, privation and trial for many of us. Let this beautiful feast enter every home with peace and love and give us strength to retain Christian patience and courage, whatever the circumstances.'

Orthodox services took place, too, in the Assumption Cathedral in the Kremlin and in St Basil's Cathedral in Red Square; and, in events which underlined the great changes that had taken place within a single year, an American evangelical choir gave recitals in the Central House of Trades Unions, St Basil's and the Central Theatre of the Red Army.

But these were the big official events. For ordinary Russians the local parish church was the centre of the festivities and the venue for me was the little Church of the Assumption of the Mother of God in the area known as the Potteries. There, one Saturday evening, the parish priest Father Valentin was permitted for the first time to perform the procession known as *Krestniy Khod* thrice round the outside of the church as midnight approached.

The Church of the Assumption, in what was the traditional district of Moscow potters, was built in 1654 and is a tiny building with a central golden onion-dome surrounded by four blue domes studded with golden stars – a little architectural gem set in a concrete wasteland of high-rise buildings.

On that Saturday evening, it was packed to overflowing. Those too late to gain entry crowded the streets outside, and Father Valentin, his face illuminated with a broad smile, told me he had never thought he would live to see this day.

Outside on the church wall, the rare icon of the Virgin and Child, in which the painter had given the Virgin three hands, was adorned with paper flowers in the white, red and blue colours of the Russian tricolour. Old women kissed the icon and whispered their prayers, while younger Russians – and there were many of them – looked on, holding thin red candles stuck through small squares of paper to protect their hands from the melting wax.

Inside the crowded church, the press of people was overwhelming. A tiny *babushka* beside me knew from her long experience exactly when to bow and when to make the sign of the cross to match the words emanating from the priests, hidden behind the ornate golden iconostasis. She clicked her tongue repeatedly at the two youngsters in front of her in their stone-washed denims, whose lack of familiarity with the details of the liturgy was all too obvious.

At the high point of the ceremony, Father Valentin, his long grey beard hanging down over his ornate scarlet vestments, led the *Krestniy Khod* out into the street followed by a platoon of *babushki*, stalwarts of the church, all determined to be first in line behind the priests and deacons. Then the doors of the church were closed on those who remained inside as the procession encircled the little church three times, before they were opened again to the words: '*Khristos voskrese*' – 'Christ is risen'. '*Voistinu voskrese*' – 'Truly He is risen'. The congregation responded with fervour, repeatedly making the sign of the cross as their little red candles glimmered.

Out on the street afterwards, tiny pinpoints of light could be seen as small knots of people, their red candles shielded by their hands from the cold wind – there had been a snowstorm earlier – made their way home to their cramped apartments for the *Razgovenye*, a traditional meal including eggs, butter and meat, as well as the high cylindrical *kulich* Easter cake.

Some kiosk traders had stayed open late for the occasion, plying their Indonesian whiskies, their small packets of Yugoslav condoms and their American cigarettes. In this manner, in the early hours of the first Easter Sunday since the end of communist rule, the old Russia collided uncomfortably with the new.

Those cosy and moving events of that first Easter night since the collapse of the communist system were not repeated throughout the former Soviet Union. A crisis of faith had arisen. Most Soviet citizens had been brought up in the traditions of atheism and Marxism-Leninism. A minority clung to those views, but for a large proportion of the population a set of beliefs nurtured since their childhood had suddenly been demolished and they were open to conversion.

Groups of evangelical carpetbaggers began to arrive from the West. Once, in the lobby of a grim hotel in the central Russian city of Voronezh, I encountered a group of young, clean-shaven Americans crowding the reception desk. My conversation with one of them went something like this:

'What are you guys doing here?'

'We've come to save Russia.'

'How long will you be here?'

'Two weeks.'

In Georgia (USSR) a planeload of Bibles had arrived at Sukhumi airport from Georgia (USA) with the purpose of 'converting' a country that had been Christian since the first century. It was a local Soviet proselytiser, however, who made the biggest impact in the course of this period of religious turmoil.

It had become the practice for many of those who once sang 'The Internationale' to learn other anthems, the most appropriate perhaps being 'Money Makes the World go Round'. Old communists had become new capitalists, and every sphere in which money could be made, from politics through business to religion, had been permeated by the former comrades.

Some of the top brass from the Soviet Union had to settle for smaller pastures, new little countries instead of the former superpower. Geidar Aliyev, for example, who once bombarded old Leonid Brezhnev with diamonds and casks of caviar from his Caspian homeland of Azerbaijan in the hope of becoming prime minister, settled temporarily for the little enclave of Nakhichevan before making his successful bid for the Azeri leadership.

Other communists in the Central Asian republics made an overnight conversion to Islam, and the president of Turkmenistan, Mr Saparmurad Niyazov, a former communist, declared himself a 'hero of the republic' having never quite made it to 'hero of the Soviet Union'.

Several Moscow banks were believed to be funded from the money stashed away by the party in Switzerland. But perhaps the most bizarre conversion to Western ways was the case of Maria Devi Christos, the self-styled 'Mother of the World'.

Her face became as well known in Moscow as that of Boris Yeltsin or Mikhail Gorbachev. She took her name from the Virgin Mary, Christ and the word Devi, which is the female personification of the Indian god Shiva. On lamp posts and walls all over Moscow, Maria – white-gowned, wearing what appeared to be a full-bottomed judicial wig, raising two fingers of her right hand in blessing, and carrying a shepherd's staff in her left hand – peered down from posters that beseeched Muscovites to join an organisation called the 'White Brotherhood'.

She had, she informed us, died, been in Heaven and had returned to us mere mortals as a joint personification of Jesus and Mary, with a dash of Indian deity thrown in, like so much ground cumin seed.

In fact, Maria Devi Christos would have us believe that she did not have a human body but only *appeared* to have one due to a mysterious combination of light. In more materialistic terms she could be described as a living hologram.

No one in the brotherhood could prove this, however, as its rules strictly prohibited coming close to the deity for fear of harmful heavenly radiation. One of the key beliefs of the sect was that the apocalypse would hit Moscow on 24 November 1993, and anyone who had not joined the brotherhood and deposited their clothes, money and jewellery by that date would be doomed.

The great city would on that day be hit by a massive earthquake, and non-members would fall down into a bottomless abyss, never to be seen again. Then the Golden Age would begin and only 144,000 members of the brotherhood would remain to enjoy the fruits of the new world.

While the Golden Age had begun for Maria in the form of two large houses in Kiev, the membership had not reached anything like the prescribed figure, and there were reports of child-stealing in order to bring the numbers up.

At one stage, the Mother of the World was reported to be in Poland, because of a criminal case brought against her husband, Yuri Krivonogov – or 'Ioan Swami', as he was now known – by the Moscow Militia. Mr Swami, by the way, claimed to be the reincarnation of 'Father the Lord, Nicholas Roerich, King Vladimir, John the Baptist, Osiris, Krishna and Adam'.

The brotherhood, not surprisingly, came under attack from established Churchmen. Never ones to mince their words, Russian Orthodox priests made their point with declarations describing the organisation's members as 'dogs with the saliva of lust', 'godless bastards' and 'stinking debauchees'.

Komsomolskaya Pravda, once the mouthpiece of Komsomol (the Communist League of Youth) and now a democratic organ, decided to investigate the background of the Mother of the World. And where better to start than in the old files of Komsomol, to which it had particularly easy access.

What they discovered was the following: Maria Devi Christos was born in Ukraine as Marina Tsvygun and began her working life as a Komsomol employee. From there she graduated to the rank of instructor at the party's regional committee, charged with visiting major enterprises in her area and telling the workers that the golden age of Marxism-Leninism was at hand and that if they didn't join they were doomed.

When the new times arrived, things went sour for a while and she quickly fell down the social scale, becoming in succession a journalist and a waitress in a Kiev café. Now, like many of her old comrades, she appeared to have found a new song to sing: at least until 24 November 1993.

As you may have gathered, the apocalypse did not occur in Moscow on the prescribed date, but Maria, in anticipation of that non-event, announced to all who would listen that the world would end in Kiev and, never having covered the End of the World before in the course of my journalistic career, I went to Sheremetyevo airport and got on a newly privatised Transaero Boeing 737 for the Ukrainian capital.

When I got there, the White Brotherhood announced that the end of the world, scheduled to take place on the following Sunday, might have to be postponed due to the actions of the local police force. Members of the sect had gathered in their thousands in the Ukrainian capital for the great occasion, but the local cops were giving them a hard time.

Originally fixed for 24 November, the Ukrainian Armageddon was brought forward by ten days for no apparent reason. Members of the cult had been demonstrating in the precincts of wonderful eleventh-century St Sophia's Cathedral in preparation for what the local authorities worried might end up as a mass suicide.

Then out of the blue, Maria Devi Christos was arrested with

her husband and taken to the city's Podolsk detention centre. Dressed in a sweater and denim skirt, she was identified when an ex-husband pointed her out to police and when members of the brotherhood began to prostrate themselves in her sacred presence. Taken into custody with her current spouse, she screamed in what appeared to be Latin: *'Vade retro Satanas.'* (Get behind me Satan.')

According to police sources in Kiev, she was under the influence of her husband, Krivonogov, who was described as a sexually obsessed hypnotist wanted by police in several countries. The couple were charged with incitement to suicide, illegal seizure of land and breaches of the country's law on religious denominations.

A basic condition for the Armageddon, however, was that Maria Devi Christos must die before the holocaust could take place. This looked somewhat difficult to achieve under the surveillance of the Kiev police force, but her husband, Krivonogov, a chemist, was rumoured to have given her a time-lapse suicide pill which could trigger the catastrophe.

As the days passed, more and more cult members converged on Kiev from other parts of Ukraine and in large numbers from Russia, where posters of the 'goddess' attracted many young people, including the son of my Russian-Irish friend Genrikh Patrikeyevich Kreitser.

While they were busy waiting for the world to end, some cult members caused havoc in the cathedral, smashing icons and spraying the church's interior with foam from fire extinguishers. Fourteen Interior Ministry riot police were injured in the incidents and serious damage was done to the cathedral's main altar.

By now nearly eight hundred members of the brotherhood

had been detained in the greater Kiev area. But thousands more were still at large, and it was announced that the end of the world would not be called off for a second time.

It was, however, the least cataclysmic Armageddon this correspondent has ever covered. About a hundred of us stood in the bright sunshine and bitter cold in the square outside the great St Sophia Cathedral waiting for the sky to fall. It didn't happen, otherwise you would not be reading this. The prediction by the 'goddess' Marina Tsvygun, alias Marina Krivonogova, alias Maria Devi Christos, that Sunday 14 November would bring the Last Judgement to St Sophia's Square, the navel of the universe, was an enticing proposition for the small crowd – composed mainly of journalists – that braved the perishing wind.

Ironically, the 'goddess' and her prophet husband Yuri Krivonogov and other members of the Great White Brotherhood sect sat in the warmth of their prison cells while we stood and froze.

There were no peals of thunder and, thank goodness, no separation of the wheat from the chaff. Two bus loads of police sat parked under a sign marked 'Parking Categorically Prohibited' in front of the cathedral's great blue-and-white-stuccoed bell tower with its golden dome.

Suddenly, a voice uttered the words '*S Prazdnikom*,' the traditional Russian greeting used on holidays of religion and communism. It was Colonel Alexander Naumov of the Interior Ministry police, with whom I had exchanged the occasional shot of vodka over the past three days.

'Nothing to report,' he told me. 'The city is quieter than it has been for weeks. The event was to happen at noon, the deadline has passed. Drop round to the station at about five for a quick one if you like.'

It all would have been so funny but for the pathetic sadness which surrounded the occasion. In a corner of the square stood a woman named Nina, who had travelled all the way from a village in the steppes of northern Kazakhstan in the hope of finding her twenty-five-year-old daughter, Natasha, who had defected to the White Brotherhood and whom she had not seen for two years.

She held Natasha's photograph in front of her like an icon, hoping someone would recognise her. 'She met these people on the streets of our village and fell under their spell. I used to argue with her. I told her this thing was one hundred per cent wrong. She said it was three hundred per cent right.

'Then she sent me a telegram for my birthday, asking me to come to Kiev and join her for the day of judgement, but I haven't found her. She had a good life, a job, an apartment and a child. I don't understand why she would do this.'

Antonina had travelled from a Cossack village near Krasnodar in southern Russia in search of her daughter, whom she would not name, and her little granddaughter, Dasha. In tears, she told of how she had found Dasha, an eight-year-old who clung to her coat tails in the bitter cold. She had gone to a Russian extrasensory mystic, who told her that her daughter and grandchild were in Kiev with the brotherhood. Little Dasha had been one of the eight hundred brethren picked up by the police that week.

As time passed, the Western journalists drifted away to their expensive hotels. Nina and Antonina and a dozen or so others stayed on in the hope of finding their loved ones.

— The 'Moscow Letter' —

In 1986 I became impressed by the political efforts of my Clondalkin neighbour, Pat Rabbitte, and decided to join the Workers' Party to help get him elected to Dáil Éireann. It was a decision I was never to live down as far as a small number of politically sectarian journalistic colleagues were concerned. None of these, it should be stressed, was a member of the staff of *The Irish Times*.

My role in the party, which I left in May 1991, was purely on a local level. It involved the writing of election literature, the selling of the *Irish People* in local pubs on Sunday mornings, the incessant delivery of literature through the letterboxes of Clondalkin, Newcastle and Tallaght in the constituency of Dublin South West, as well as chairing meetings of the constituency council from time to time.

After Pat had been elected to the Dáil in 1989, I was approached to stand in the local elections and declined. I was also, incidentally, approached by Fine Gael and declined to stand for them as well. I had joined the party purely on the condition I worked locally and that no pressure would be placed on my journalistic work.

There was nothing out of the ordinary about this in *The Irish Times*. The current editor, Geraldine Kennedy, had been a Progressive Democrat TD; her predecessor, Conor Brady, had been a member of the John Marcus O'Sullivan branch of Fine Gael; and before that it was well known that Douglas Gageby was not unsympathetic to Fianna Fáil. Three senior journalists, John Horgan, James Downey and Don Buckley, had stood for election for the Labour Party.

In all cases they were meticulously on their guard not to allow their political beliefs to impinge on their editorial integrity. Dick Walsh, who had been political editor, was seen as sympathetic to the Workers' Party, as was Mary Maher, but neither of these were members. In later years attempts were made by controversialists such as Vincent Browne and Kevin Myers to suggest that Workers' Party members and sympathisers had an undue influence. Browne even wrote that they were 'embedded' in *The Irish Times*.

Comparisons were made between a group in RTÉ headed by Eoghan Harris and those associated with Dick Walsh in *The Irish Times*. It is enough to say that while the staff of *The Irish Times* clubbed together to commission a bust of Walsh to be put on display in its new office block in Dublin, the likelihood of RTÉ staff doing the same for Harris in Donnybrook is extremely remote.

Conor Brady, no supporter of the Workers' Party, and who had a much better handle on what was going on in his own paper, made the following comment to staff at one of the general meetings he held: 'I have never encountered any conscious or deliberate attempt by any *Irish Times* journalist to distort or misrepresent anything.'

In my own case, I remember scrupulously writing a story in such a way that those speaking on behalf of the different parties were listed in order of their party's representation in the Dáil. Pat Rabbitte, as the member of the smallest of these, was placed last. The result, of course, was that there was pressure on space and Rabbitte's contribution was the only one not to appear in the paper.

My brief period in the party, however, gave me an advantage over many colleagues in learning how political parties worked and how the Workers' Party had a number of different strands of opinion attempting to get their views accepted as policy. There was a certain amateurism in the journalistic appraisal of the party as a monolithic, often Stalinist, bloc. The Soviet embassy, interestingly, had a much clearer view of what was going on there.

In my trawls of the Communist Party archives in Moscow, I came across an assessment of the Workers' Party's internal politics that was given in February 1986 in a non-confidential document from the Soviet embassy's second secretary, Mr D.S. Molodtsov. The party, he wrote, contained at least two tendencies. One deserved to be called Marxist-Leninist and the other 'would be more correctly determined as a Social Democratic tendency'.

'Such a situation,' he wrote, 'was connected with the fact that the Workers' Party crystallised from the left wing of Sinn Féin, a petty-bourgeois nationalist party, where Marxists played a certain, but not dominant, role.'

He identified the 'chief ideologist' of the social-democratic tendency as the trade unionist Des Geraghty, and said the party's international secretary, Seán Ó Cionnaith, was standing on 'solid Marxist-Leninist ground'. The party was later to split on lines quite close to those identified by Molodtsov, although there was also an element of North–South division involved.

As for the monolithic nature of the Workers' Party, that was shown to be false when, about a year after I left, it split into different factions. Still, there was a good bit of mischievous fun in the Clondalkin branch, which frequently and openly opposed the thinking of the general secretary, Seán Garland. We made a name for ourselves when a motion was proposed at an *Ard Fheis* to call for a ban on all trade with 'totalitarian regimes such as that in South Africa'. Our amendment to ban all trade with 'totalitarian regimes such as those in South Africa and North Korea' proved so controversial that the original motion was withdrawn.

I left the party before that split took place and before I became Moscow correspondent of *The Irish Times*. I had no personal animus against anyone in the Workers' Party, but there was a great deal of friction between various individuals and groupings, which made me feel quite uncomfortable. Pat Rabbitte, by the way, gave me an interesting piece of advice. He told me that I should never join the Labour Party, as the internal machinations there would drive me crazy.

Pat later became the leader of the Labour Party and resigned after the 2007 general election. His advice in retrospect seems ironic, but I took it. I don't know if he advised others in the same way, but it was interesting to look at what happened in Clondalkin at the time of Democratic Left's formation as a breakaway from the Workers' Party. There were just three active members other than Pat Rabbitte when the split came: Seán Kelly, a brilliant Cork computer expert; Sinéad Butler, a superb linguist; and Donna Conlon, a sound and highly intelligent working-class mother. All took the same line as I had done and opted out of active politics rather than join Democratic Left, stay in the Workers' Party, or eventually join Labour.

The most controversial document regarding Ireland to emerge from the archives of the Communist Party of the Soviet Union became known as the 'Moscow Letter', and was the subject of a libel case in which Proinsias De Rossa was awarded record-breaking damages against the *Sunday Independent*.

This letter, also from 1986, purported to be a request from the Workers' Party to the Communist Party of the Soviet Union for a grant of £1 million to set up a party school. The letter also referred to previous funding of the Workers' Party through what was termed 'special activities' and which had now been abandoned.

Unfortunately for me, the story broke in the London *Independent* on the day before it was to appear in *The Irish Times*. The reason for this was that it appeared in the '*Indy*' on the one weekday in October 1992 when *The Irish Times* was not published. My report, in far greater detail, had been with the editor's office in Dublin for approximately two weeks before that, and appeared the day after the non-publication day.

The letter had, by the way, emerged as a photocopy, in which the alleged signatures of leading Workers' Party members, Seán Garland and Proinsias De Rossa, were almost illegible. My later attempts to view the original and get a clearer photocopy met with some difficulty due to problems within the Communist Party archives themselves.

A new electronic system for finding files was in operation, but a directive had been received from the office of President Yeltsin forbidding its use. One can only assume that Mr Yeltsin wanted to make it difficult for people to find certain files concerning himself. In any event the archivists did their best not only to find the original letter but to dig up anything they could that concerned Ireland.

By mid-December I was called to the archives, where a package of documents had been prepared. It was obvious that the Soviet embassy in Dublin had been working hard on all fronts. Each Soviet embassy at the time was working for at least three masters. The ambassador usually reported to the Foreign Ministry; a KGB operative posing as a diplomat would report to the Lubyanka; and a third party would report to the Communist Party.

The reports to the Communist Party were the ones that I was allowed to view and to have photocopied. They were so detailed that they even included a copy of Dr Garret FitzGerald's speech to the Fine Gael *Ard Fheis* in 1986.

I now had a good photocopy of the letter in which the two signatures were absolutely clear. I faxed this to Dublin with the following advice. I knew that a handwriting expert would be called in, so I pointed out that what they had received was a fax copy of a photocopy of the original letter. I suggested, therefore, that they should do one of two things: they could send a handwriting expert out from Dublin to examine the original in the archives or they could get a Russian handwriting expert to make a similar examination.

My advice was not taken and, instead, an expert made his judgement on the fax copy of the photocopy. I returned to Dublin with the package of documents from the archives. Due to my experience of the previous burglaries, I did not want to leave them in the Moscow office. I handed them over to Conor Brady for safekeeping but, unfortunately, he was unable to find them at a later date when they were badly needed.

This arose many years later when my Moscow days were over and a further investigation into the Moscow Letter was made. Conor O'Clery and Denis Staunton, then the paper's Berlin correspondent, were sent to Moscow to meet Seán Garland, who had promised to provide new information on the issue.

They met Garland in the Shamrock Bar in Moscow. He was accompanied by Yevgeny Lagutin, a former member of the international department of the Communist Party of the Soviet Union. Lagutin told them he had known a great deal about the letter, as he had been assigned to translate it into Russian. He claimed not only that De Rossa had signed the document but that he had actually typed it on a typewriter supplied by the staff of the Oktyabrskaya Hotel, where both men had been staying.

Staunton and O'Clery produced a report of the meeting but the editor (Conor Brady) believed that there was not enough evidence to proceed. I was then sent to Moscow to meet Denis Staunton and Lagutin and ask further questions. On the night of my arrival, I received a phone call from Dublin and was told that I was not to discover anything that contradicted the evidence given by Garland and Lagutin. I regarded this as extremely unethical and decided to try to find out as much evidence as I could without prejudice either to Garland or De Rossa.

Staunton and I met Lagutin in the Metropol Hotel in Moscow. What he told us was largely a reiteration of his earlier interview, but there were some points on which the two interviews did not coincide. In casual conversation after the formal taped interview had ended, I expressed surprise that the Workers' Party had asked for as much as £1 million. Lagutin seemed genuinely surprised and said he did not know anything about such a sum.

Back in Dublin, I attended a special editorial conference.

Conor Brady had been in touch with some Special Branch contacts, who asserted that Garland and De Rossa were in Moscow at the time the Moscow Letter was dated.

I raised the matter of the phone call I had received and said that I would research the matter honestly and would come up with whatever I could find, whether it supported Garland's claims or not. At this stage some differences arose concerning strategy on the matter. Conor Brady and Paul Gillespie, the foreign editor, were keen to pursue it to the end, while Pat O'Hara (deputy editor) and Don Buckley (duty editor) urged extreme caution.

Over an extended period, Denis Staunton and I were sent to Moscow to talk to people who were members of the Central Committee at the time of the letter. We had some difficulty in tracking these people down. Some, we discovered, were already dead. Others, such as Eduard Shevardnadze, were no longer in Moscow. Those we did manage to find, such as Anatoly Chernyayev, Vadim Zagladin and Karen Brutents, were all strongly connected with former president Mikhail Gorbachev. None of them seemed to know anything about De Rossa. All of them knew Garland, and said that the only other Workers' Party man they knew personally was Des O'Hagan, a leading party member from Northern Ireland.

On Staunton's recommendation, *The Irish Times* employed a man who had researched the archives for German newspapers in order to obtain fresh copies of the letter. This person, an elderly man whose surname Bezimensky translated into English as 'Nameless', came up with copies of the relevant documents marked 'Not for Publication'. I recognised them as genuine.

Previously, I had had no particular reason to read the Russian translation of the Moscow Letter in any great detail. This time

I read it closely. There was an annotation at the end that said, in Russian, 'Translated by Lev Ponomaryov'. This was a damning discovery, because according to the document itself, Lagutin's claim to be its translator and therefore to have known its precise provenance was shown to be false.

The Irish Times' pursuit of the matter, therefore, came quickly to an end. A number of other journalists had worked on the story in Dublin and elsewhere in Ireland. Memos had flown in all directions as was the custom in *The Irish Times*, and I retained copies of them and of the documents retrieved from the archives by Bezimensky. On my retirement I gave these documents to John Horgan, who is now the press ombudsman. He in turn gave them to Professor Eunan O'Halpin of Trinity College, Dublin and they are currently in that university's archives.

The Moscow archivists, by the way, were able to show by certain markings that the photocopy of the Moscow Letter that had caused the initial stir back in Ireland had been released from the office of the Information Minister, Mr Mikhail Poltoranin, a close associate of Mr Yeltsin.

Mr Poltoranin, incidentally, while officially described as a democrat, would hardly have qualified on that score under any close examination. He was a professed admirer of one of the most reactionary figures in Russian history, Konstantin Pobedonostsev. He also claimed that twenty years previously he had predicted the demise of the Soviet Union. This was not done by means of political science, he wrote, but by his conviction that the future could be foretold by the behaviour of fruit flies.

All this emerged in an interview with one of Moscow's new glossy magazines, *Moscow Magazine*, and he went even further by suggesting he knew when the end of the world was going to take place. He was, he told his interviewer, '... an earnest believer in cosmogony and, interlarding Kant's ideas with the latest data of special analysis, I set the time boundaries for the end of the world on Planet Earth as a whole.'

He concluded coyly by saying, 'I shall not go into details here as this goes beyond the subject of our conversation.' The end of the Soviet Union and its evil influence would, he said, be replaced by a new cluster of fruit flies. A great Muslim empire would take shape, grow strong, and sprawl over half of the world, compelling 'civilisation to throw vast resources into the furnace of nuclear confrontation'. He also said that Russia must lead the way to the future expansion of a new super-empire, which, in alliance with many non-Muslim countries, would create a balancing counterweight.

Mr Poltoranin's hero, Pobedonostsev, had a particular abhorrence of parliamentary democracy, and this concept was quickly taking root in the Yeltsin camp. Parliament, led by Mr Ruslan Khasbulatov, was getting in the way of Yeltsin's followers. It contained a large number of hardliners from the communist and extreme right-wing camps.

But not all of those who stood out against the president and occupied the White House parliament buildings in October 1993 were hardliners, and the Western press, which by now included a large number of Yeltsin's cheerleaders, had to tailor their ideas to the developing situation. The *Economist*, for example, which had previously described Khasbulatov as a free-market reformer, now branded him as a hard-liner. I was reminded at the time of a description of the magazine by an eminent person far detached from the political left. It was, he said, 'the best-informed news magazine in the world except on subjects I know something about'.

In the end the Yeltsin forces stormed the parliament build-ings, shelling it from the banks of the Moscow River. A march by parliamentary supporters on the TV Centre at Ostankino had earlier resulted in large-scale bloodshed and was in the main reported as the heroic defence of the centre against blood-thirsty communists. Sixty-one people died that night. Only one of them was a soldier defending the TV station. The other sixty were either journalists, passers-by or members of a raggle-taggle mob of elderly communists led by what my colleague Bruce Clark of the London *Times* described as 'bumbling blimp General Albert Makashov'.

I had been at another march earlier that day at which gunfire had echoed around the parliament buildings. I had considered following the remnants of the demonstration to Ostankino, but changed my mind at the last minute as my deadline was approaching and our photographer Sasha Meshcheryakov told me he had a direct-line number to one of the journalists at the station, so I could keep in touch while I was writing my story.

It was a fortunate decision.

Later that evening, the bodies began to arrive at the mortu-ary of the Sklivosovky Hospital, just one hundred metres from my apartment. One of them was that of Rory Peck, who came from an Ango-Irish family in Prehen, just outside Derry city.

No one was sure how many died in the White House itself. In an attempt to find out more, I interviewed some of the firemen who had been called to put out the blaze. They spoke of being ordered to wait an inappropriately long time before entering the building and being ordered not to enter a certain floor, where they could hear a great deal of shooting going on.

The whole business was quite peculiar. People were being killed at the White House and at the TV station. Yeltsin and his friends were trying to convince everyone that a civil war was in progress. Yet outside of those two small locations, all of Moscow was absolutely normal, with people going about their everyday lives unconcerned.

With Helen Womack of the London *Independent*, I made an attempt to enter the White House, but it ended quite dramatically. There were groups of protesters with banners attacking President Yeltsin and excoriating the foreign media for their reportage. Farther down the side street leading from the American embassy to the White House, there was a barricade manned by armed troops and led by a Russian-army major.

We tried everything to persuade him to let us through. Helen even flirted with him, but to no avail. I began to address him as colonel, but even that promotion failed to move him. We decided, therefore, to try to sneak around via the courtyards of some apartment blocks and past the Mir Hotel into the confines of the White House. We both knew the area very well, for it had been our daily chore to visit the White House in the days leading up to the shelling to check on developments.

As we made our way through the maze of buildings, getting closer to the smouldering building, our journey came to an abrupt end. We were thrown to the ground by a group of blackened-faced soldiers, who first of all thought we might be some kind of provocateurs. We showed them our identifications as officially registered foreign correspondents and we got off with a mere scolding. We were told that we were very stupid people to be where we were, as the place was full of snipers. I suppose they were right.

The parliament having been summarily dealt with, President Yeltsin turned his attention to setting up a Constitution that would place an unprecedented amount of power in his hands.

By the end of the year, a new basic law was passed by referendum, allowing the president to rule by decree. The new parliament, the State Duma, was not enabled even to discuss any presidential decrees, let alone modify them.

He could choose the prime minister, the head of the Central Bank and key members of the judiciary. He could also, in a bizarre constitutional move, dissolve parliament if it passed a motion of no-confidence in the government. Perhaps most importantly the procedure for impeachment of the president was so complicated that it was virtually inoperable. Western governments almost unanimously and, it must be said, short-sightedly, backed the Yeltsin Constitution. The same governments, and frequently the same political personalities, today claim that the Russian president has too much power. This change in attitude may be connected with the fact that Russia is now a far more powerful state than it was in those days.

In the immediate aftermath of the shelling, a curfew was introduced in Moscow, during the course of which strange events took place. There were those who took advantage of the situation and none more so than that enterprising Glaswegian, Jacko, whose bar in the Leningradskaya Hotel was just a few hundred metres from the *Irish Times'* office. Jacko hit upon the idea of giving drinks away for nothing for part of the day and naturally his place became packed with customers. But many of those who imbibed unwisely discovered that they were still on the premises when the curfew began. They were now trapped until after dawn, and Jacko began to charge them a great deal more than usual for their beer and spirits.

The curfew was used by others to round up Azeri traders in the capital and send them on a free fifty-three-hour train ride to Baku. The man mainly responsible for this was General

Alexander Kulikov, who had been placed in charge of the city for the duration of the state of emergency.

Then, when the state of emergency ended, the mayor, Yuri Luzhkov, took over where the general had left off. He promised citizens even greater protection against those who had been undermining the city's morals in a sinister horticultural manner.

The city would be cleansed, Mr Luzhkov told the state-controlled news agency ITAR-TASS, by 'enhanced police patrols', volunteers, public organisations and 'democratically minded youth'. He also intended, with Mr Yeltsin's backing, he said, to introduce a visa system for Moscow, which marked a return to the old communist regulations and the even older ones of Tsarist times.

He expressed the view, too, that the removal of the Azeris and others with darkish skins would help oust those who sold 'exotic fruits' and make room for 'honest traders from Tambov, Lipetsk, Bryansk, and other places, who sell traditional Russian produce like cabbage and potatoes'. But Mr Luzhkov's proposals held out the prospect of certain problems. If a youth, for example, cornered you in some dark alley in the dead of the Moscow night, how were you to know if he or she was 'democratically minded' or just a thug or, even worse – and in the language used at the time to describe Mr Yeltsin's enemies – an 'undemocratically minded, morally degenerate, revanchist bandit'?

You might question the young person on his or her dietary habits. You could try the following: 'Do you eat exotic fruits?' If the answer was, 'This produce is non-Russian', your interlocutor would be democratically minded. If he or she added, 'I prefer good Russian cabbage and potatoes sold by honest traders', then you would be talking to someone whose democratic credentials were impeccable. It might be advisable, for safety's sake, not to have on your person any incriminating materials such as yams, mangoes, papayas, pomegranates, pineapples, coconuts, mandarins, sweet peppers, saffron, nutmegs, cinnamon, or garam masala.

Better still, you could carry with you real evidence of your support for democracy in the form of a sack of spuds as well as some cabbage and beetroot. In order to do this, you would probably have to queue for some time before meeting an honest trader from Tambov, for which you should have counted your blessings. You would also have been well advised to count your change, for Tambov was a city not noted throughout the vast Russian Federation for 'honest trading'. The denizens of that city were not known throughout Russia and Ukraine as the 'Tambov Wolves' for nothing.

Some wishy-washy liberals, exotic non-Russian organisations such as Helsinki-Watch and Amnesty International, were quite worried about what form the new citrus-free Russia would take, now that the patriotism of certain fruits and vegetables had been called into question. One of the country's leading TV personalities, Mr Alexander Lyubimov, a hero of the glasnost era, was axed for broadcasting his own views on the matter rather than those of the state.

In one respect, worries that Russia was about to become a Latin-American-style dictatorship were, without a shadow of doubt, unfounded. If Mr Luzhkov had his way, the last thing Russia would become was a banana republic.

With my US colleague Ken Fireman, I did a tour of the police stations near the different market areas of Moscow to discover that the cells were packed to overflowing with men from the Caucasus. As well as the Muslim hordes from Azerbaijan and

Central Asia, there was a sprinkling of Christian Ossetes and Georgians. As one Muscovite put it: 'They all look the same.'

These developments did not bode well for the future of democracy in Russia, but I was not to be in Moscow much longer. One morning I received a phone call from Paddy Smyth, who was on the foreign desk in Dublin, to tell me that Jarlath Dolan, who had been appointed as correspondent in Johannesburg, had been killed in a car crash near the town of Colesberg in the Northern Cape.

Jarlath had frequently stayed with me on his visits to Moscow and had studied Russian at Trinity with a view to succeeding me as Moscow correspondent. While Jarlath had wanted to come to Moscow, I had hoped to take over where I had left off in South Africa in 1990. There was a great irony involved in this, for if both of us had got what we wanted, Jarlath might have been safely ensconced in Moscow rather than meeting his death in an over-turned car on a dirt track near a remote South African town.

As it turned out, I had been back in Dublin on a break when the African job had been advertised internally in *The Irish Times* earlier in 1993, and I wrote out my formal application and left it with the personnel department as the advertisement had requested. Usually an applicant from the staff is called for an interview before being declared successful or unsuccessful. In my case, however, receipt of my application was not even acknowledged. I discovered later that the interview panel was told I had withdrawn my application.

Jarlath was a good colleague so I didn't make a fuss of the matter. Now that he had lost his life in such tragic circumstances, I simply concentrated on the job in hand in Moscow where the country was still lurching from crisis to crisis.

There were, however, breaks from the pressure – especially

in the large Irish community, many of whom lived in the same foreigners-only compound as I did. Clare McGill from Bangor in County Down had taken over as Irish Trade Representative and had a really swish apartment overlooking two of Moscow's Stalinist skyscrapers built in what Lena described as the 'late repressionist style'.

Éamonn McCarthy from Whitehall in Dublin, who was involved on the administrative side, also had an apartment in the building. Éamonn, a true Dublin character, was extremely popular with the Irish community and known to them as 'the real ambassador', just as Jack Lynch had become known in Ireland even when out of office as 'the real Taoiseach'. Éamonn fancied a pint and spent a fair amount of time in a well-known spot called Night Flight, which had one of the hottest reputations in a city that had developed a reputation as the hottest spot in Europe. Éamonn, however, was not particularly interested in that sort of night life and liked the place mainly because the bar stayed open late.

There was a celebrated story that he told about himself. Moscow in midsummer had the climate of a Rome or a Barcelona. The dawn rose out of clear skies each day and this had greatly impressed Ambassador McCabe. One morning, when the embassy staff gathered for coffee, the ambassador regaled the assembled company with his description of having been on the embassy's flat roof to experience the wonderful occasion of the Moscow sunrise.

He then turned to Éamonn and asked him, 'Have you ever seen the sun rise over Moscow?'

The reply was almost instantaneous: 'I have, Ambassador. Every morning on the way home from Night Flight.'

On one particular evening I was asked to dinner by members of the embassy's secretarial staff, and on the way back to my apartment I did my usual check of the wires and messages from Dublin on the link to my office computer via the Sprint network. There was a message from Conor Brady asking me whether I was prepared to go to Johannesburg to cover the process leading to the end of apartheid which had already begun before Jarlath's death.

It was a strange turnaround. Not long before, my application for the Johannesburg job had not even warranted a reply, but now I was being offered the job without even an interview. I was to learn later that I had not been the first to have been offered the Johannesburg posting after Jarlath's death. Conor Brady had contacted Suzanne Breen of the Belfast office to ask her to take up the job. This decision was made to sort out personal difficulties between members of the staff in Belfast.

Many of the best decisions made by *The Irish Times* were made for reasons of office politics. The opening of the Moscow office was one of them. When Conor Brady had won the battle for the editorship of the paper with James Downey, it was obvious that the presence of both in the same office in Dublin would cause severe problems in the editorial area.

To avoid this, James Downey was offered the job of London editor, and in order to get the current London editor, Conor O'Clery's agreement, the latter was offered his choice of posting. O'Clery, astutely and with great prescience, proposed that the paper open a bureau in Moscow. He put his case well, pointing to the seismic political changes there, and after negotiations with the commercial management this move was agreed.

It wasn't especially flattering to be the third choice for Johannesburg, but I had been offered the job I wanted. There was to be no interview, as the appointment was to be made on an emergency and temporary basis and, as such, was cleared by the NUJ chapel in Dublin. Jarlath had been appointed as Africa correspondent to cover the entire continent, while my appointment was simply to cover South Africa's progress towards democracy in the lead-up to the first democratic elections in April 1994.

I had a short space of time to welcome my replacement in Moscow, Deaglan de Bréadún, and prepare for my departure for Johannesburg in January. I came home for Christmas and then returned to Moscow to hand over to Deaglan, to introduce him to as many contacts as I could, and to say goodbye to my friends and colleagues in the Russian capital. Deaglan's introduction to Russia was far different from my own. I had arrived in midsummer and he had come in the blizzards and snowstorms of the Russian winter, the climate that had devastated both the Napoleonic and German Nazi armies.

My farewell party was held in Rosie O'Grady's pub on Znamenka, the former Frunze Street, right beside the central headquarters of the Red Army. My friends and colleagues Will Englund and Kathy Lally from the *Baltimore Sun* and Robyn Dixon of the *Sydney Morning Herald* hosted dinner for me later that night at the Slovenian restaurant in the Moscow Commercial Club; and for a week or so I prepared to show Deaglan the ropes before my departure.

The following night I was woken from my sleep by a phone call from Anita in Dublin. Her mother, who had been living with us in Clondalkin for almost twenty years, had died in her ninety-third year. She had become part of the family since Anita's father had died and provided a wonderful link between our daughters Ruth and Deirdre and the Ireland of the early twentieth century. Her stories, her lore of a rural Ireland of long ago, had connected my daughters to a culture that had almost died out and to a past that many of their generation knew little about.

My stay in Moscow was now cut short. I returned for Anita's mother's funeral, and in January, having observed the end of the communist system in Russia, I was on my way to witness the end of the apartheid system in South Africa.

A number of people from Moscow and Dublin had arrived there before me. Kader Asmal was already there as a leading member of the ANC. Another ANC member and friend from Dublin was less well known but had endured a horrific series of events on the road to apartheid's end.

This was Marius Schoon, an Afrikaner who found himself in Dublin as a refugee. He had been imprisoned by the apartheid regime for more than a decade, and in the course of his incarceration his first wife took her own life. On his release, he married again to Jeannette Curtis and went into exile in Angola with her. They had had two children by the time the forces of law and order, South-African style, decided to send them a parcel bomb. Marius was out of town when it arrived. Jeannette opened it and she and her little five-year-old daughter Katryn were blown to pieces. Little Fritz, playing under a table, survived.

Marius was an official of the South African Development Bank when I arrived for my second tour of duty in a country that was already totally different from the one I had covered four years earlier.

Back in South Africa, too, were my friends Thabo from Guguletu and Tsede from Lesotho. Things had changed for them, too. Thabo Ntsome had reverted to his real name Andile Apleni, but his relationship with Tsede had broken down in a most unusual way. After his indemnity from arrest had been confirmed by the South African embassy, he set out for home for the first time in many years. Tsede made him promise to stay out of political activity, mainly because she was worried about his safety.

He told her he would, but very shortly after his arrival in South Africa an event took place that polarised politics there even further and resulted in Tsede breaking up with Thabo. On 10 April 1993, Chris Hani, the leader of the ANC's armed wing, of which Thabo had been a member, was assassinated in the town of Boksburg. His killer was a right-wing Polish immigrant called Janusz Walus, who had been given the murder weapon by the South African Conservative Party MP Clive Derby-Lewis.

Hani was a charismatic leader, second only in popularity to Nelson Mandela amongst the young black population. His funeral received widespread coverage throughout the world. On Russian TV, one image was repeatedly shown: it was Thabo dressed in the ANC colours, giving the clenched-fist salute.

This meant only one thing to Tsede. Thabo had broken his promise. 'Those South Africans,' she said, 'when there is trouble they run towards it. In Lesotho when there is trouble we back away.'

She broke off their relationship and I was never to see her again. I learned later, from Thabo, that she had married a lawyer and was practising medicine in Bloemfontein.

— 'Nkosi Sikelel' iAfrika'— 'God Bless Africa'

I had been told before I went back to Johannesburg that the house Jarlath Dolan had rented might not be all that suitable for my requirements, particularly as Anita was due to spend a good part of the time in South Africa. During my time in Russia she had commuted from Dublin, as our daughters were still at college in Ireland at that time. As it turned out, the house itself was fine. There *was* a problem, though. It was completely unfurnished.

Poor Jarlath had not even moved in before he lost his life in that motor accident. There was a cooker all right, but no beds, tables or chairs and, crucially for any journalist, no telephone. In fact, the only item other than the cooker was lying in the middle of the floor of the main room where Jarlath had obviously left it before setting out on his last journey: a bullet-proof vest, which had a rather consoling label attached that read 'Made in Northern Ireland'. It was, however, exceptionally heavy, and I felt it might be better to be able to run away than to stand and watch bullets bouncing off the flak jacket.

As it happened, my mind was made up for me by my South African colleagues, who told me that under no circumstances should I wear the bullet-proof vest, since it was precisely the same colour as that worn by the South African police force. I would, if I wore it, make myself a target, and those who took pot shots at the cops would not aim for my torso, which the vest protected, but for my head.

Things were happening quickly and it had been my intention to hit the ground running. It was not possible to work from the house, so I booked into the Sandton Sun Hotel for a while. I picked this place because the development minister, Tom Kitt, was staying there at the time during the course of an official visit, which I covered for *The Irish Times*.

I immediately set out to order a bed for the house, which was situated in the trendy neighbourhood of Melville, now something of a media ghetto. The house lay near the South African Broadcasting Corporation's headquarters at Auckland Park and was therefore convenient for local, as well as visiting, TV people.

Once the bed was installed, I moved into the little cottage in Melville and got to work on getting the place furnished. Soon I had a washing machine, a dishwasher, curtains to preserve one's modesty, a table and chairs, knives and forks, a TV and a bed for the second of the two bedrooms.

I had promised myself a dishwasher, since I did not have one in Moscow, and it arrived early and was installed by a local plumber. It was then that I ran into my first problem. I searched everywhere for dishwasher powder or tablets but could not find any. There was a simple explanation for this. White South Africans used a very different type of dishwasher to the one I had bought. Their favoured brand was not a Zanussi or an Indesit or a Whirlpool: it was known simply as a black woman.

The main room of the house was painted a dark-maroon colour and it needed brightening up. This was where Michael, the painter, came in. Michael was a Xhosa from the Eastern Cape and he got to work instantly on cheering up the place. He also found Anna, who came a couple of times a week to clean up, and Peter, who looked after the little garden. Having a gardener might seem like something of an extravagance but I learned quickly that it was a necessity because of the effect the weather had on the garden. It is midsummer in January in South Africa, and the climate at that time of the year is remarkable. The sun shines right from dawn but, during the day, the clouds build up and every afternoon almost without fail there is an extremely spectacular high-veld thunderstorm that dumps gallons of water everywhere. Then it clears up, the sun comes out and the great weather machine starts working on producing the next day's tropical downpour.

The city is situated at almost 6,000 feet above sea level, so when the storm arrives you are almost in the middle of it. The air is thin with less oxygen than there is at sea level and water boils at a lower temperature than elsewhere. This latter effect exasperated the chef at our local Italian restaurant, Nino da Genova, as he found it extremely difficult to cook pasta to perfection.

I discovered the need for a gardener after a two-week trip to Cape Town. With so much sunshine and so much rain the growth was phenomenal, and when I returned, the backyard had reverted almost to jungle. Peter would come in once a week to cut back the growth. He did similar work elsewhere in the area to help provide for his family in the horrible and distant township of Sebokeng. He was needed, too, when I received a note from my next-door neighbours. It was couched in terms that had never been addressed to me before or since, and certainly not during my time in Ballyfermot. 'Mr Martin,' it read, 'your bougainvillea is encroaching on our front garden. Please get your servants to cut it back.'

Anna lived locally in one of the little huts white people kept in their gardens to house their servants. There was a hut in my garden, too, but I used it as my office, as there was little room to work in the house itself, which consisted of one large room encompassing the living room, dining room and kitchen; two bedrooms; a bathroom-toilet; and a back *stoep*, or veranda.

There was also a garage or carport with an automatic door that would not open. Car theft was at that time, and still is, a major problem in Johannesburg, so it was necessary to get the door fixed as soon as possible rather than leave the mini-car out on the street to be stolen.

All this work was done as fast as possible, but instead of travelling around the country as I had hoped, I spent part of each day in those early weeks waiting for household items to be delivered. The most difficult job was getting the phone installed. The system was similar to that in the Ireland of the 1970s, which meant you simply had to wait until the phone department was ready to deal with you – and that could take some time. So each day I did my interviews and so on, wrote my reports on the laptop computer and then drove to Patrick Laurence's house to send the article over to Dublin.

I also needed a bank account, but I discovered that South

African banks at that time did not appear to want your money. There was an incredible amount of red tape in order to prevent people from taking money out of the country, but for some reason this also made it difficult to bring hard currency into South Africa – a country that badly needed the US dollars *The Irish Times* was prepared to pay. Eventually, I found a sympathetic bank official at Nedbank in Parktown who was prepared to circumvent the bureaucracy and open an account for me.

I also spent some time trying to get Peter and Anna to change the ways that had been drummed into them by their other employers. At first Anna called me 'master', as most white South African employers insisted. After I kept refusing to be addressed that way, she got round to calling me by my first name. It was more difficult, after Anita arrived, to get Anna and Peter to have lunch with us, but eventually they got round to that, too.

My colleagues from the international press and broadcast media included Fergal Keane of the BBC and his wife Anne O'Flaherty. They had inherited a posh mansion in the exclusive northern suburbs from their BBC predecessors and entertained frequently. John Carlin of the London *Independent* had worked on a freelance basis for *The Irish Times*, David Beresford was the long-term *Guardian* correspondent and had spent quite some time in Northern Ireland, where he wrote *Ten Men Dead*, an account of the hunger strikes. Patrick Laurence, who had been our paper's stringer in South Africa, was an extremely helpful friend and colleague, as was his wife Sandra. Anita and Sandra got on particularly well, and our friendship with the Laurence family has lasted to this day.

The Johannesburg lifestyle was particularly seductive and very different indeed from Moscow. The British girls' public school,

Roedean, had a Johannesburg offshoot, and St John's College was the local equivalent of an English boys' public school. Life was comfortable in the northern suburbs with their English-speaking inhabitants and British-sounding place names such as Parktown, Rosebank, Sandton, Atholl and Saxonwold. The latter, I learned later, had been founded by a wealthy German immigrant and had been called Sachsenwald until all things German became unpopular during the First World War.

There was also evidence of an Irish presence, and one of the northern suburbs was called Killarney. In another prosperous area, called Parkview, the sumptuous houses on their own grounds nestled in roads such as Kilkenny, Carlow, Wicklow, Cavan and Derry. It was Derry, mind you, and not Londonderry, so it appeared that the local politician or more likely the builder who founded the place did not come from the Ulster unionist community. It was in a store in Parkview, by the way, that after a month's search I finally found my supply of dishwasher powder.

Life was so comfortable that I found it necessary to pinch myself into reality by making as many visits as possible to the black townships, where the vast majority of South Africans lived. In the immense area of Soweto, an acronym for South Western Townships, the accommodation ranged from fairly acceptable housing in older established areas, such as Orlando, where Nelson Mandela's little house stood, to squatter regions, such as Johnson's Stop. Here, entire families lived in cardboard and corrugated-iron lean-to hovels. The stench from open sewers assaulted one's nose, and white visitors were looked at suspiciously by little groups of unemployed men who hung around playing cards.

Early on I witnessed a remarkable exception to this state of affairs, when I accompanied an elderly nun from County Kerry to Johnson's Stop. On our arrival, the men stopped playing cards. One of them, who appeared to be their leader, broke away from the group and ran forward. I was on my guard immediately but I needn't have worried. He simply ran towards the old nun and threw his arms around her in a huge embrace.

Visiting townships such as Soweto and Alexandra in Johannesburg, Mamelodi in Pretoria, and Guguletu and Langa near Cape Town not only kept one in touch with real life in South Africa but gave one an advantage over white South Africans, who frequently confronted visiting journalists. One of their more frequent accusations was that we didn't know enough about their country and had come over to give it a bad name.

More than ninety per cent of white South Africans had never – whether from fear, prejudice or inertia induced by their affluent lifestyle – been in a black township. Responding to their allegations with the question, 'When were you last in a township?' usually softened their cough for them.

In my early weeks in South Africa, I concentrated on providing background on the main ethnic groups that made up the population. Working on this proved illuminating for myself, also. The white community, apart from recent immigrant groups of Greek, Italian and Portuguese origin, was divided between the Afrikaner majority and the English-speaking minority. The latter still regarded themselves as essentially British, and one of the more striking examples of this was to be seen at the 'Proms' in the Johannesburg City Hall, where 'Land of Hope and Glory' was sung with gusto and brought the audience to its feet. The British were considerably the wealthier of the two main white groups, and if there were any poor whites to be found they were almost certain to be Afrikaners. Many of the British South Africans were able to hedge their bets on the arrival of majority rule by getting British, Australian and frequently New Zealand passports. The number of Irish citizens was quite small, at around 5,000 people.

Afrikaners did not have the luxury of dual citizenship. They could not go to the Dutch, German or French embassies and ask for a passport on the grounds that their ancestors had arrived at the Cape more than three hundred years ago. They truly were the white tribe of Africa.

The mixed race, or 'coloureds', had a great deal in common with the Afrikaners as Afrikaans-speakers and adherents of a branch of the Dutch Reformed Church. The other large ethnic minority was composed of the descendants of indentured workers from India, who had come to work the sugar plantations in Natal. There was little or no friction between South African Indians of Muslim and Hindu origin, and there was also a very strong tradition amongst the better-off members of the community to send their offspring to Dublin to study medicine at the Royal College of Surgeons.

I remember speaking to two Indian doctors near Durban. When they heard my accent, one of them broke into a big smile and uttered the totally unexpected phrase, 'Janey Mac!' For many of these South African Indians, their period in Ireland was the first time they had experienced any kind of personal freedom. Under apartheid, they were forced to live in certain areas and if they developed a relationship with a member of the opposite sex from another ethnic community they could be arrested under legislation known by the sinister title of the Immorality Act. My own GP in Clondalkin, who had married an Irishwoman, could, if he returned home with her, be arrested as 'immoral' for living with his wife.

His brother-in-law, Rafiq Bismillah, who worked at the Baragwanath Hospital in Soweto, the largest hospital in the world, spoke to me of his days as a student on Stephen's Green and its legacy in South Africa. Every St Patrick's Day, he said, he and a group of doctors who had all studied together in Ireland would hire a room in a hostelry in Johannesburg. There they would talk of their student days, drink pints of beer and sing Irish ballads in celebration of their lost youth.

There were divisions in the Indian community as there were in the other South African ethnic groups, but these divisions were slight. The vast majority were united against apartheid and only a tiny minority supported a plan by the apartheid regime to set up racially based parliaments, including one for South Africans of Indian origin. One person who did accept this racist proposal was a man whose name was once exceptionally well known in Ireland.

Shan Mohangi was found guilty of the particularly grue-some murder of his girlfriend Hazel Mullen in 1960s. After a short time in prison, he was deported to South Africa and later became a member of the puppet parliament set up for Indians by the racist regime. As a member of this assembly he was unique in that he crossed the floor of the house three times in one day, moving from one undemocratic party to another.

In the majority African community there were strong politi-cal divisions. These were largely reported as difficulties between Zulus, on the one hand, and other ethnic groups on the other. In fact, most of the very serious violence took place between Zulus of differing political traditions in Natal. The urbanised Zulus in the townships around Durban were, in the main, supporters of the ANC while the traditional Zulus from rural areas gravi-tated towards the Inkatha Freedom Party of Chief Mangosuthu Buthelezi, who was chief minister of the autonomous region of KwaZulu-Natal and had played a cameo role in the movie *Zulu*.

This political rivalry became extremely bloody, and there were murderers on both sides. For quite some time in the build up to the election, Nelson Mandela's plea to the population of Natal to end their violence fell on deaf ears. Mandela, a Xhosa, had less influence in Natal than in other parts of South Africa in those days, but as time went on the vicious infighting died down.

I travelled to Ulundi, the Zulu capital, to interview Chief Buthelezi. The journey involved arriving at the Prince Mangosuthu Buthelezi airport then travelling down the Prince Mangosuthu Buthelezi highway to the centre of town. I stayed at the Holiday Inn on Princess Magogo Street, which was one of the few places in town not called after Chief Buthelezi. It was, in fact, named after his mother. Next morning, Chief Buthelezi met a group of seven journalists at the Prince Mangosuthu Buthelezi Conference Centre.

The Chief, or Prince as he liked to be called, was the uncle of the Zulu monarch, King Goodwill Zwelethini, and he received us in regal fashion and, at least in the early stages of our visit, with some dignity. Things took a turn for the worse, however, when the woman from the *Chicago Tribune* asked an important question. The Inkatha Party at this stage had refused to take part in the April elections and she wondered if this was a tactical error on Inkatha's part. If they boycotted the vote, she posited, would the ANC not then win a majority of seats in the area and gain control of KwaZulu-Natal?

Prince Buthelezi exploded. 'This is the question of an ANC spy,' he roared. His handlers, a group of right-wing whites, told us that the chief minister had an urgent meeting elsewhere and he was ushered out of the room That was the end of our engagement with the ANC's leading black opponent. As it turned out, he relented on his anti-election stance very late in the day and Inkatha's name and symbol had to be added to the ballot paper in the form of a sticker. In the end, Buthelezi became the country's minister for home affairs.

Having experienced the Prince's tantrum, I almost got myself into the same trouble the following day, when a large group of locals staged a pro-Inkatha demonstration in the centre of Ulundi. Between their assembly point and the police station, where the march was to end, lay a triangular piece of waste ground opposite the hotel on Princess Magogo Street, and I decided that this would be a good place from which to view the march.

It had been a strong belief amongst rural Zulus that they should be allowed to carry their traditional weapons and they did so on this occasion. The men carried spears and clubs called knobkerries, and even some of the women had planks from which large nails stuck out.

All appeared well until the crowd approached the piece of waste ground, chanting and waving their weapons about. Then they speeded up their pace. Finally, they began to run and someone decided they should take a short cut through the waste ground. Within seconds I was being carried away in the stream of demonstrators. I asked one of them what the song was that they had suddenly begun to chant in harmony. He eyed me ferociously and said: 'The song says no white man should be here.'

The old Dublin excuse for leaving someone quickly came into my head. 'Here's me bus,' I said, and made it quickly across the road to the hotel lobby.

Patrick Laurence and I travelled back towards Durban, where a big pro-ANC demonstration was due to take place the next afternoon. It was quite impressive and fortunately did not engender violence. On our way we called into Empangeni, where another ANC demo was scheduled. On this occasion, however, hardly any demonstrators turned up. It was clear that there were parts of the region where ANC support was minimal.

One place where support was much higher than anyone in the white community expected was in the nominally independent state of Bophuthatswana, run by its South African-appointed dictator Lucas Mangope. Bop, as it was mercifully known for short, was what was known as a Bantustan: as part of the grand design of apartheid, certain tribal regions were given a technical independence that was recognised only by the South African regime.

Thus, there was a South African embassy in the capital Mmabatho and a Bop embassy in Pretoria. The South African ambassador acted effectively as Pretoria's governor of Bophuthatswana, from whom 'President' Mangope simply had to obey orders and ensure that the fortune that he and his family amassed from this arrangement was securely invested abroad. He also, of course, had to ensure that he remained as 'president', and did so through a repressive police force.

Mangope, thoroughly corrupt as he was, wanted to ensure that Bop would be excluded from any democratic elections that were to be held in South Africa. He failed completely, and when Nelson Mandela arrived in Mmabatho to address a vast attendance in the local stadium, the game was already up for Mangope.

Mandela's magnetism was amazing, and the day he arrived in Mmabatho the city's entire population and that of neighbouring Mafikeng turned out to greet him enthusiastically. They also celebrated the demise of Mangope in similar fashion, and the South African authorities, recognising the reality of the situation, announced the end of Bop's independence and admitted that their ambassador was now officially the territory's administrator.

It was in the ambassador's residence that I witnessed a scene of considerable pathos on that day. A photocall had been arranged for pictures of Nelson Mandela with the South African ambassador-turned-administrator in the garden of the embassy residence. The two men stood side by side, and then an intruder arrived and interposed herself between the two men. It was Winnie Mandela. Not only did she and Nelson Mandela not speak to each other, but they did not even exchange glances. Her estranged husband, the future president, simply looked down at his shoes for the entire process of the photocall.

That day in Mmabatho marked the first realisation throughout South Africa that the ANC would win an overwhelming majority in the elections. Up to then, whites had convinced themselves that the black electorate and especially their own servants would act differently. This was borne out to me most strikingly in the town of Bethlehem in the Orange Free State. There, as elsewhere in South Africa, every white household had a black maid who called her employers master and madam. The masters and the madams were convinced that their maids would not descend to vote for the troublemakers of the ANC. They had good steady jobs as domestic servants and were happy with their lot.

The maids thought very differently. I met a group of them at the bus stop on their way from Bethlehem to the local township of Bohlokong. First I had to establish my credentials. I showed my passport to let them know I was not South African. I mentioned the magic word 'overseas'. This to many South Africans, deprived of a basic education as they were by their masters, represented a sort of enchanted mythical place where there was no apartheid.

Once they were convinced that I came from that great place called 'overseas' they vented their feelings in no uncertain manner. The 'madams' got it hot and heavy for their condescension and their selfishness. Every black woman at that bus stop was going to vote ANC and of that there was not the slightest doubt.

The great day dawned on 27 April and, in an unusual gesture, *The Irish Times* asked me to write a front-page editorial. It was published under the headline 'Nkosi Sikelel' iAfrika' – 'God Bless Africa'. This is what I wrote:

Tonight at midnight, at public buildings throughout South Africa, but more significantly at the parliamentary and administrative capitals of Cape Town and Pretoria, a short but highly emotional ceremony will take place.

The orange, white and blue flag of the Republic of South Africa will be lowered to the strains of 'Die Stem van Suid Afrika' ('The Voice of South Africa'). Then a new flag which combines the colours associated with black and white political movements will be raised.

The singing of the haunting anthem 'Nkosi Sikelel' iAfrika' ('God Bless Africa') will usher in an era of great opportunity for a country which has the potential to emerge from the darkness of apartheid and become a beacon of hope in a continent plagued by disease, famine, poverty and an increasingly hopeless anarchy.

This potential exists surprisingly, despite the history from which South Africa is emerging; a history of brutal oppression which began almost immediately after the arrival of the first settlers from the Dutch East India Company in 1652.

The next colonial masters, the British, informally introduced racial segregation and when the time came for them to leave in 1910, they handed their power over to the country's white minority.

There followed a period of repression, increasing in its brutality over the years and punctuated by massacres of blacks. As early as 1921 police shot dead 183 members of a black religious sect which had declared its independence.

The National Party came to power in 1948 and introduced

its policy of apartheid which institutionalised racism, stripped people of their homes and land, and sent a shock wave of abhorrence throughout the civilised world.

Even the scene at the final session of the racially structured parliament yesterday as white deputies voted in amendments to the constitution to allow participation of the mainly Zulu Inkatha Freedom Party, carried the aura of a past which all but a few misguided neo-Nazis in this country want to forget. All this has come to an end.

The last words spoken in the chamber, where apartheid's great architect, Dr Hendrik Verwoerd, was stabbed to death by an usher in 1966, came from the Speaker, Mr Eli Louw, who ended the session by saying: 'I wish honourable members well', surely the most anticlimactic exit for a political system which was internationally despised.

Yesterday I met a woman who has lived through most of this trauma. Her name is Elizabeth, she is 95 years old and lives in the Alexandra township in Johannesburg.

Her story echoes those of many throughout the dark years from which South Africa is about to emerge. Her family bought land in Alexandra from the local landlord, Mr Papenvus, in 1912 when Elizabeth was a 13-year-old girl. This land was taken away by the apartheid regime purely because Elizabeth and her family were black.

'Now my land is covered in shacks, that's what they did with it. Life was very heavy. We had to carry that pass all the time, maybe it is going to be better now. I am praying that it will,' Elizabeth told me.

Today, for the first time in her long life, Elizabeth will go to a polling station, put a cross beside the party of her choice and slip her folded ballot paper into a box.

'Amandla!' (Power), she exclaimed to me. 'Ngawethu!' (It will be ours), I replied. And then Elizabeth pulled herself up to her full four feet and 11 inches and told me with a broad African laugh: 'When I am finished here I am going to Ireland and I will do my power there too.'

As that editorial ran off the presses, I was on my way to Cape Town to join my old friend from Moscow days – Andile Apleni, alias Thabo Ntsome. I met his parents at their little house in Guguletu, and then we went to the polling station. A long line of thousands of would-be voters snaked through the township's dusty paths. I stood with them and waited until Thabo reached the polling booth and cast a vote for the first time. Inside were two Irish observers, the Fine Gael TD Norah Owen, and the anti-apartheid activist Garry Kilgallen.

The country in fact was awash with Irish observers. They included my *Irish Times* colleagues Mark Brennock and Frank McDonald, as well as former *Irish Times* journalist Helen Shaw, who was to become head of radio at RTÉ.

There had been some controversy early on when a group of Irish observers at a rally in Soweto wore ANC tee shirts and danced around during a speech by Nelson Mandela. They had to be told to be quiet because Mr Mandela was speaking in Xhosa and their merrymaking was blotting out the translation of his words. I mentioned this incident in my report of the meeting, not as an important story, but buried in the middle of the article. I felt their behaviour compromised what should have been seen as their total impartiality and obviously so did the Irish government agency that sent them. Officials were dispatched from Dublin to question the observers. Just one man admitted honestly to wearing an ANC tee shirt and he was sent home. He was not one of those I had referred to in the article. They remained as observers.

Most observers worked conscientiously and with great efficiency over a long number of difficult hours. But one of them, a leading Irish parliamentarian, showed how seriously he considered his task by arriving with his golf clubs. He was quickly disabused of his leisurely approach and also of his idea that he could avoid observing in black areas.

Of the parliamentary observers I saw in action, Nora Owen and the independent Dublin TD Tony Gregory impressed with their dedication to duty. They were there also in Cape Town on the memorable occasion when the old flag came down and the old anthem was played for the last time. Also in the great throng that witnessed the historic moment were the Irish journalist Lynn Geldof and my friend from Moscow, Thabo, now free to call himself Andile once more.

He and I had wondered in our Russian days if this moment would really arrive and would we be there to share it. We spoke about it over pints of Guinness at the Shamrock Bar on the Novy Arbat and when we went for walks in the gardens of the Novodevichy Monastery.

In those days, Thabo had just qualified as a major in the Red Army after a six-year stint at the imposing Frunze Military Academy. This had been his first step towards the conventional world. Earlier, he had been a guerrilla in the training camps of the ANC's military wing, Umkhonto we Sizwe, for four years in Angola.

As we sat and talked in the bleak depths of the Moscow winter, Thabo dreamt aloud about his beautiful city of Cape Town, about when he would be allowed to return home to see his parents and brothers and sisters again, and about the advent of democracy in his country.

Now Thabo's hour had come. His country had changed irrevocably, but so, too, had he. First of all, he was now at home at last; secondly, he was no longer Thabo, for he could use his own name again. Thabo had become Andile and, in an example of the potential that the new South Africa might hold, his whole purpose in life has changed.

Whereas once Thabo had donned his khaki uniform, shining

boots and his cap with its hammer, sickle and red star to attend his courses with what was once the most powerful military machine on earth, Andile now emerged from his hostel in the mornings dressed in a smart suit, shirt and tie. The ex-guerrilla and former Soviet officer now pursued a course in business studies at the University of Cape Town. He did not need to be a soldier any more.

While these great events were taking place at the Cape, strange things were happening at my little house in Melville. Now that the election had taken place, observers were demobbed and the relevant authorities had ceased to pay for their accommodation. One of them, Una Keating, a lawyer from Dublin, stayed in my house while I was down at the Cape. I had made the mistake of leaving the remote control for the garage door beside the TV, and Una used it, unsuccessfully, in her attempts to change channels. Unknown to herself, she happened to be opening and closing the car-port's door, which led through the secure high wall and into the front garden and the backyard. At that time, white South Africa, as it had been for decades and still is today, was obsessed with security. Notices with the words 'Armed Response' appeared on the walls of houses to indicate that security companies had been hired to shoot intruders on sight.

As well as genuine fear, there appeared to me to be an element of guilt involved in this display of insecurity. If the danger from blacks was not as real as it seemed perhaps in the minds of those holed up in their luxurious fortresses it deserved to be.

There was no 'Armed Response' notice on the Melville house, just a little plaque installed by the owners that read 'Beware of the Dog', and everyone in the neighbourhood knew there was no dog. That night, as passers-by walked down the street, the garage door was going up and down at a furious rate as the TV channel steadfastly refused to budge.

In the morning, Una luxuriated in the bath, and a black face appeared pressed against the frosted-glass window. She screamed. 'I have only come to read the meter,' the man told her. She asked how he had gained entry and was told that the garage door had been wide open all night.

Back in the Transvaal, Nelson Mandela was memorably installed as president in the presence of political leaders from all over the world. Meanwhile, South African airforce jets screamed overhead to honour a man who was once the state's imprisoned enemy.

As for me, my task was coming to an end. I had come to South Africa on an emergency basis and I was ready to return to my previous duties. The position as Africa correspondent was now advertised, and most of my colleagues were surprised that I did not apply. I was now in my fifties and felt that I would not physically be able to cover the entire continent from its southernmost point. Perhaps a younger person would have the strength and stamina to make the vast journeys to places such as Senegal and Nigeria in the west, or to Sudan and Somalia to the far northeast, some of which were closer to Dublin than Johannesburg.

My colleagues paid me what I considered to be a great compliment. I was told that no applications for the post were received because it was presumed I would apply. When it became known that I did not apply, it was necessary to advertise the post again.

The little house in Melville witnessed a huge farewell party. Anna and her husband John, a diffident Shangaan man from the Mozambique border, helped prepare the food and drink. A big crowd from the dangerous township of Thokoza hired a bus to attend. Fergal Keane and Anne and John Carlin and other colleagues joined in.

Fergal and I made a promise that we would watch Ireland's World Cup games on TV together back in Ireland, perhaps in the relaxed atmosphere of the County Clare, where Anne came from. This was not to be. Fergal recounted in his book how he saw the games in Rwanda at the home of a man who supported that country's appalling genocide. I watched the Irish play in unusual circumstances, too. I was back in the former Soviet Union, in Kiev, the capital of Ukraine. The only place where Ireland's games could be seen on satellite TV was in the bar of a sleazy nightclub run by a former RUC special operative, who had been given a new identity.

— Rip-off Russia —

Back in Ireland, I took my holidays and packed the bags again
to return to Moscow, where my colleague Deaglan de Bréadún
had been standing in for me. Things were quieter there for the
moment, and I began to settle back into the very different lifestyle. I had enjoyed the work in South Africa, but the unreal
luxury in which the white community lived and its contrast
with the abject poverty endured by the majority was something
I found very difficult to come to terms with.

There were times, too, at dinner parties in Jo'burg's northern
suburbs when I wished I was back in Russia. Talk centred on
house prices and whether or not young sons should be packed
off to public school in England. Late into one dinner party, as
the suburban chatter deepened into the vital area of the price
of the latest BMW, I remember thinking how different things

might be at this stage in Moscow. The vodka would be flowing. Someone would be reciting from Pushkin or Tolstoy, songs would be sung. A strange melancholy took over. I was feeling homesick not for Dublin and the Irish, but for Moscow and the Russians.

Back in Moscow things *had* changed. Where once little knots of people stood to examine the little Volvo 440, now big Mercedes limos with smoked-glass windows and no licence plates blasted their horns to get me to move out of the way as I drove along the Garden Ring Road. My friend Sasha, a doctor who worked in the accident-and-emergency service, used to deal mainly with household injuries. Now he was dealing increasingly with gunshot wounds.

Elsewhere things began to get worse. There were indications of increased tension in Chechnya, but no all-out conflict had yet begun. Things were not well in the army, and a young journalist investigating corruption in that area died in extremely suspicious circumstances: Dmitri Kholodov worked for the popular newspaper *Moskovsky Komsomolets*, and was told that a briefcase of documents awaited him at the Kazan station's left-luggage department. Its contents, he was told, would be extremely interesting.

The young man went to the station, collected the briefcase and returned to the office. The briefcase was booby-trapped. Opening it cost Kholodov his life. I went to his funeral at the Palace of Youth on Komsomolsky Prospekt and was roughed up by the Moscow police on my way in. Not punched or anything as serious as that, but jostled and pushed around. Lena and Ken Fireman were also roughly treated.

In Russia, coffins are traditionally left open when people pay their respects, but Kholodov's body was so badly mutilated it was wrapped up in cloth. A veil prevented his face from being fully seen.

Attempts to make money out of foreigners gathered apace, and one morning when I arrived in the office I found Lena in a quite-agitated state. The *Irish Times'* bank account, from which her wages were paid, had been frozen by the authorities in the tax inspectorate. Unlike the taxmen in Ireland, many of Russia's inspectors were armed with sub-machine guns rather than pocket calculators. It was with some trepidation, therefore, that I set out for the inspectorate's headquarters on Ilyinka Street, just across from the building that used to house the Communist Party archives.

There, an official explained that *The Irish Times* should have its accounts audited in order to show that it was not making a profit in Russia. The suggestion that the paper would be in a position to earn money was a ludicrous one, but I had little choice but to conform with the request. I had all the bank chits showing that there was money coming in from Dublin every month and that nothing was going back. So I volunteered to have an audit done by KPMG, the international accountancy practice which dealt with the newspaper's accounts and, as it turned out, had an office in Moscow, in which one of its accountants was Irish.

The offer was refused and I immediately began to smell a rat. The tax official took a business card from his pocket and told me that I had no choice of accountant. I must have the audit done by his friend. I sensed a rip-off and I was right. The price the taxman's pal quoted to unfreeze the bank account was considerably larger than the amount of money in the account.

I pulled as many strings as I could and was pleasantly surprised

that the Foreign Ministry of the Russian Federation was prepared to come to my rescue. They issued me with a letter that
outlined the bona fides of *The Irish Times* as a genuine newspaper
that did not make a profit in Russia and that to force it to pay
such a sum for an audit was against all international norms.

It was with some confidence, therefore, that I set out for
Ilyinka Street again, armed with a letter bearing the stamp of
the Ministry of Foreign Affairs. I showed it to the taxman. He
read it. Then, with utter contempt, he crumpled it up and threw
it in a waste-paper basket.

It was becoming obvious that I was getting nowhere and that
if the Foreign Ministry could be treated in such a way, *The Irish
Times* could be treated with even greater disdain. I knew that
if we decided to pay up this time other occasions would arise
in which even more money would be demanded. An unend-
ing series of extortions loomed, and Dublin felt there was only
one option. It was with great sadness that I had to tell Lena
and Valeriy that *The Irish Times* had decided to close down its
Moscow office.

The tax claim was not made against me as a person, as I had
fulfilled my obligations to the Russian authorities; and in any
case I was not worth extorting money from. In this regard there
was no problem about my continuing to report from Moscow.
It was decided, therefore, that I would cover situations from
Ireland and would fly over and back as the occasion demanded.
There were frequent and inexpensive Aeroflot flights from
Shannon to allow this to be done at a cost considerably lower
than maintaining a Moscow office and running the risk of being
bled dry by the authorities.

It was with great reluctance, however, that I began to pack my
bags, and there were quite a few of them after all those years. I

was also in for two surprises. The first came from Dublin in the form of a phone call requesting me 'on your way home' to cover a summit of the Commission on Security and Co-operation in Europe (CSCE) in Budapest. I organised my ticket to Dublin via the Hungarian capital and didn't relish dragging all my Russian belongings with me 'on my way home'.

Then, the night before my departure, my friends Will Englund and Kathy Lally from Baltimore, Maryland, invited me to dinner to wish me farewell. They would, they said, meet me outside the Turgenevskaya Metro station. One of the few Moscow tramlines ran nearby and I was taken aback to see a large group of people waiting for me. Not far away was a tram decked out in fairy lights with a bar installed at one end of its passenger compartment and a large table of *zakuski* (elaborate Russian hors d'oeuvres) set out at the other.

My friends and colleagues, Russian and foreign, had managed to hire and deck out a Moscow tram in which to hold a farewell party. The vodka and champagne flowed as the tram glided its way around Moscow clanging its bell at pedestrians and cars that got in its way. There was a stop at the tram drivers' rest rooms at Chistye Prudi for calls of nature.

Robert Haupt of the *Australian Financial Review* fell asleep and for some reason woke up every time the tram, on its many circuits of the city, passed the statue of the writer Alexander Griboyedov in the little park at Chistye Prudi. 'Griboyedov!' he would cry on seeing the statue before falling asleep again.

Amongst the revellers were Boris Ryzhak, his wife Masha and their son Yasha, who had become a journalist. Boris and Masha had a *dacha* out to the north of Moscow, where I was always made welcome. Boris once illustrated the inflation that had troubled Russia in a way that struck me forcefully. He had decided to buy a small pedal-operated car for his little son Gleb's birthday. A search of the city ensued and in a suburban store he found a little red pedal-operated Moskvich. A price was agreed and Boris burst into uncontrollable laughter. Asked why, he explained that only two years earlier he had paid exactly the same price for a real Moskvich.

The party went on into the early hours of the morning and I was in a decidedly shaky condition when I set out for Budapest and the last summit the CSCE was to hold before it changed its name to the OSCE (Organisation for Security and Co-operation in Europe). It made this change despite strong protests from the Maltese delegation, which explained that OSCE in Maltese is a very rude word indeed. Small countries are rarely listened to in these circumstances, and OSCE it remains to this day.

The meeting was to become far more important from an Irish point of view than anyone had anticipated. When Albert Reynolds arrived, all was quiet. But all hell broke loose following a report in that morning's *Irish Times* by Geraldine Kennedy that sent the government into crisis.

Then Albert went missing. The world's leaders lined up for the 'team picture' and he was not there. The world's leaders came down a staircase in dribs and drabs on their way to the auditorium where the major speeches were made but there was no sign of Albert. The TV reporter Tommie Gorman and I stood at the bottom of that staircase intent on collaring him, and we waited and waited.

We could have interviewed Bill Clinton. He had come down the stairs and looked around to see if anyone wanted to talk to him. We hid from his view. It would have been discourteous in the extreme to tell the president of the United States that we didn't want to speak to him because if we did, we might miss Albert.

Then François Mitterrand came down the stairs. His final illness had begun to ravage his body. His face was so white it was
as though no blood coursed through his veins. We ignored him.

Two large heavy feet thumped their way down the steps. A
red face exuded either bonhomie or rage. It was difficult to tell
which, for Boris Nikolayevich Yeltsin had just had a flaming
row with Bill Clinton. We avoided him.

In the auditorium, Silvio Berlusconi was telling the assembled leaders that corruption was a bad thing. We didn't listen.

Then John Major arrived and stood at the bottom of the
steps. He turned his back on us and we breathed a sigh of relief.
There had been rumours that Major had his hair cut by his wife.
When he turned his back on us we could see that the rumours
were true.

At last, at the top of the staircase there was movement.
A group of suited men were clearly in a hurry. It was our lot.
Ambassador Ted Barrington led the pack. 'The Taoiseach is busy.
He must go in and make his speech.' The group rushed past and
Gorman and I rushed after them. Confusion reigned. Instead
of entering the auditorium on the right to the applause of the
assembled leaders, they turned left. They found themselves in
the kitchen of the adjoining Novotel. A large Hungarian chef
was honing his cleaver against a steel sharpener. He shouted
something unpleasant at them and they left.

'There'll be no dissolution,' Albert shouted to us as he disap-
peared out the door and into the area reserved for official delegations. He had vowed that the Dáil would not be dissolved
and he kept his word.

That was all we got from him. I wrote my article and headed
back to the Grand Hotel Hungaria, which had seen grander days.
It was now approaching midnight and I had missed an arranged

get-together with Robert Haupt and another Australian journalist, Mike Brissenden. My stomach was rumbling with hunger and, amazingly, the restaurant in the basement was open.

I ordered my meal and suddenly found myself surrounded by a Hungarian gypsy band. Its leader asked me what country I came from. I told him. He leafed through a little book of sheet music and opened it. It seemed that two pages had become stuck together in their alphabetical order. The band struck up a rousing version of the Israeli song 'Hava Nagila' in my honour. It felt as though my day had been scripted by Federico Fellini.

So it was that I returned to Dublin after many years' absence to a job that was not specified. The one thing that I realised *was* certain after I arrived in the office was that I would have no desk. It became my destiny to hang around and wait until someone else got up and left their designated work station. I would then pounce, take over their terminal, log on to the system and work until the proprietor of the desk returned.

Because I needed somewhere to sit down, I vowed to return to Russia as frequently as possible so that I could find a place to put my laptop. The *Irish Times'* office and apartment in Moscow had now been allocated by Boris Spartakovich to Robyn Dixon of the *Sydney Morning Herald*, so I had to find somewhere else. Sonya Kishkovsky of the *New York Times* came to the rescue. She had friends, Nikita and Tatyana, who lived just off Tverskaya, the city's most important street. The apartment next to theirs had been unoccupied for over a year. They contacted the owners and it was agreed that I could have it on short-term rental during my visits to Moscow. In a city that was now rated as the most expensive in the world, the nightly rate of $40 was the best bargain in town.

There was a kitchen, a living room, two bedrooms, a bathroom and a toilet. And it was in one of the most sought-after locations in the Russian capital. It was from this house on Tryokhprudny Pereoulok that I operated the transient *Irish Times'* bureau for some of the most important stories that broke in the latter part of the 1990s.

Things had been getting very tough in Russia. Murder and mayhem had become accepted tools of business. The killing of entrepreneurs was so commonplace that hardly an eyebrow was raised. But the gangland execution of Ms Larisa Nechayeva, financial controller of the Spartak football club, marked an unwelcome milestone in what experts saw as a trend towards the criminalisation of the entire economy of the largest country on earth.

Under Soviet power, criminal gangs restricted themselves to local and regional activities. The Russian criminal fraternity, like the honest citizenry, was hampered by severe restrictions on freedom of movement, the absence of a convertible currency and, to put it mildly, a shortage of victims worthy of exploiting. The criminals had to become very efficient to operate within such strict confines.

When the old order ended, they moved quickly. Suddenly private commercial activity of all sorts was allowed without any regulatory legislation. Sharp practices were permitted simply because there was no law there to be broken.

New banks sprang up overnight, and new bankers were shot dead with such frequency that their demise merited little more than a paragraph in the press. The killing of Mr Ivan Kivelidi, one of the country's leading businessmen, made headlines not because of his status but because rather than being shot in the usual way his vodka was spiked with poison at a business lunch.

Paul Tatum, the American who, as mentioned before, claimed he owned forty per cent of a plush Moscow hotel simply because he had put up forty per cent of the money did not understand the business practices of the new Russia. He stepped into a hail of automatic fire at the Kievskaya Metro station and grabbed media attention not because he was a murdered businessman but because he was a murdered American businessman and, until then, Westerners had been regarded as 'safe'.

New ground was being broken all the time. Among the items stolen in one week by criminal gangs far too close to the surface of society to be described as an underworld was a three-engined, 150-seater Yak-42 jet liner. The hoods were even bold enough to advertise their occupations by the types of tattoos they sported: a spider's web for a drug dealer, a heart split in two for a regional boss, and a stylised eagle for an important chieftain.

The mafia was now moving into the sporting arena, as instanced by Ms Nechayeva's murder. Increasingly, sport was a business and where there was money to be made the mafia was to be found. Rivalry over sponsorship deals was cited as the most likely reason why what was planned as a quiet weekend in the country ended in a bloodbath that killed Ms Nechayeva and her friend Yelena Rudzate and left her brother Grigory Sorokin badly wounded.

When Valentin Sych, president of the Russian Ice Hockey Federation, was murdered, it was claimed he died because he would not share out the proceeds of fees gained from the transfer of Russian players to the lucrative leagues in North America. Russian stars in American and Canadian teams started asking for official protection when visiting Moscow.

Even amateur boxing was tainted. Sports journalists at international tournaments witnessed a new breed of boxing 'official', namely new and conspicuously wealthy male 'administrators' who had replaced the old-style boxing types and were joined at the hip to glamorous young women in ankle-length sable coats.

Among the old hands who left the scene were referee Vladimir Dadiev, who was found shot dead in the bath of his Moscow apartment following rumours that he was about to expose a fight-fixing scandal. Dadiev's son had earlier been gunned down in a Moscow restaurant in what may have been a mistaken attempt to kill the son of Vladimir Ivanchenko, the president of the Russian Amateur Boxing Federation.

Sport, crime and politics became linked for the first time, when a bizarre chain of events led to the dismissal of Mr Yeltsin's close confidant, General Alexander Korzhakov, a former KGB officer who led the presidential bodyguard. Presidents need bodyguards, but there were questions raised as to whether Yeltsin needed a bodyguard of sixteen thousand men. One of Korzhakov's men, Colonel Valery Streletsky, ordered the detention of two members of Mr Yeltsin's campaign team who were found to be leaving government buildings with a suitcase containing $500,000.

Streletsky had just taken over as deputy head of the National Sports Fund (NSF) from Mr Boris Fyodorov, who retired for health reasons after he had sustained bullet and stab wounds in a Moscow laneway. The NSF had been making large sums of money due to a special dispensation which allowed it to import alcohol and tobacco tax free. This privilege was withdrawn and the fund's then-head, Mr Yeltsin's tennis coach, Mr Shamil Tarpishchev, removed.

The detention of the two men with the bag of money was immediately interpreted as an 'attempted coup' by a compliant Russian media. As a result, General Korzhakov lost his job.

Rumours abounded that some sort of computer fraud would be used to ensure that Boris Yeltsin would be re-elected in 1996. Robyn Dixon and I wanted to find out if this was possible, so we spoke to a person who had links to the security services. We did not want his opinion on what was going to happen – we just wanted to know if it was technically possible to rig the results.

He said it was possible but highly improbable. The KGB had been broken up into a number of different organisations. The FSB looked after internal matters. On the international espionage front it was the SVR that was in charge. There was another group called FAPSI in charge of electronic surveillance, and they had the technology to ensure that the man they wanted would be elected. But they were not going to do anything like that because they were seriously divided about who they wanted to win.

Our man then took on a very serious demeanour and said there was something important that we should know. There were people who wanted to prevent the election from taking place and would go to extreme lengths to do so. We should watch out for two things. Firstly, there would be an attempt at destabilisation in the form of a bomb on the Metro. Secondly, there were those who would damage Yeltsin's health so the president could become seriously ill towards the end of the campaign.

That gave us something to think about and we went our separate ways to consider the situation. I sat down and wrote for a while and then the phone rang. It was Robyn Dixon, who said: 'Have you heard the news? There's been a bomb on the Metro.'

Things were to get even creepier. Towards the end of the campaign, Yeltsin vanished. He failed to show up at the photocalls that had been arranged. On polling day he didn't appear at the voting station to cast his vote. No one knew where he was, not even those you would imagine might be really in the know. One Sunday morning I went for a stroll at Novodevichy Monastery with my colleague Michael Foley, who was visiting from Dublin. Also out for their morning constitutional were the US ambassador Thomas Pickering and his wife Alice. He asked me if I knew anything about Yeltsin's whereabouts. I was reluctant to tell him the story of the president's forecast illness. It just sounded too much like a typical Russian conspiracy theory. I just said that I knew nothing. 'Neither do we,' he replied.

As it turned out, our spooky informant had been right. Boris Yeltsin has suffered a major heart attack some days earlier. No one reported it. There were no questions asked in the media. The whole business was hushed up and Boris Nikolayevich Yeltsin was re-elected president of the Russian Federation.

He now had to go through a quintuple bypass operation and I was anxious to find out what this entailed in Russia. In fact, I had become quite interested in heart problems, for my friend Robert Haupt had died suddenly on a visit to New York. I contacted Leo Bokeria, one of Russia's leading surgeons, to get as much information as I could about the sort of operation Yeltsin was about to undergo. To my amazement, he invited me to come along to his hospital and watch a heart bypass operation being performed.

When I say 'watch the operation' I am not talking about sitting in an enclosed gallery above the theatre. That sort of thing doesn't happen in Russia. I arrived at the hospital, scrubbed up, put on a green gown and the rest of the gear and went down to the theatre. Some poor guy was stretched out on an operating table and the junior surgeons opened his chest.

Then Leo Bokeria arrived like the virtuoso conductor of a symphony orchestra. He wore those little back-to-front opera glasses that surgeons wear and started to work. Before he did what he had to do, he instructed me that I was not to touch anything green. I looked down and saw a green tube near my right foot. It appeared to be coming from somewhere inside the patient. I looked out for any other green things that I shouldn't touch and suddenly caught a glimpse of my face. It was the greenest thing in the room.

On one of my subsequent trips back to Moscow some terrible events took place. Two major apartment blocks were bombed in the middle of the night. The first one at the distant suburb of Pechatniki appeared at first to have been damaged by a gas explosion; but when another block on Kashirskoye Chausee was blown up, thoughts turned to sabotage.

As it turned out, An Taoiseach Bertie Ahern was due to visit after the second explosion, so it was a particularly busy time. There was a breakfast briefing that Bertie gave to a group of international journalists in the Metropol Hotel. That it was well attended by representatives of the leading world newspapers and agencies was a tribute to the organisation put in place by the embassy. But when the Taoiseach said at the beginning of his address that he had learned of a third explosion, this time in an apartment block in a provincial town, a number of journalists got up and left in order to get onto the story as quickly as they could.

The Taoiseach's visit did, however, give me an advantage over some of my international colleagues: as the only Irish newspaperman in town, I was admitted to the Russian White House where he was meeting the then Russian prime minister, Vladimir Putin. I asked Mr Putin about the latest developments on the bombings and he replied immediately that there was evidence of Chechen involvement. What struck me most of all was his obvious anger at what had happened.

Vladimir Putin was not the sort of man who showed his emotions openly. The one consistent criticism of him that one heard from ordinary Russians was that he appeared to be something of a cold fish. On this occasion, however, he was almost in a rage.

He has been accused by enemies in the West – notably those close to the exiled oligarch Boris Berezovsky – of having staged the bombings in order to resume Russia's war against the Chechens. His behaviour on that day was not that of a man who had calmly laid such an evil plan.

Other visits back to Moscow had brought other results. I travelled to Samara in the hope that I would get admission to a hospital where wounded young conscripts had been brought from Chechnya after they had suffered a rout by better-equipped and better-trained Chechen fighters.

Things were so bad that one soldier from Moscow told me how his armoured personnel carrier had been towed into battle by a civilian truck. Soldiers' mothers had marched on Grozny to get their sons back and had succeeded, but Samara was different. The local regiment had almost been wiped out, and there were reports that the military hospital was full of the wounded.

I arrived with two colleagues, Will Englund and Robyn Dixon. We were refused entry at the hospital gate and, turning round on the heavy snow that had fallen over the icy ground – a treacherous combination – I slipped and broke my arm. Soon I was in the hospital, not so much as a journalist, but as a patient.

I had to wait a while, mind you, in the local officers' club, where in order to kill the time I was treated to an exhibition of poisonous snakes. Then the ambulance arrived and I asked the doctor what he thought of my now badly swollen limb. He told me he knew nothing about accidents and emergencies because he was a psychiatrist. It was a rule in Russia that a fully qualified doctor should be on board every ambulance and he was taking advantage of this to make some extra money.

In the hospital they diagnosed that my wrist had been broken. They set it in plaster, leaving a little gap because they knew I would be flying back to Moscow and they said that it was like an expansion joint to allow my wrist to swell in the pressurised cabin of the big Tupolev 154.

All around were wounded soldiers who told of their experiences in Grozny. Some, like me, had their arms in plaster; others lay pale in their beds and one young lad, shot in the neck, was *in extremis.*

Back in Moscow, my usual apartment was undergoing renovation and I had been renting a small place from an elderly *babushka* called Marina Ivanovna. When she saw me with my arm in plaster she left the apartment and returned about ten minutes later with a bottle of holy water with which she doused me from all angles.

She told me she was against the Chechen war and had her own wartime experiences. Her mother had died not long before the German invasion in 1941, and the family was living in a village near Smolensk in western Russia, right in the path of the invading forces. 'My father,' she said, 'called us together and said that since our wooden house was the largest in the village the Germans might make it their headquarters. "What we will do now," he said, "is burn down our house."'

The family moved into the forest and joined up with a group of partisans, until one day they heard an artillery battle in progress, at the end of which there was a loud hoorah. '*Oni nashi*,' ('They are ours') her father shouted, and they went in the direction of the hoorah and found the Red Army and safety.

Mr Hitler had obviously made a mistake in taking on people of that resilient nature, but Marina Ivanovna had learned that wars were awful things and was on the side of the soldiers' mothers, who wanted their sons back.

I went to an American clinic in Moscow about my arm, where I was warned that the Russian military doctors had made a mess of setting the fracture. My friend Sasha, the Russian doctor, disagreed. It was, he said, a Colles fracture, named after a nineteenth-century Dublin surgeon called Abraham Colles. Sasha apparently knew his history as well as his medicine.

Back in Dublin, I went to see a leading specialist at the paper's expense. He asked about the American medics and I told him who they were. He had my wrist X-rayed once more and came to the following conclusion: the Americans did not know what they were talking about – it was indeed a Colles fracture and the Russian army doctor had set it perfectly.

— 'A State of Chassis' —

Russia was still quite an important source of news, but there were other parts of the Slavic world that were making the headlines. I was a frequent visitor to Belgrade, where hundreds of thousands of people were demonstrating against the government of Slobodan Milosevic. Serbia and Serbians have been getting particularly bad press in recent years, so it is worth remembering that for a considerable period of time the people of Belgrade were brave enough to stand up to Milosevic's repression and the rigging of elections.

On my first visit to the city, I had to travel to London to get my visa and was helped by Zhivko Jaksic, an anti-Milosevic Serb in Dublin. On arrival at Belgrade airport, a large man stopped me on the walkway from the aircraft to the terminal building. He spoke to me in Russian and asked to see my passport. It was a way of letting me know that they knew who I was and why I was in town. The official passport control took place later, after my bags came up on the carousel.

Serbia was the only country I have visited in which the ordinary inhabitants referred to their government as the 'regime'. There was a very real feeling of repression in the air, but also a sense of bold determination on the part of the people. The TV news broadcasts were almost comical. There would be hundreds of thousands of protesters in the centre of the capital and not a mention of it on the main bulletins. Instead, there were the latest speeches of the leaders of the regime and the occasional story about factories increasing their output. The same was true of the major pro-regime newspapers.

But there were brave voices. The publication *Nasa Borba* (Our Struggle) was on the streets giving the anti-Milosevic point of view, and Radio B92 was doing a similar job. There was also a pop song called 'Baba Yula', which excoriated Milosevic's wife Mirjana as a *baba*, or peasant woman. It was banned, but one could hear it blaring from car stereos on the streets of Belgrade.

When NATO bombed Belgrade, these were the people I felt for. My colleague Lara Marlowe, who was in the city, reported that NATO's claims of pinpoint accuracy were far from true. The most glaring botched attack was the one that destroyed the Chinese embassy.

At the time, I was in Belarus, giving a course on journalism for an organisation sponsored by a number of groups. One of these groups was NATO. I was to have returned to Ireland to give a paper to the Royal Irish Academy (RIA) but was ordered to stay on to cover Russia's attitude to the Belgrade attacks. I felt quite uncomfortable doing this since my trip to Moscow and onwards to Minsk had been paid for by one of the belligerents. I offered to return to Dublin for the day of my proposed paper at the RIA and to return to Moscow immediately at the expense of *The Irish Times*, but this was refused.

Not all that much happened in Moscow except for a failed rocket attack by a passing car on the US embassy. I got there quickly and just as quickly got into trouble. The embassy was surrounded by a crowd of right-wing demonstrators, many of them carrying the banners of the so-called Liberal Democratic Party led by the madcap neo-fascist Vladimir Zhirinovsky. Just as I arrived, my mobile rang with a call from RTÉ. Some of the crowd heard me speak in English and I was quickly surrounded by hostile people. I told them, in Russian, that I was from Ireland, and it worked. An elderly man immediately explained that Ireland was not a member of NATO, and the atmosphere cooled appreciably.

There were demos taking place all over Eastern Europe at that time, and perhaps the most good-humoured of these was in Bulgaria, where students led the marchers against a government that had let them down. In some Eastern European countries, the issue was lack of personal freedom, while in others it was grinding poverty. In Bulgaria it was both. There was, all the same, a sense of humour there that had not been apparent elsewhere.

On the route from the impressive centre of the Bulgarian capital to the parliament stood the mausoleum of Georgi Dimitrov, the communist leader. It was designed in a similar style to the Lenin Mausoleum in Moscow but had been done on the cheap. Instead of the polished marble of its Moscow counterpart, the Belgrade mausoleum was built of concrete blocks. As the thousands of demonstrators marched past the mausoleum, the student leaders would stand on top, taking the salute in the style of Stalin and his comrades at the May Day parades in Moscow in the old days – this despite the fact that Dimitrov's body had been removed by this stage.

I found the Bulgarians to be extremely friendly and hospitable people, with a definite southern touch to their character. The Bulgarian and Russian languages are to a large extent mutually understandable, so I was able to get on quite well with those involved in the anti-government protests.

Things were very different at my next port of call. In March 1997 Albania descended into chaos and I came closer to losing my life than at any stage in my career. Arrival at the Albanian capital Tirana's little airport presented a very sad picture. In the forecourt outside the main building hundreds of men begged to be allowed drive passengers into town. I engaged the nearest one and we drove away past a little white mosque set in green countryside – Albania is one of only two countries in mainland Europe with a Muslim majority (Bosnia-Herzegovina is the other).

Shortly after this, the green became speckled with grey, as bunker after paranoid bunker built on the orders of the Stalinist dictator Enver Hoxha began to appear. Hoxha feared invasion from the West. He feared invasion from the East as well. He also feared an uprising of his own people.

He built bunkers in which his loyal followers would fight to the death. There were seven hundred thousand of them in a country one-third the size of Ireland, and their greatest concentration was around the capital. They were shaped like the ancient monastic beehive huts of western Ireland, but larger. Hoxha had long gone, and no one now feared invasion. The bunkers were used by Europe's poorest population either as hen-houses or as sites for mushroom growing.

Hoxha's fundamentalist strain of communism had withered

away and had been replaced with an authoritarian capitalist government that was now on the verge of collapse. The promise of wealth under a capitalist system had been reneged on by ruthless operators who had impoverished the people even further.

Pyramid schemes had flourished and, as is the way with these schemes, the tiny numbers who got in early made lots of money and the news spread of great wealth to be made in the new world of capitalism. And, as is also the way with pyramid schemes, the vast numbers who came in later lost everything they had. It is easy to condemn or to ridicule those in the West who fall for such scams, but one could only feel sympathy for the poor Albanians, who had been so isolated from the rest of the world that they knew no better.

By now the schemes were collapsing all over the country and an armed rebellion was in full swing in the south. Raids were taking place on government arsenals. A million rifles were believed to be in the hands of the people, and in a land where ancient family feuds were endemic this could mean very big trouble.

My taxi driver was unable to help me gather much information. He merely signalled that he spoke only Albanian and drove on. We arrived at my destination, the Austrian-run Rogner Europapark Hotel, and I paid him in dollars, for which he was immensely grateful. Then, in a sudden movement, he leaned towards me and whispered the Italian words '*Il nostro presidente e pazzo.*' ('Our president is mad.')

There were signs, if not of madness, of a new dictatorship emerging. The country's only independent newspaper, *Koha Jone*, had ceased publication after its newsroom had been burned down by what appeared to be armed civilians, but were more likely members of the secret police in civilian clothes. On certain sections of certain streets, the footpaths were deserted and pedestrians walked on the road. There was an unwritten rule that you could not walk near government installations.

On the avenue of the Martyrs of the Nation (formerly Stalin Avenue), citizens of Tirana strolled in the sunshine. A glass-and-concrete wigwam that was once the mausoleum of the dictator Enver Hoxha was now a 'palace of culture' and known to locals as the 'Pyramid', after the pyramid-investment schemes.

At the end of the avenue the Restorant Pizzeri Kumanova, run by Albanian refugees from the Serbian province of Kosovo, plied its trade where the huge statue of Stalin once stood. Across the street the great effigy of Lenin had been replaced by the Admiral Poker Machine Club.

Around to the right and down a dusty, potholed laneway a crowd of men hung out in front of Berisha's Democratic Party headquarters. One, a fierce-looking peasant in his seventies, refused to give his name. He carried a Kalashnikov. He said only that he would defend himself against 'the communist bandits'.

Close to the central Skenderbeg Square, the city's largest mosque prepared for the afternoon prayers of the Muslim sabbath. More than seventy per cent of Albanians are, theoretically at least, adherents of Islam.

About a hundred men at a street corner were trading in a sort of informal bourse. The houses and farms of the disinherited were being bought and sold. Two of the more primitive-looking marketeers told me to move on. I did.

Around the corner to the right, in the shadow of the Tirana International Hotel, where the world's TV crews were stationed, stands a pleasant tree-lined square. The large grey house with a top-floor balcony was once the home of a young man called Zog, who in the distant past was the local correspondent of the

London *Times*. Zog was the sort of person who saw his chance and took it. When political convulsion broke out, the story goes, Zog's editor telegraphed him demanding to know why no reports were being sent. His reply contained just two devastating words: 'Am king.'

There was nothing regal about the large crowd nearby at the headquarters of VEFA Holdings, one of the investment schemes still able to pay out some money. Here, the faces were taut with anger and frustration. Men and women waited for the daily list of numbers to be read, identifying investors who would get some of their money back.

Ferit Duru, aged seventy-five, hoped to get some cash. He looked older than his years and was bent from hard work; his face, with its high cheek bones and skin turned almost to leather, was that of a quintessential Balkan peasant.

The end of communism benefited him at first. He became a private farmer, a landowner, a man of property. Then the pyramid fever caught hold. Investors were promised incredibly high interest rates and Ferit thought that this new capitalism was the thing for him. 'I sold my house. I sold my farm and my cattle and my sheep. I sold everything for $35,000 and put it all in VEFA. I come here every day to see if I am going to get something back.' A man in his sixties, who identified himself only as Dishnitsa, had saved $7,000 sent to him in remittances from two of his sons who worked in Greece. But he seemed resigned to all of it being lost.

There was no sign of resignation, however, in the face of Ismet Vruxhe, a wild-eyed man who sold his house and stood to lose $14,000. 'If VEFA collapses, there will be fighting here in Tirana like there is in the south and I will be one of the fighters,' he told me.

Back across Skenderbeg Square, past the former party building with its mosaic of heroic Albanian revolutionaries, and down another dusty road, Gilda Kromic, an elegant lady in her seventies, broke from her prayers in the Church of the Sacred Heart (about ten per cent of Albanians are Catholics). She sprang to President Berisha's defence. 'He brought us democracy. All the things that have gone wrong are the fault of the communists. They have been digging holes in the roads and water pipes to make life difficult and put the blame on our president. They started these pyramids themselves to cause trouble. I would have nothing to do with them … everything I have I earned by my own sweat. Those who are against our president are nothing but dirty communists.'

Just fifty yards away, a former gymnasium was now a home to the Albanian Orthodox Church, whose adherents comprise twenty per cent of the population. Peter Rama had called in to pray. He was a dapper man in his eighty-third year, his shoes burnished to a brilliant shine. 'Berisha is for his people. Those who are against him should be calm and stop fighting. Our Holy Orthodox Church tells us it is our duty to support our leaders.'

On the way back to the hotel, the youngsters thronging the cafés and bars in the Park of Youth seemed closer in their views to old Peter Rama than to anyone else. They looked calm, as though they knew nothing of the fighting which raged in their country.

But appearances in Albania can be deceptive. Outside the headquarters of the SHIK (secret police) near the Park of Youth, burly men in leather jackets bearing the trademark moustaches of their occupation wandered everywhere. Everything was under control. Literally.

Day by day, as the fighting moved northwards, Albanians

who spoke English approached journalists in the lobby of the Europapark Hotel offering their services as fixers and interpreters. I employed a man in his forties who knew all the political machinations and was soon to know even more. One morning, he came to me and told me he was worried that he might not be able to work for me any more. He had, he told me, been given a job in the Foreign Ministry. I persuaded him to continue and he agreed on the condition that we would meet in an unobtrusive little café each day. The result was bizarre. At these morning meetings he would say things such as: 'Madeleine Albright rang last night and this is what she said …' or 'The Italians have a ship in the middle of the Adriatic and they are flying representatives of the government and the opposition out there for talks. The ship is called the *San Giorgio* …'

Our relationship continued for days on this basis and I was on the inside track. A trip south to Elbasan, an appalling town dominated by a sprawling Chinese steelworks, showed that the armed conflict was getting closer. Just on the other side of town I arrived on the scene of a gun battle. The shooting was coming to an end and the secret police were about to claim victory. On the way back over the hills to Tirana, small children stood at the roadside selling bunches of wild violets to passers-by. Nothing could have been more peaceful.

Then the violence hit Tirana and I was left stranded. I was scheduled to go to Helsinki to cover a summit between Bill Clinton and Boris Yeltsin, which, in world terms, was considerably more important than this little sideshow in Albania. While Dublin was deciding whether I should go or stay, the choice was made for us by the rebels.

They began to open fire on civilian aircraft at Tirana airport. The airport was closed and the foreign population of the capital was in panic. Evacuation was now the main story and I finally got word from the editor's office that I was to go with a group of evacuees who would meet at the British embassy.

The scene there was one of efficient organisation, as names were taken of the British, Canadian, Irish, Hungarian, Argentinian, Dutch and other civilians anxious to leave. The story was that the British would get the evacuees to the port of Durres and from there the Italians would take people to safety.

As we stood and waited for instructions, a bizarre and curiously Irish incident occurred. There was a loud burst of gunfire and we threw ourselves to the ground. The firing ended, and as I stood up I saw a tiny nun in a brown habit approach me. Her question stunned me: 'Are you a cousin of the Fitzpatricks in James's Street?'

She introduced herself as Sister Veronica Gibbons from Dublin. She said she recognised me from my picture in *The Irish Times* and knew my cousins, who had run a shop in James's Street.

Next we were addressed by a military type who described himself as Front-End Charlie (FEC). He had, he said, entered Albania clandestinely after the airport had closed down and would be in charge of our convoy, leading from the front. There would be wireless communication between him and a Rear-End Charlie to ensure the safety of the convoy, and all would be well.

Thus began a nightmare journey. In the course of it, the face of an evil man became imprinted on my mind for life, after which I would never take a national stereotype for granted again.

A series of minibuses had now been lined up and we boarded in the order allocated to us. FEC got into the first vehicle, which revved up, and off we went. Within eight hundred metres the entire operation had been botched. The final six minibuses became detached from the rest of the convoy and got lost. Naturally, I was in one of the lost minibuses.

We regrouped, and as the Albanian drivers knew the way to Durres we decided to make a run for it without military assistance. We were fortunate in that a large Welsh policeman with an Irish name had some organisational experience in this sort of thing, and set up a means of communication between the first and last minibus through a type of semaphore using pieces of cloth.

Off we went again with the Welsh policeman in charge of our minibus, accompanied by two of his compatriots. We also had a Scots banker with thousands of dollars hidden in his socks; Sister Veronica and a Scottish nun from the same convent; Tom Englishby from Navan; and myself.

Disaster struck just outside Tirana. We ran into a scene of utter pandemonium: hundreds of people were looting bags of meal and flour from a large grain store. Many of them were armed with the Kalashnikovs that were being stolen daily from the government arsenals. Our way was blocked and then a man who appeared to be the leader of the looters stood in front of our minibus with a large crowbar in his hand. His face was the most evil I have ever seen and from time to time it returns to me in flashbacks.

He wanted money and he got some. He wanted more than that and he took the Albanian driver's gold wedding ring. Then something distracted his attention and he let us go.

There was just one further shock before we got to Durres. Up in the hills, in a place miles from anywhere, we ran out of petrol. My language was now of a kind that the two holy nuns could not have been accustomed to, but the problem was not as bad as I anticipated. One of the Albanians went off into the countryside and returned soon after with a large canister. Off we went again.

We arrived at the port of Durres and made enquiries after Front-End Charlie. We were directed through a decrepit area of dockland and there he was with the rest of the group. He told us that he had got us safely to Durres and there were to be no complaints. We did not complain, but we knew we had got there ourselves. We were also soon to discover that we were at the wrong dock.

The Italians were planning to arrive at another section of the port to pick up a hundred or so people who had already been waiting eight hours to be evacuated. We were supposed to be there to wait for evacuation in the next batch. FEC decided that the Italians should come to us on the wrong dock, so he lined up the minibuses and told them to flash their headlamps on and off in the direction of the sea.

A bizarre system of communications was now set up. First of all, FEC asked if anyone had a mobile phone that worked in Albania. He was given one by a Dublin building worker. What happened next was farcical. FEC wanted to get in touch with the Italian mother ship, the *San Giorgio*, to let them know where we were. He rang the British embassy in Tirana, who rang the Foreign Office in London, who rang the Foreign Ministry in Rome, who rang the *San Giorgio*.

The captain of the *San Giorgio* then rang the Foreign Ministry in Rome with his reply, and the message was relayed by the Foreign Office in London, who rang the embassy in Tirana, who then rang Front End Charlie on the Dubliner's mobile phone.

The message, not surprisingly, was that we were to go to the other dock and wait our turn. So off we went to the other dock to find that things were getting nasty. The group that had been waiting eight hours was being threatened by an armed group of Albanians who like most of their compatriots would give an arm and a leg to get to Italy.

It was a frightening situation, but also a sad one. Here was a group of people prepared to kill in order to get away from their homeland. Some of them may indeed have been criminals, but others were women and children trying to get to a country where they might have a decent life.

Next up was Front End Charlie again. We were not to worry. The Italians would be here in seven minutes. No one knew where he got the information from, but he was wrong. Five hours and thirty minutes later, they arrived in a squadron of landing craft – and then the dangerous part began.

Armed Albanians tried to force their way on board. The Italian marines resisted. There was a deafening outburst of machine-gun fire and the frightening noise of thunderclap devices used to scare the enemy. They scared me, too. I lay on the ground with my head covered by my laptop. I knew that would be no protection but it was simply a natural reaction. Occasionally, I looked up and saw that the Italian marines were firing directly into the air, the muzzles of their sub-machine guns were perpendicular to the ground and the red tracer bullets were streaming skywards.

Yet three Albanians were killed just a few metres away from where I lay. I can only assume they were shot by their own side. The armed Albanians were using these weapons for the first time. They had no training and little control over where their bullets were going.

As the Italians withdrew with the first batch of evacuees, things were now getting extremely tense. There were still groups of armed Albanians around and three of their friends had lost their lives. If anyone was a target, it was us.

I had my Sony shortwave radio and listened to the BBC
World Service. Their reporter Paul Wood was telling the world
that it was too dangerous to go to the docks in Durres – something that did little to boost our confidence. There were reports,
too, from Tirana that the Americans had taken the direct route
to evacuate their citizens. No trips across hostile territory for
them. US navy helicopters were airlifting the Americans out.

Striking news also came from the German embassy compound. In order to get their citizens out safely, German soldiers
had opened fire in a military operation for the first time since
the end of the Second World War.

Meanwhile back in Durres, the docklands were, as Paul
Wood had said, too dangerous. Gunfire was constant. Much
of it was coming from a neighbouring area, where stores were
being looted. Some of it was coming from our own area. Armed
Albanians were gathering in conspiratorial groups and glaring
in our direction.

The battery on the Dubliner's mobile phone was running
low. The British evacuees were talking about what they wouldn't
do for a plate of fish and chips. Churchill's name began to come
up in their conversations. An American woman, a Protestant
missionary, had been struck a glancing blow by a ricochet bullet.
Then something totally unexpected took place.

A large van containing a group of extremely big, tough-
looking men arrived. They were Croatians who had been working on a nearby oil rig. Their arrival had three positive results.
Firstly, they had a car phone, which was run off the van's batteries; secondly, they placed themselves menacingly between us and
the Albanians; and thirdly, they handed out bottles of decent red
and white Croatian wine. The three journalists – myself and two
Dutch colleagues – were glad of the unexpected refreshments.

The Dublin building workers joined in. The British chose to talk once more of fish and chips and Churchill.

FEC told us there was good news. HMS *Birmingham* was on its way and, in the meantime, a small group of five or six SAS men would arrive shortly to protect us.

Then, as dawn came up, the shapes of landing craft could be seen on the horizon. It was the small group of SAS men, cunningly disguised as two hundred and fifty Italian marines. As they drew closer, we prepared ourselves for another gun battle between the Italians and the Albanians. But we were in for a surprise. An Italian officer stepped up onto the dock and made an announcement that completely defused the situation. All Albanians who wanted to go to Italy would be taken there provided they were not armed.

Guns were flung into the sea and we began to board the landing craft together. I am not the sort of person who takes to hugging Italian marines as a rule, but I was sorely tempted to do so that morning.

As the Albanian shore receded there was an overwhelming relief. One young Englishwoman expressed her disappointment that HMS *Birmingham* and the SAS had not arrived, but she was not volunteering to go back to shore and wait.

We arrived at the *San Giorgio* and were split up into groups and given fruit salad and little boxes of Italian red wine before being transferred to its sister ship, the *San Giusto*. There we went through passport control and were put on a lower deck that was set out with little tables and parasols, rather like the *terrasse* of an Italian restaurant. There was food and wine and relaxation, but no communication with the outside world.

The two ships then patrolled up and down the Adriatic as parties of marines went ashore to rescue people at little coves and ports along the shores of Albania. It was late at night when we arrived at Brindisi and an announcement was made: 'Order of disembarkment: first, Italians; second, citizens of the European Union; third, non-European citizens; last, Albanians.'

Soon we were ashore. The gunfire still rang in our ears, but we were in the delightful land of Italy. Myself, Tom Englishby and the big Welsh policeman booked ourselves into a hotel for the night and onto an Alitalia flight for Rome the next day. In the morning we heard British evacuees on the World Service blame the Italians for all the problems that had arisen, but we knew better.

The sound of the gunfire lasted in our ears for days, even when we got to Rome, where I stayed a couple of nights with my brother in Trastevere. At Dublin airport I was met by Anita, Ruth and Deirdre, who were very relieved to see me. I had brought a spent rifle cartridge into which I had placed a single rose in memory of the closest shave I have ever had. It still stands on my mantelpiece at home in Dublin.

After my adventures in the warmth of the Mediterranean, I was soon off to the chill of Helsinki on the Gulf of Finland. There, Presidents Clinton and Yeltsin held successful talks, and the Russian leader behaved himself impeccably. The day after the summit the international press drifted homewards. I stayed on a further day to cover the bilateral meeting between Mr Yeltsin and the Finnish president.

Yeltsin arrived and had obviously had a few drinks on board. I sat with the Irish ambassador, Dáithí Ó Ceallaigh, and we both almost collapsed on hearing him say that Russia was about to join the European Union.

Back in Dublin, a very strange thing happened. I went with

some Eastern European friends, including Zhivko Jaksic, to the little Orthodox Church in Arbour Hill for the ceremonies that mark the Orthodox Easter. When they ended, a Frenchman came up to me as he recognised me as the journalist who had been in Albania. He introduced me to his wife, Elvira, a concert pianist and member of the Albanian Orthodox Church.

It was a pity, I was told, that I had not interviewed President Berisha during my stay, but he had obviously been too busy to talk to journalists during the disturbances. They assured me an interview with the controversial leader was possible, and a week or so later a fax arrived from the Albanian ambassador in Paris stating that His Excellency Dr Sali Ram Berisha would meet me at his palace in Tirana on the afternoon of a specified date.

So, very soon I was back in Tirana. It was a different place. The airport was now open and Turkish peacekeeping troops patrolled the streets, but the locals were still not allowed to walk on the footpaths outside government installations.

I was ushered into the presidential palace and led to an ante-room. Dr Berisha's secretary explained that there was no need of a translator as the president spoke perfect English. This turned out to be something of an exaggeration. Dr Berisha's English was less than perfect and difficult to follow. I sat there with a number of thoughts on my mind, or should I say some thoughts on many numbers. I was adding the price of the air fare to the cost of overnights at the Europapark and meals and taxis. I had nothing to show for it after an interview I didn't understand and couldn't transcribe in a way the readers of *The Irish Times* might understand.

An old memory came to me of the comedian Professor Stanley Unwin, who had invented his own language that had a strange resemblance to English. He had begun his version of the story of Goldilocks in the following way: 'Once apollytito and Goldiloppers set out in the deep dark of the forry. She carry a basket with buttery-flabe and cheese flavour.'

I was relieved that Berisha's English was a bit better than that, thanked the president and went back to the Europapark. I worked for nearly four hours to transcribe the tape and make some sense of it.

Not long after this, Berisha lost the presidency in a general election. He tried and failed again in 2001. Not one to give in easily, Dr Berisha, politician, heart surgeon and mangler of the English language, after the elections of 2005 and after deals with smaller parties, is now prime minister of Albania.

— Hints of Crisis —

There were some early indications that *The Irish Times* needed to cut back on spending, but in my case they were so ludicrous that I paid little attention. My visits to Moscow were usually on Aeroflot from Shannon, and on my return to Ireland I would fly from Moscow to Shannon on Aeroflot and from Shannon to Dublin on Aer Lingus. Then, out of the blue, an edict was issued that I was to save money by travelling overland from Shannon to Dublin.

This usually entailed a mixture of taxi, bus and train in getting from Shannon to Ennis and onwards to Limerick station to take the train to Dublin. Frequently, the Aeroflot flight from Moscow arrived when onward overland connections were not possible and this meant spending the night in a hotel in Limerick. Either method of getting from one place to another was considerably more expensive than flying, but at least it gave the bureaucrats at head office a feeling that they were doing something to justify their existence and their extremely inflated salaries. My response was to move from Aeroflot to Scandinavian Airlines, changing planes at Copenhagen, and arriving at Dublin instead of Shannon. This was more expensive still but no objections were raised.

On my return from Albania I had lost all my clothes other than those I was wearing. All evacuees had been told to bring just one bag and I took the *Irish Times'* laptop as it was the most valuable. The paper agreed to pay for replacement clothing. Then something strange happened that changed the course of my journalistic career once more.

Eoin McVey, one of the burgeoning number of managing editors, decided to write to the editor Conor Brady to say that I was costing the paper too much and that I might be better employed as editor of the website and associated publications. He typed out his memo and then put it into the computerised system for Conor Brady. But he made a very important mistake. Instead of addressing it to the editor he addressed it to me.

When I received the message I went to Conor Brady in his office to let him know what had happened. He thought for a moment and asked me would I like the job. I thought about it, then reflected on the Albanian bullet case with the rose in it on the mantelpiece at home. The likelihood of being shot at would diminish and there would be the added bonus of having a desk to sit at. I said yes, but added that I wanted to continue my interest in Russia.

Hands were shaken and I moved from the *Irish Times'* building in D'Olier Street to Ballast House with the grandiose title of editor of the electronic publications of *The Irish Times*. I spent two years there with a team of very bright and capable young journalists. There were problems regarding editorial independence, with some members of the commercial side of the house trying to have items published without my seeing them. On one occasion, two journalists from the paper were asked to work on a supplement on education, but when they realised I had not been informed they pulled out.

Eoin McVey, by the way, had been profusely apologetic about his memo in which he said I had cost too much. I had been annoyed at it, since the Albanian trip had almost cost me my life; but these things happen in newspapers and it must be said he was of great assistance in helping me avoid commercial intrusion into the editorial side in the electronic division.

I spent two fruitful years in the job, in the course of which the website, Ireland.com, won numerous Golden Spider awards as the best in Ireland, both editorially and commercially. It was my policy to give the young web journalists their heads and intervene only when necessary. They were extremely successful, and a high point came in 1998 with the winning of the Swiss-based IP Top award for best content against first-class world opposition, including the vastly better-funded BBC News website. Major McDowell sent over a bottle of vintage champagne from his 'bunker' in D'Olier Street. It was already chilled, and without much deference to grand style it was imbibed from plastic cups.

Conor Pope, now deputy editor of the website, produced a superb series on the Peace Process in Northern Ireland, which was a finalist in the Editor and Publisher Awards in the United States. Out of hundreds of entries it was the only non-US one to make it to the top three at the awards ceremony in Atlanta, Georgia.

After my two years in Ballast House overlooking O'Connell

Bridge, I was called in once more by Conor Brady, who asked me to take over the world-news section. This was to be a fairly difficult task as it involved a great deal of diplomacy, which had never been my strong point. There were already two journalists in the foreign area with positions of responsibility. Paul Gillespie, the foreign editor, and Patrick Comerford, the foreign-desk editor, did not get on well and were known to more sardonic members of staff as Iran and Iraq.

The initial plan, proposed to Conor Brady by senior editor Peter Murtagh, was to give Paul Gillespie another title, allowing him to continue his input into the paper's editorial policy, with the title of foreign editor devolving to myself. I knew how much Paul was attached to the foreign-editor title and said this to Conor Brady. He asked me if I could come up with a title for myself and I said I would work with the title international editor provided that I had complete control of the foreign coverage. In this form the situation was put before the NUJ representatives, who agreed that no interview process was necessary since the post was a new one.

At that time a new system of running the newspaper was being put in place, with four journalists manning the News Centre from which the direction of the paper's coverage would be determined. The four were Cliff Taylor, the former business editor and now editor of the *Sunday Business Post*; Peter Murtagh, a former news editor of the *Guardian* in London; Peter Thursfield, the pictures editor; and myself.

The News Centre experiment was barely put into operation when the paper ran into severe financial difficulties. At that stage the centre was running in tandem with the traditional news-desk operation as a transitional measure. There had been some rumours of financial difficulties, and union representatives had been told of unfavourable projections in the middle of 2001. But no one outside the top management was sure what was going to happen until November of the same year, when matters reached a crisis point.

The terrorist attacks in New York and Washington on 11 September of that year had an adverse effect on world economic conditions and also on *The Irish Times*. The paper, however, had been in trouble for quite some time before that. The 'dot-com bubble' had burst more than a year earlier, and the Irish economy had a larger dependency than most on companies involved in information technology.

The *Irish Times'* revenues were heavily dependent for many years on recruitment and real-estate advertising, and these had already suffered erosion for some time prior to 11 September.

As these traumatic changes were taking place in the economy, important changes were taking place in *The Irish Times* itself. Louis O'Neill had been succeeded as managing director by Nick Chapman, who had come to Ireland from the BBC. Chapman, described by Conor Brady as the 'quintessential, decent Englishman' was not cut out for the office politics that now dominated the paper. If Irish mainstream politics could be described as a 'shark-infested swimming pool', the situation in D'Olier Street deserved to be portrayed as a 'shark-infested wash-hand basin'.

The infighting started as soon as Chapman arrived and he became known as 'the man from the mainland' and 'the English Impatient'. It was said that Chapman referred to our neighbouring island as the 'mainland'. This sort of reference, which is deeply insulting and condescending, would certainly have got people's backs up. I must say I never heard him use the term.

His arrival, however, agitated the sharks considerably. The in-house favourite for the MD job, Maeve Donovan, had been overlooked and those who supported her candidature were furious. I always got on well with Maeve and telephoned her office and left a message of commiseration when I heard she had not got the job. Chapman arrived as I was preparing to leave as electronic editor, and at that time I had considerable contact with the commercial side of the house. Right from his arrival, the antipathy of some senior commercial executives was palpable. Chapman gave them some opportunities in the form of a certain personal gaucheness.

There was a typical incident when Mrs Mary O'Rourke, the government minister involved in the information-technology area, came to the *Irish Times'* table at a luncheon in the Clontarf Castle Hotel and was introduced to Chapman. He remained seated while shaking her hand instead of affording her the courtesy of standing up.

Well, the commercial executives at the table behaved as if they had just won the Lotto. A piece of valuable anti-Chapman material had fallen into their laps and they were absolutely thrilled. They could hardly wait to get back to the office to spread the good news. The process of undermining the new MD was under way.

On the editorial side, Conor Brady – known to the commercial people as 'The Prince of Darkness' – wooed Chapman openly. Lunches were held at which he was introduced to editorial executives on extremely friendly terms. The result was that tensions on the commercial side, with whom he had his closest dealings, increased even further. He became seen as an editorial Trojan Horse installed in the fastnesses of the once-impregnable commercial city.

There was also to be investment in new technology in a part

of Dublin known as City West. The old press that had produced the paper in D'Olier Street was on the verge of collapse. It had not been designed to bear the brunt of printing the large-sized editions of the paper that had evolved at the end of the twentieth century. A new press was badly needed and it was decided to finance the project out of the company's own resources.

The convergence of such expenditure with the downturn in revenue resulted in near calamity. On 1 November the paper carried a report that representatives of management would meet the unions shortly to brief them on what was described as 'difficulties arising from the economic downturn'. The term 'downturn' was something of an understatement. The company had made a record profit of £14.7 million (€18.6 million) the previous year and now it appeared to be heading for disaster.

On 6 November the company issued the following statement:

> Senior management met representatives of the unions representing staff at *The Irish Times* today and were told of the urgent need for measures to maintain the company's competitiveness and efficiency.
>
> Representatives of the company's Joint Consultative Council were also present. Other management members and editors were briefed simultaneously.
>
> A drop in revenues, in the wake of the world economic downturn, combined with steeply rising costs, means that the company faces unacceptably severe losses unless extensive savings can be achieved quickly.
>
> Union representatives were provided with information on the company's financial situation.
>
> The union representatives were told that the company is seeking to shed 250 jobs from its workforce of more than 700, including some subsidiary operations. In addition, extensive non-payroll savings will have to be implemented.
>
> In accordance with the partnership agreements which operate between the company and the unions, consultation will take place immediately on achievement of these objectives.

Seamus Martin

Management has told the union representatives that The Irish Times Ltd is happy to have an early assessment of the company's financial circumstances by an agreed and suitably qualified third party.

The company's aim is to spread job losses proportionately between editorial, commercial, production, central service departments and at all levels.

The company is examining the matter of terms for departing employees. It is hoped that as many as possible of the necessary 250 job losses will be voluntary. If the required savings are not secured by voluntary partings, it will be necessary to have involuntary partings.

The union representatives were told that the company's financial circumstances were such that monetary compensation for departing staff would not be at levels comparable to those which have been made available in the past.

The meeting was told that managers and editors would immediately begin a process of consultation in departments in order to ensure that the newspaper's traditionally high standards and range of services can be maintained.

The editor, Mr Conor Brady, told the meeting that while he deeply regretted the necessity for the measures now ahead, he was confident that *The Irish Times* would maintain its unchallenged place as the leading newspaper in the country in terms of its authority, its depth and its range of editorial content.

The newspaper's character and ethos would remain the same, he said. '*The Irish Times* will remain independent of all external interests. It will remain primarily concerned with serious issues. It will continue to provide the most comprehensive news coverage and the most informed opinion and analysis.'

Also at the meeting were the Chairman of The Irish Times Ltd, Mr Don Reid, Commercial Director, Ms Maeve Donovan, Director-Human Resources, Mr Michael Austen and the Director of Finance, Mr Liam Kavanagh. Mr Alex Burns of KPMG, who is acting as a consultant to the company, was also present.

As the company is now entering into consultative procedures with the unions, no additional details of measures to be taken will be made available until further notice.

Editorial executives were being briefed separately and in this case the ice-cold words of the meeting with the unions were replaced by sincere emotion. The 'executive editor', Pat O'Hara, was almost in tears as he spoke of the crisis that had afflicted the newspaper in which he had begun his career as a copy-boy. In the newsroom there was turmoil verging on open revolt, and for those of us who had worked in the old *Tribune* at the time of its demise there was a sense of déjà vu, except on this occasion it was not a fragile infant publication that was in danger of folding but a major force in Irish publishing that had been in existence for well over a hundred years.

The following day, Conor Brady gave an interview to Cathal MacCoille on RTÉ radio. He had been working on it with communications experts in order to be able to give the smoothest possible performance. In my view, Brady did not perform as well as he should have done, as I think the following transcript shows:

> *C MacC*: What's it like to go before your own workforce and tell them one in three will have to go?
> *CB*: It's dreadful Cathal. It's a terrible pass we have come to and I understand the anger and the upset. I'm angry, I'm upset and apprehensive. But what I would say to our people … to our workforce and to my colleagues is that we have a job to do. We can put our shoulders into this job and if we succeed in doing it we can come out of this with two out of three jobs in *The Irish Times* secure for the future … and with the newspaper … its ethos, its quality and its role in Irish society preserved [indistinct].
> *C MacC*: We'll come back to what the unions are saying about that in a moment but how will the readers notice the fact that two out of three are gone, I mean what way will their product be less attractive, less satisfying for them?
> *CB*: Well there are going to have to be modifications. We are at the moment in the process of consulting with my senior editors and with my colleagues. We are also consulting with the

workforce … until we've gone through that, it would be very wrong to say that this is going to change or that is going to change. It's going to take some little time. There's obviously going to be some attenuation of services but we also have the advantage of putting in extremely efficient publishing technology, which means we can put more journalists out front where they should be, fewer journalists in administration, more journalists in actually producing pages, that kind of thing. I think that we … I have little doubt, I have little doubt that people will notice some changes in the paper but I am equally certain that the headroom that *The Irish Times* has over its rivals as this country's finest newspaper is going to be well preserved.

C MacC: The unions are saying they are going to oppose compulsory redundancies.

CB: Yes.

C MacC: And can what needs to be done, be done without compulsory redundancies?

CB: Well I understand why the unions had to take this position at the beginning. I think that when they sit down and look at the books, and the books are being opened to them, I think they will understand and I think they will recognise – it's not for me to prejudge their position but I believe that any [indistinct] person will realise the urgency and the gravity of it. Our problem is two-fold, we have a historically very high cost base. We have been endeavouring to get that down, to manage it down in a structured and progressive way and we were overtaken by events …

C MacC: We'll come to that. What about the deal, which will ultimately affect whether compulsory redundancies happen or not, the deal that people will be offered, the redundancy terms – can they be as, can they be at the same level as they have been until now?

CB: That is a matter which has to be negotiated between the unions and the company. My opinion from what I know of the … of the realities of the financial situation is that they can't be.

C MacC: Can I put it to you and this is a view that has been expressed to me, and expressed on air, indeed, by your own staff, that we are hearing criticism of the way the company was run, management decisions made, which if you were writing about another company in your financial pages, you'd be saying this company was badly managed, serious mistakes had been made, and the implication is, and some columnists would write it, heads would have to roll.

CB: Well I think, I think, we have a board and we have a trust, I think the board and the trust will and are squaring up to their responsibilities. They have to. Nobody's trying to run away from that responsibility ... it is quite clear that the processes put in place to reduce our cost level were not sufficient. They weren't put in in time, speedily enough. I would stress again that we were overtaken by world events. Very few people, very few commentators were able to predict as we went into 2001 the cataclysmic speed at which so many disasters were going to impact on the economy and we were not alone in this ... world, all over the western world, media companies were finding themselves in this very same situation.

C MacC: Your friendly rivals in the Star had a headline saying: 'Sack the bosses. Outrage at *Irish Times*. 250 jobs are slashed.' We have a lot of people, a lot of workers are going to think that way. Somebody ... some of you guys should go, because of what happened because suddenly ... because times are bad but they're not this bad in other newspapers.

CB: Well I accept that they're not this bad in other newspapers but they've been very good in *The Irish Times* for a very long time and we didn't get a lot of calls for people to go at that stage. Now I think that this thing ... there are questions to be asked, there are questions to be answered and I think responsibility has to lie where it must lie. I don't know that anybody wants to run from that responsibility.

C MacC: Could some of these redundancies be averted if the featherbedding that as I say, some of your own wor– ... some of your own staff talk about. They say, too many company cars, too many inflated salaries, maybe too many staff in some areas. Is this a fixed number of redundancies, could it be lower than this if you cut costs elsewhere including in the upper reaches of the company ...

CB: We are cutting costs elsewhere ...

C MacC: Salaries?

CB: And the cuts which are going to go in place, the cuts which are going to go in place have to be agreed and negotiated all round and I can assure you of this: what we are putting in place will be spread proportionally right across the organisation horizontally and up and down the organisation.

C MacC: Are you taking a cut?

CB: That is a matter that is yet to be decided.

C MacC: But you said up and down the company. I mean ... I mean ...

CB: We are not talking about pay cuts at the moment to anybody. We are talking about taking people out. We are talking about reducing costs right across the organisation. Everything has to be negotiated and will be negotiated.

C MacC: So in other words your pay and conditions are on the line here?

CB: My pay and conditions are a matter that I have to discuss with *The Irish Times*, with the company ... at the end of all this there are people who may not have jobs, there are people who will have to reduce their expectations. All of us, including myself

[*C MacC begins to intervene ...*]

CB: Let me finish, let me finish, let me finish. All of us including myself will have to reduce our expectations severely and I certainly will not shed, I will not shy away from my share of responsibility in that –

C MacC: I simply asked the question, I don't mean it personally, I simply mean that if a company sends out signals from its upper reaches saying that we're taking pain, we're taking cuts we're, I don't know, offloading some of our benefits or whatever and therefore we're making an effort that's obviously going to improve morale and if you don't send out the message people are going to feel ... all the load, all the pain is at the lower reaches of the staff.

CB: I have said and I say again our reductions in services and our cuts will be proportionate across all departments and they will be spread vertically throughout the organisation from the very top to the very bottom.

C MacC: What about ... the way in which, I know you are bringing a very expensive printing plant on line and you're doing it with all, within your own resources without borrowing. Do you think now in reflection with money being so cheap that you should have borrowed?

CB: Well one way or the other we would have got into borrowing. If we had borrowed for City West we would still be in the situation where we would have to ... we would have actually added to our cost base so the gap between income and expenditure would have widened ... [indistinct] whatever way we did it we would have been into borrowing. There has been comment about City West that this was in fact the root of our problem – City West was not at the root of our problems. Our problem is a gap between daily spending and daily income.

C MacC: A final question – you are going to be talking to the unions, how long is it going to take? How long … when do you have to have decisions made about how many people are going to go and in what circumstances …

CB: Well we've opened discussions with the unions yesterday, there'll be another meeting with them in the next few days. We would expect … we would hope that we will have the … outline of the programme agreed and in place within a matter of a short number of weeks.

Some of what Conor Brady said at that interview added to the fury of the staff and some of his other statements that morning were used as ammunition by them as time went on. His use of the phrase 'taking people out' was particularly ill-chosen. It sounded like a mafia boss talking about eliminating his rivals. It was something he was to apologise for later, but by now the damage was done. His use of the form of words 'I certainly will not shed …' before changing to 'I will not shy away' was taken as a Freudian slip.

His apparent prioritising of job cuts over reduction in salaries and other expenses was seen as a move by the higher-ups to save their own privileges at the expense of the main body of journalists. His loss of composure in that section of the interview in which he was questioned on the sort of cuts he would have to take in salary, bonuses or conditions fuelled suspicions that he was to retain all his perks while others lost their jobs.

Conor Brady was to make further statements that would haunt him. There would, he told editorial executives, be 'equality of pain' in the cuts that were to be made, a statement that was frequently to be thrown back in his face.

As had happened at the *Tribune* and, I presume, in other companies that have faced the possibility of liquidation, the turmoil amongst the staff had its own therapeutic value. People need to work the anger and bitterness out of their system. The endless crisis meetings would take their toll on people's energy, and gradually the tumult would subside as they came to terms with the reality of the situation.

The same did not apply to journalists in rival publications. There had been a maxim in the newspaper business that 'dog does not eat dog', but in this case the *Irish Times'* dog was surrounded by beasts of a different species. The vultures were circling.

Other newspapers were quick to decide that the *Irish Times'* difficulties stemmed from vanity and featherbedding. They blamed the very existence of the paper's foreign-news section, the plethora of 'assistant editors', the salary structures and the perks. *Schadenfreude* – the enjoyment obtained from the misfortune of others – reigned supreme.

Much of the criticism was valid but some also showed a certain laziness and latching onto certain 'facts' without looking further into the situation. Perhaps the most common criticism was that the paper had eighteen assistant editors. At first glance this seemed to be correct, but in reality the paper had just one journalist, Dick Walsh, with that title. The other seventeen were on the same pay scale and included the finance editor, the features editor, other heads of department and some senior correspondents. The official term for this level of payment was grade E.

The number of 'assistant editors' was seized on by certain commercial executives, too, as an example of featherbedding on the editorial side. It was also used, with partial and temporary success, to drive a wedge between the NUJ representatives in the group of unions and their colleagues in the print unions and SIPTU.

The internal and external critics failed to see where the featherbedding really was. What they did not focus on was the number of executives employed at higher levels and, in most cases, on considerably higher salaries than those described as assistant editors. I should declare my own interest here at this stage. The post of Moscow correspondent had been advertised internally at grade-E level and, having been successful at interview, I moved to that grade in 1991, remaining on that level until I retired in 2002.

Way above the 'assistant editor' grade was a group of eighteen senior executives. Conor Brady, as editor, was at the top of the list, followed by the executive editor, Pat O'Hara. After this came five journalists at managing-editor level. These included Eoin McVey, who looked at budgets; Joe Breen, who oversaw presentation and design; Gerry Smyth, who oversaw features; Seán Olson, who was given the title of associate editor for reading the paper in detail and reporting his views to the editor; and finally Cliff Taylor at the central desk.

Some of these journalists acted in a supervisory capacity over those on grade E. They spent a lot of time ambling round their domains looking over the shoulders of those at work in producing the paper. For this reason they had become known as the 'floorwalkers' by some, and the 'store detectives' by others.

Below the managing-editor group was a team of twelve 'duty editors', a title invented in RTÉ and introduced to *The Irish Times* by Conor Brady. Amongst these were John Armstrong and Eugene McEldowney, who alternated in the demanding job of night editor; Don Buckley, like Arthur Hunter in the old days of the *Irish Press*, was designated day editor; Peter Murtagh ran the opinion page, which appeared opposite the editorial and letters page; and Paul Gillespie, who was now in charge of policy. Also on this grade was Maev-Ann Wren, who had been away from her duties for a number of years due to illness.

The list of editorial executives supplied by management at the time showed a number of anomalies. The finance editor and the deputy finance editor, for example, appeared to be on the same scale, and a number of journalists who bore the word 'editor' in their titles did not appear on the list at all. These included the property editor, Jack Fagan, the London editor, Frank Millar, the environment editor, Frank McDonald, and the obituaries editor, Seán Hogan, who was known in the trade as 'the Grim Reaper'.

It was clear that management had lost track of the number of its executive employees and there were certainly others, such as the diarist Kevin Myers and some 'star' writers, who were paid above the 'assistant editor' grade.

All of these were entitled to office cars of varying marques and models, depending on their seniority in the *Irish Times*' hierarchy. At the apex of this motorcade were the editor's stately Jaguar and the Northern-registered Mercedes of Major Thomas Bleakley McDowell. After that came a dazzling array of BMWs, Alfa Romeos and other premium makes until one reached the lower orders, such as myself. I had been entitled to an office car ever since my appointment to Moscow in 1991, but I didn't succumb to the temptation until my own car died of old age. When the company was being reorganised in 2002, I was driving an *Irish Times*' 1997 Opel Vectra that had turned pink with oxidation.

There appears to have been a similar amount of feather-bedding on the commercial side, too. A partial list of office car holders was purloined by the pedestrian journalists, who found that it ran only as far as those staff members whose first names began with *S*. Starting at Adrian and ending at Siobhán, a total of 122 cars were accounted for. And that did not include the Toms and Vincents and Victors and Williams. I don't think there were many staff members called Xavier, Yves or Zoltan, though there may have been a motorised Yvonne or Zoë somewhere.

The idea of renting out the Phoenix Park to hold an *Irish Times* grand prix with Conor Brady's Jaguar in pole position had been discussed on several occasions amongst those with a taste for subversion. But there were so many cars that a series of eliminator heats would have been necessary.

Also in the firing line along with the 'assistant editors' was the foreign department, and the shots fired in this direction betrayed the provincial mentality of those firing them. A fairly typical example came in a special feature article in *Magill* magazine in January 2002.

The anonymous author wrote: 'Where a daily newspaper would normally have no more than one editor in charge of foreign coverage, *The Irish Times* has a Foreign Editor, an International Editor, an International Business Editor and a Foreign Desk Editor as well as a London Editor and correspondents overseas.'

In fact, *The Irish Times* did have only one editor in charge of foreign coverage at that time and that was myself as international editor. I started work early in the morning and set the agenda before handing over in the late evening to the foreign-desk editor, who worked into the early hours.

After I left for home I was on call in the event of the breaking of major foreign stories. Paul Gillespie had retained the title foreign editor, although he was no longer involved in the area of foreign coverage.

As for Conor O'Clery, as international business editor he was not involved in foreign pages in any way and was employed as a member of the business section. The suggestion that the London editor and the foreign correspondents were in any way 'in charge of foreign coverage' was patently ludicrous.

Foreign coverage had long been an item that distinguished *The Irish Times* from other newspapers in Ireland. For decades after independence, Irish newspapers had relied on British sources for their view of the outside world. Other countries also relied on British sources for their views on Ireland.

Attempts had been made to overcome this dependence. The Irish News Agency was set up in the 1950s to provide a view of Ireland through what had become known as the 'paper wall'. Douglas Gageby had worked there with Conor Cruise O'Brien, and when he became editor of *The Irish Times* he attempted to provide a more international view of world affairs. He commissioned the news service of Agence France Presse to counterbalance the British-angled coverage provided by Reuters, and he also appointed Fergus Pyle as the paper's first foreign correspondent.

Under Conor Brady, in addition to the offices in London and Brussels, resident foreign correspondents were appointed to Moscow, Paris, Berlin for a brief period, Johannesburg, Washington and Beijing. Not all of these bureaux were in operation at the same time, and even before the crisis Moscow, Johannesburg and Berlin no longer had staff correspondents.

Within *The Irish Times* and in rival Irish newspapers, a colonial attitude prevailed in which the idea of this country providing its own foreign news was not only opposed but was openly mocked. Those who adopted this attitude were dubbed the 'little Irelanders' with some justification by Brady; but there were a few 'little Englanders' about as well, who regarded British coverage as superior to that which came from Irish sources. I was reminded that this attitude existed in other spheres when listening to the chief of staff of the Defence Forces, Lieutenant General Dermot Earley, being interviewed on the *Tubridy Show* on RTÉ radio in July 2007. A large number of listeners who phoned in questioned the idea of the republic having its own army. The colonial mindset lingers still.

Because of his setting up of foreign bureaux, there were those who accused Brady of a certain *folie de grandeur*, and some charged him with thinking he was editor of the *New York Times*. In fact, the paper's corps of foreign correspondents was always smaller in number than those employed by newspapers such as *Berlingske Tidende* in Denmark, and never approached that of the serious British, French or US dailies.

There was, however, a strong US influence in Brady's *Irish Times*. Some editorial executives were sent to the Poynter Institute in Florida for management courses. The strict separation of 'Church and state', as the editorial–commercial divide was known in the United States, was a major element in his editorial policy and stemmed more from the American than the European newspaper tradition.

Brady's attempt to bring in an ethics code to limit the acceptance of gifts and free travel, including facility visits by foreign governments, was also of American provenance. Although it was accepted by the NUJ chapel, it was strongly opposed in certain quarters and gradually fell into abeyance.

It could be argued, too, that the preponderance of executives on the top rungs of the editorial ladder mirrored the organisational pattern of leading US newspapers. This was resented on the commercial side, but there were US influences there, too, with leading executives pining for the powers vested in that purely American newspaper official, the 'publisher', who could intervene in the editorial process.

— The End is Near —

As the crisis of 2001 and 2002 developed, Conor Brady found himself under attack from almost all sides. The commercial side of the house had been his enemies for years, but now most of his journalistic staff had turned against him. They felt that they had contributed greatly to the paper's success without being rewarded in the way that a small group of their colleagues had been.

They also felt that now the crunch had come, the favoured few who had reaped the benefits would retain their rewards while the axe would fall on the rest of the staff. To a very large extent they were correct in that judgement.

At this stage, a number of forces came into play. One of them – on the journalistic side – was unusual in the context of newspapers in the English-speaking world, though a more advanced version was in existence at *Le Monde* in Paris. This was the editorial committee, a group of journalists elected by their peers which began its existence during a previous crisis that had almost brought the paper to its knees in the 1970s. The driving force towards the creation of this committee was the political correspondent Dick Walsh, who believed passionately that staff members should have a say in the running of the company.

A major oil crisis had induced an economic downturn, not unlike that experienced in 2001. The editor at the time, Fergus Pyle, had been courageous and backed his journalists in reporting the existence of a group called the 'heavy gang' within the Garda Síochána. But circulation and advertising revenue had begun to fall dramatically, and a group of senior journalists within the NUJ chapel met to evaluate the situation.

They met the chairman, Major McDowell, and later had two meetings with Douglas Gageby (who had retired as editor of the paper) in hired rooms, firstly in Blooms Hotel and later in the Royal Hibernian Hotel in Dublin. The group felt that Douglas Gageby should be asked to return as editor and that he should stay long enough to get the paper back on its feet.

When he heard that this view had become prevalent, Major McDowell agreed that from this point on, certain conditions would apply to the appointment of the editor of *The Irish Times*. In the first place, a period of at least six months' notice would be given when a change of editor was proposed. The post of editor would be advertised internally and externally, and when a shortlist was drawn up it would be presented to a representative group of journalists. If someone on the shortlist was unacceptable to this group then the chairman and managing director would be informed, and unless there were special reasons for proceeding with it, the candidature in question would end.

This was initially described by Major McDowell as a 'negative veto', but he felt later that the word 'veto' was too strong and the term 'negative sieve' came into being. The informal group was now becoming a formal one, and it drew up its own 'constitution' by which it was elected by a secret ballot of the entire membership of the NUJ chapel.

A document was drafted setting out the criteria on which the group's decisions would be based. Other functions were added to the committee's duties, the principal one of which was to provide a representative to monitor each interview panel for editorial posts in *The Irish Times* and the *Irish Field*.

The group became formalised as the editorial committee and performed an essential role in relations between the management and the NUJ chapel. It began as, and has remained, a committee of the NUJ chapel; but since it was not involved in the sphere of industrial relations it was removed from areas of potential confrontation. The issues with which the committee was involved were professional rather than industrial. It dealt with editorial standards and not with wages and conditions. Its representatives at job interviews were there to ensure that each applicant knew his or her rights and received equal treatment.

The editorial committee also had become increasingly aware of the top-heavy management structure that was developing in the paper in the late 1980s and 1990s. Addressing the editor on behalf of the committee, Mary Maher gave a stark warning at a meeting in 1989: 'According to the Father of the Chapel's figures, there are 5.6 journalists for every senior person of E grade and above, and only 2.1 journalists for every person of D grade [head of department] or above. Is this a top heavy structure?' In the intervening twelve years between that meeting and the crisis, the trend towards top-heaviness increased rather than decreased.

When the crisis arose in 2001 the editorial committee faced

what was probably its sternest test, and was involved in meetings with Conor Brady and also with the board. The committee at that time was headed by Kieran Fagan, who was responsible for training in the newspaper and regarded as a close associate of the editor. Other members included the columnist Mary Holland; Denis Coghlan, the chief political reporter; Alison O'Connor from the newsroom; Dick Ahlstrom, the science correspondent; Deaglan de Bréadún of the political staff; Joe Cully from sports; Dick Walsh; and myself. Dick had been suffering from a serious illness for some time and was not able to attend all editorial-committee meetings.

One of our meetings with Conor Brady was bizarre. He spoke about his house in Monkstown and pointed to Denis Coghlan saying that it was similar in size and location to his. Denis immediately disagreed.

Brady was asked about his salary – about which there were many rumours at the time. Some newspapers had published the sum of €250,000 and he replied that we could divide that by two and still subtract a bit.

His response to our questions generally elicited the truth, but we did not get the whole truth. This may have been because our questions were not probing enough. In mid-November, after the meeting with the editorial committee, the *Sunday Business Post* reported that *The Irish Times* had bought the house in Monkstown for Conor Brady in 1988, two years after he had become editor, and that he had bought it from the company for £130,000 in 1990. It also wrote that he had bought the adjoining mews from the company nine years later for £105,000.

In a statement on this issue, Conor Brady said: 'At the end of 1988 The Irish Times Ltd purchased the house in which I now live and the adjoining mews building. An independent, profes-

Seamus Martin

sional valuation was made on behalf of the company and I purchased the house at market value. I later leased and then purchased the mews in 1999. The same procedure was followed with regard to valuation and again I purchased at market value.'

I would not venture to dispute Conor Brady's statement, but the entire business of the house and the mews were critical in causing a lack of trust in the negotiations between management and the group of unions in the attempts to get the company back on the rails. The union representatives, John White, Fergus Farrell of the GPMU, Jack Nash of SIPTU (now a member of the Labour Court), and Séamus Dooley and Mary Maher of the NUJ had been under the impression they had received full disclosure of all salaries and perks. They had not been told about these two items. When they discovered the details they were outraged that they had been kept in the dark.

Conor Brady's failure to give these details during the meeting with the editorial committee did not serve to engender a feeling of trust between the two sides; and when fairly accurate details of that meeting appeared in the *Magill* article, only one member of the committee, Joe Cully, raised serious objections to what he regarded as a breach of confidence.

Conor Brady had a very strong sense of the history of *The Irish Times* and its previous editors. He was, after all, a history graduate. He bore little resemblance to the great Bertie Smyllie, whose portrait hung on the wall of his office. Smyllie was a huge man, almost twenty-five stones in weight, who wore a green sombrero, carved a fingernail into the shape of a nib to write with, and frequently chanted his editorials in operatic recitative.

Brady's editorship, to put it mildly, was less colourful. He was, however, strongly influenced by Gageby, whose protégé he had been. But there were dissimilarities here, too. Gageby, a former army officer, occasionally resorted to barrack-room language when annoyed. Brady did not. Where Gageby used the heavy-duty machine gun and the occasional artillery shell, Brady went for the stiletto. One staff member put in this way: 'The difference between the two was that Gageby did his own bullying while Brady employed others to do his bullying for him.'

Brady also frequently referred to the actions of another predecessor, the ascetic John Edward Healy, who ensured that the paper was published for most of Easter Week in 1916 and who himself stood outside the Kildare Street Club to sell copies of the paper. Brady was especially aware of this in 2001 when, during a forced absence in the US, he learned the paper would not be published on the national day of mourning in Ireland for those who had died in the terrorist attacks on 11 September. I understand that the editorial committee had backed his views that the paper should have been published; but while Brady was in California at a wedding and unable to return, I was even farther away with Anita on holidays and meeting old friends in Cape Town.

The status of the editor in relation to the managing director was something that exercised his mind frequently. He also had a sense of class distinction within the paper and occasionally referred to some of his lower-ranking colleagues as the 'helots'.

At that meeting with the editorial committee, status came up again in Brady's account of what was happening. The editor's car was bigger than the managing-director's car, he told us; and when there was a board meeting, the editor sat to the right of the chairman, indicating that he was more important in the scheme of things than the managing director, who sat to the editor's left.

Later, when the committee went on to meet the board, there

was a surprise in store. The *Irish Times'* boardroom was placed away from the rest of the D'Olier Street premises in a dismal outbuilding set in a yard to the side of the main office. It faced out on to D'Olier Street through windows made of one-way glass. Those in the boardroom could see out on to the street but those on the street could not see into the boardroom.

The room itself was divided into two areas. One contained the table at which board members sat, and the other was set out as a type of ante-room. It had a fireplace surrounded by a high, cushioned fender on which, in the manner of an old-style English gentlemen's club, board members could sit and warm their bums beside the fire. Hanging above the fireplace was an etching of Queen Victoria and, across from it, an oil painting of Douglas Gageby, who was no lover of royalty. There was also a framed copy of the *Magna Carta*.

As the board members assembled and took their places, there was a sharp intake of breath from the editorial-committee members when Conor Brady sat down to the left of the chairman, Don Reid, and the favoured place to the right was occupied by Maeve Donovan.

The editorial committee made its points clearly. We felt that the entire structure of the company should be changed. In 1974 the self-perpetuating Irish Times Trust had been set up in order to prevent its takeover by hovering foreign magnates. It was ostensibly a charitable foundation and the paper was frequently accused of hypocrisy on this count, since no charity had benefited from the trust's activities. In fact, its charitable function only applied should the trust be wound up.

More importantly, the trust was under the virtual control of Major Thomas Bleakley McDowell, a monocled, moustachioed relic of another era when, as Myles na gCopaleen frequently put it, the firm (meaning Ireland) was under different management. There were rumours as to the major's actual rank. Some of the comments on this were vicious. I once spoke to Hugh O'Neill, now Lord Rathcavan, at his large country house at the foot of Slemish Mountain in County Antrim. Hugh had been the paper's business editor and was reminiscing about his days there. He asked after Valentine Lamb, the editor of the *Irish Field*, and he asked after Mary Maher. Then out of the blue he said, 'How is McDowell?'

I asked if he meant the major.

'Major? Major?' replied O'Neill, who had been an officer in the Irish Guards. 'The only time I ever saw him in uniform was when he was a ticket collector in Northern Ireland Railways.'

There was little doubt from this response that O'Neill and McDowell, though both from Ulster unionist backgrounds, were not the best of friends. McDowell, however, actually had been a wartime major in the British army.

He was also the only 'A' member of the trust. All the other governors were 'B men', so to speak. This distinction would have come into play in the event of a motion being put to remove the 'A' member. In this case, as the articles of the trust so quaintly put it, the 'A' member would have 'one vote, plus a number of votes equal to all the other votes cast'. He would therefore constitute a one-man majority. There was also a bizarre clause which excluded certain people from being governors of the trust. These included anyone who had been declared a bankrupt, who had been certified as insane, who was more than a mere member of a political party, who was a minister of religion, and so on. The clause finished with the proviso that none of the above should apply to Major Thomas Bleakley McDowell.

The major, it should be said, had never in this long association with the paper attempted to interfere with its editorial independence. Also, his undisputed business acumen had been of great benefit over the years.

But times had changed, and members of the board of the newspaper as well as union representatives and members of editorial committee were agreed that the structure of *The Irish Times* should change as well. It was time not only for new corporate governance but also for new blood.

While the groups may have had a single objective, they went about it in different ways. The board, led by Don Reid, had access to the major and the governors of the trust, while the editorial committee had not. A meeting of the trust was due to take place shortly, and the editorial committee decided to set up shop in the hotel where the meeting was scheduled in order to inform the governors of its views.

This decision led to a crucial meeting that almost split the editorial committee. Its chairman, Kieran Fagan, called an urgent meeting in a small room at the back of the front office in D'Olier Street. He told those present that he had spoken to a very senior executive of the paper who had told him our proposed action at the meeting of the trust should be called off. It would, we were told, endanger the fragile moves to persuade Major McDowell to step down. He was asked several times who this 'senior executive' might be, but he would not reveal the person's name. Everyone present was clear in their own minds that the person concerned was Conor Brady, with whom Kieran Fagan had been closely associated in the eyes of the majority of the committee and also in the eyes of the editorial staff in general.

It was an extremely tense affair, with Mary Holland and Denis Coghlan insisting that the proposed contact with the trust should go ahead at all costs. Kieran Fagan was asked to contact the executive in question and ask him to appear before the committee in person. Kieran left and arrived some time later with Conor Brady.

Brady put his case and left. Most of us were furious at what happened and this was reflected in the vote that took place. In my own case I felt that despite my anger at the way this meeting had been arranged, we should reluctantly call off the action. If there was the slightest possibility that it might upset the apple cart we should abandon our proposed action.

A vote was taken and those in favour of the action were narrowly successful. It was decided, however, that since two members of the committee had been absent that we should meet again in the afternoon. The two men, Deaglan de Bréadún and Dick Ahlstrom, had been out on jobs that morning and when they returned a full meeting was called. The arguments for both sides were put and a motion to call off the proposed attempt to meet the members of the trust was carried, with both Ahlstrom and de Bréadún voting in favour.

Although I had been in favour of calling off the action, I was furious at the way Kieran Fagan, as chairman of what was an NUJ committee, had acted on behalf of the editor on this issue. I did not know why Conor Brady could not have met us in the first place instead of using our chairman as his surrogate. I asked Kieran Fagan to meet me privately and I told him I thought he should resign as chairman of the editorial committee.

At a meeting the following day Mary Holland acted to calm the situation down and Kieran remained as chairman for the rest of the committee's term. What we did not know at the time was that there was a fourth group exerting pressure to get Major McDowell to give up the post of 'A' member so that new structures and acceptable corporate governance could be put in place.

The group of unions representing the broad range of staff at the paper had come to an agreement that a team of consultants should examine the financial situation on its behalf.

This group of experts consisted of the consultants Farrell Grant Sparks, as well as Paul Sweeney, the economist. Sweeney – known for his left-wing views – and Greg Sparks were the leading personalities involved, and the team quickly became known as Marx and Sparks.

Greg Sparks and Paul Sweeney met the editorial committee briefly at the Temple Bar Hotel in Dublin to explain what they were going to do, and it was at that meeting that I, for the first time, heard the term 'forensic accountants'. These experts were to be employed to dissect the accounts of *The Irish Times*, and there was to be no room for rumours or guesswork in future.

The consultants gave no indication that they would be involved in an attempt to persuade Major McDowell to depart gently from the scene. I have since discovered that of the groups involved in attempting to do this (the board, the editorial committee, the group of unions and the new consultants acting on the unions' behalf) it was the consultants who were successful in the end, despite claims to the contrary by board members.

'Marx and Sparks' used Alex Burns, a partner in the accountancy firm KPMG, as the person to persuade McDowell that the changes had to be made. The paper was in danger of folding and obviously Major McDowell did not want to be the key person in the Irish Times Trust to oversee the death of a great Irish newspaper. Alex Burns' task may not, therefore, have been as difficult as it might have appeared at first sight.

Burns, according to those involved, was extraordinarily nervous about being asked to perform this task. The consultants were, after all, acting on behalf of the group of trade unions.

The end result that they wanted, however, coincided with the end result that the board also desired. It was, according to all concerned, a very delicate situation and, in hindsight, it appears that Conor Brady may have been right in his judgement that the action planned by the editorial committee could have jeopardised the plans.

Christmas was now on the horizon and on 21 December the news of Major McDowell's retirement appeared in *The Irish Times*. In recognition of his contribution to the paper, the report said, the boards of the trust and the company had awarded him the title of 'President for Life'.

It was understood, the report continued, that Professor David McConnell of the genetics department at Trinity College was to be appointed as chairman of the trust 'in the coming days'. As part of a restructuring plan a number of other trustees would step down, and in a separate development the chairman of the board of the company, Mr Don Reid, announced he would retire the following April.

It was a sad end to the career of a man who had played his part in building up *The Irish Times* as a truly national paper from a position in which it had been the house organ for the minority Protestant community in the Republic. Despite its rightful claims to represent the entire island of Ireland, the paper's sales in the unionist areas of Northern Ireland were minimal.

'Marx and Sparks' set to work on investigating the books of the company in the following way: they were interested solely in what could be done to ensure it would be a viable proposition in the future. Allegations of the company's funding of the lavish lifestyles of leading personalities in the past were of little interest to the consultants other than that they wished to ensure no excesses would occur in the future.

A team of young forensic accountants led by Derek Donoghue was sent into action. They spent a week at KPMG studying not only the audits of *The Irish Times* carried out by that company but also the notes written into the margins by the junior auditors. In this way they found out more about the *Irish Times'* accounts than was probably known by the paper's executives.

A room was set up for the consultants in the *Irish Times* building and they began to burrow into the company's documents. There was some resistance initially from the commercial side of the house. This was based, it should be stressed, not on a desire to keep facts hidden but on worries about the amount of time being taken, since the consultants were charging on a daily basis. It was quickly realised, though, that the consultants needed to get to the bottom of the paper's financial situation regardless of the cost.

While they did not say anything openly, the consulting group came to the conclusion that the corporate governance and the accounting procedures in the paper were in a total mess. This conclusion was conveyed to management. There was hardly any need to convey it to the unions, who knew from their own experience that this was the case. The next step in the process was that of restructuring the entire framework under which the company, editorially and commercially, was run. The consultants expressed some worries that this restructuring might go too far and, in retrospect, there are indications that this may have been the case.

In the end, it was the union side, and the consultants engaged by the unions, who devised the corporate-governance structure and overall rescue strategy – not management. This was an important and rare development. Normally, union financial advisers merely react to and in some circumstances modify management plans.

Progress was being made in turning *The Irish Times* into a normal company that used open and accepted methods of corporate governance, including adherence to the Combined Code of Corporate Governance as put forward by the Institute of Directors. This included the setting up of a remunerations committee to oversee and provide transparency in the area of payments to board members.

— Farewell to *The Times* —

The newspaper remained in a state of flux for some time but, in the grand traditions of the trade, the daily miracle took place without fail, and the paper came out on time, with good professional reporting and writing. This occurred against a background of a series of meetings to restructure each editorial department. A restructuring committee was set up by Conor Brady representing a broad editorial cross-section – with one important exception. There was no representative from the foreign section.

This committee was headed by Cliff Taylor and included Geraldine Kennedy, who was seen to be the other main contender for the editorship if and when Conor Brady departed. I can only speak about the meetings with the committee that dealt with the foreign area, and these were extremely emotional and included some very tough exchanges of views. Major cuts were proposed and resisted. Don Buckley, the editor's enforcer, took the lead at every opportunity and attempted to act as chairman. He met stern resistance, particularly from the very experienced sub-editor Paddy Woodworth, who gave absolutely no quarter.

What became obvious at an early stage was that Cliff Taylor was showing himself to be the very decent person everyone knew he was. Geraldine Kennedy avoided even attending meetings with the foreign staff, and a smaller group, including Don Buckley and Peter Murtagh, began to push their views forward.

Cliff Taylor was seen as the favourite for the editor's job, and because of this a number of people whom he could have done without jumped on his bandwagon. Rightly or wrongly, his candidature became associated with this group and they may have cost him the editorship.

When it became known that Brady would depart as editor, the group made the cardinal error of attempting to run the show themselves. They became known very quickly as the 'junta'. Buckley regarded himself as a consummate operator in office politics, but he was no match for Brady, and when the junta attempted to take control, Brady toppled them.

In the end, the junta dived for cover under fire from Brady, and this whole episode was regarded by many as being instrumental in Geraldine Kennedy's successful bid for the editorship. The more ambitious junta members had, one argument goes, ruined Taylor's chances of the job. Another theory was that in management's eyes Taylor appeared weak by allowing Buckley to push himself to the front.

After the proposed restructuring had been decided, mainly by those whose jobs remained safe, it was time to inform those whose positions were for the axe. Miriam Donohoe was taken back from the Beijing bureau, where she had proven herself as a first-class foreign correspondent. This was expected, however, because the cost of the bureau was exceptionally high. It was particularly expensive because Miriam's children had to continue their education and English-language schools in the Chinese capital were extremely costly.

It had been decided also, by whom I don't know, that Lara Marlowe's position in Paris was in jeopardy. Buckley was told to inform her and he did so in such a manner as to leave her in tears. When I questioned him about it, he told me that the telephone line had not been up to standard and he had to deal with the matter abruptly. Whatever his qualities, Buckley was no candidate for the diplomatic corps.

In the end Lara held on to her job. She was a journalist of far higher quality than many of those who had the temerity to decide on her future. This was borne out later when her work for *The Irish Times* led her to be installed as a Chevalier of the Légion d'Honneur.

In the background, the 'Marx and Sparks' consultants were beavering away, and the group of unions was in constant meetings with management. One of the main issues being discussed was that of the vast array of office cars. Senior executives were determined to hold on to these perks, which they regarded as part of their remuneration packages. Only one them, Geraldine Kennedy, was in total agreement that the cars should go.

The subject of the cars became known as the 'decommissioning issue', and in the end the cars stayed because they were part of each executive's contract of employment. More important, however, was the question of the large number of executives and supervisors, the dreaded 'floorwalkers' and 'store detectives'. These were reduced fairly significantly in number, and those who stayed did so with an increased workload.

The group of unions in general, and the efficiency and professionalism of the NUJ's Séamus Dooley in particular, put the fear of God into the *Irish Times'* management. Even today, the very mention of Dooley's name in an e-mail to an *Irish Times* executive can evoke a hysterical response.

There was one more controversy concerning Conor Brady. It took place after he left, when it was disclosed that he had been given an annuity of €100,000 as part of his severance deal. I was not alone at being infuriated at this. I sent him an e-mail asking how this squared with his earlier statements on 'equality of pain'. He replied as follows:

My so-called 'Secret Deal'
My parting arrangements were proposed to me in a letter of offer on April 23rd 2002. They were proposed to the board by Don Reid (Chairman) and approved by the remuneration committee on April 19th. Present at the committee which approved the agreement were Don Reid, Alex Burns (auditor), Maeve Donovan (Managing Director), David McConnell (Chair of Trust), Donal Nevin (Vice Chair of Trust).

The letter of offer was signed by Don Reid and Maeve Donovan. It became legally enforceable when I returned my acceptance in writing, on May 10th.

I sought no confidentiality, other than the non-publication of the date of my planned retirement (October 2002). This was to enable me to retain effective command of the editorial departments during a period of difficulty and re-adjustment.

It was assumed from the beginning that this arrangement would be reported in the annual accounts. This advice was furnished to me by my accountants, Messrs Sheehan Quinn, Blackrock, Co Dublin.

My Terms
I received precisely the same terms as everybody else '6 weeks pay per 1 year of pensionable service'. I received no allowances for 9 years of 'broken' service during which my pension fund was afforded full contributions.

I asked that the same 'additional service' terms be applied to me as were on offer to other staff members who were within 10 years of retirement (i.e. 55 or over). I was within 5 years of my retirement age (60). This was refused.

I offered to serve on to full pensionability. Subsequently, the company offered me an 'exclusionary contract' to pay me an annual sum to 65 years which would be equivalent to that payable by way of pension. By this device, the company would save considerably, in not having to top up the pension fund in advance.

Reluctantly, I accepted. I am disadvantaged by this, in that my wife and children have no residual benefits in the event of my death.

My actual 'pension' is 26% of pay. This is the lowest pension pro rata to salary of any employee over 50 years of age who left in the period March–August 2002.

I have no other benefits in cash or kind from *The Irish Times*.

My 'Exclusionary Contract'

My 'exclusionary contract' prohibits me from undertaking any work for any newspaper in competition with The Irish Times.

Since standing down as editor, I have had:

- an offer to edit a Sunday newspaper
- an offer to write a weekly column in a UK broadsheet selling into the Irish market
- an offer to write a weekly column for an Irish Sunday newspaper
- an offer to act as a consultant to a newspaper planning to enter the daily Irish market

I have been unable to accept any of these. It causes me little difficulty. I cannot envisage myself taking up arms in competition against the newspaper which I did so much to build up over the years.

In a memorandum produced by the deputy managing director, the late Michael Austen, in 2003, certain details of remuneration of non-executive directors were disclosed. The annual salaries for the following positions were:

Managing Director €296,000

Editor €296,000
Deputy Managing Director €222,000
Finance Director €178,000
Executive Editor €125,000
Managing Editor €112,000

Directors' fees and bonuses are not included in these figures, which have risen considerably in the intervening years.

Conor Brady had left the paper as an editor whose support from the staff had lessened significantly. Perhaps this was inevitable at a time of such crisis; but he departed with important valedictory words that journalists in *The Irish Times* and elsewhere would be well advised to read over and over again.

> Never forget that we work for the readers. We work for the 320,000 people who turn to this newspaper every day to know what's going on in this society and in the wider world. If we look after the readers, they will look after us. If we take them for fools, or if we underestimate their ability to discern fact from supposition, analysis from polemic, they will cease to have faith in us.
>
> Never forget the privileged position we hold as part of the most respected newspaper in this society. And never forget those less privileged than we who count on us to keep the focus of public thinking on the inequalities and the injustices in this society.
>
> Journalists are privileged people. That obliges us to keep the focus on the marginalised, on the people who can't get their cancer treatment because they live in the wrong place, on the mothers who can't get the right education for kids with learning difficulties, on the immigrants, on the widows, on the addicts and the alcoholics, on the victims of abuse, on those who think that life isn't worth living any more.
>
> And we have to keep pouring out the boiling oil on those who evade their responsibilities, those who exploit their positions and those who victimise the weakest in society.
>
> I would ask you to beware of three things. Beware the mindset

of partition. It's deeply rooted in this community and it has to be resisted always. This was a 32-county newspaper for 100 years before there was a Border. This is too small an island to allow one part of it to fester forever in sectarianism and hate.

Beware the mindset of metropolitanism; the conviction that civilised life doesn't exist beyond Templeogue and Malahide. Don't let *The Irish Times* go back to being a newspaper for the Dublin middle classes.

Beware the 'Little Irelanders'. They are trivial people. They're everywhere and they are dangerous. The global village is a full and present reality. The great issues of our time are not whether Bertie will marry Celia or if a particular politician is gay or straight.

The great issues are the poisoning of the planet, the spread of nuclear weapons, the tide of AIDS and the economic stagnation of the Third World, with the accompanying evils of hunger, disease and ignorance. It's our job to be out there, reporting them.

And don't let anybody tell you that this newspaper is overreaching itself. Don't let anybody tell you that the difficulties of the past year grew from the fact that the journalists of *The Irish Times* built a newspaper that was too broad or too deep in its reach.

I have had many open and public disagreements with Conor Brady in my time, notably when he wrote what I felt was an intemperate and biased editorial against Nelson Mandela during the latter's visit to Dublin. I bearded him in his office and told him in no uncertain terms what I thought. One of his managing editors who was present slipped out of the room.

But, by God, I agreed wholeheartedly with every word he said in his valedictory and I know he believed fully in what he said. Unfortunately, as he said those words, his standing with his own staff had diminished for other reasons. That diminution, however, does not make the principles he outlined any less important.

His successor, Geraldine Kennedy, has been a colleague since the 1980s. She supported me very strongly when I was under pressure in the old *Tribune* and I welcomed her appointment as the first woman editor of *The Irish Times*. Her political views and mine do not coincide; but if we have anything in common it is that neither of us would let those views influence our judgement of a good, strong news story.

As I write this I am officially an *Irish Times*' pensioner. From my retirement lump sum, I was able to pay off the small amount remaining on the mortgage on the family home in Dublin. I managed to buy a second house with a little vineyard in southern France for €79,000. It could be said, I suppose, that, as in Conor Brady's case, *The Irish Times* has bought me a house. I don't feel there has been 'equality of pain', though, for I am convinced that there has been more pain for many of those who stayed on than there has been for those who left.

I maintain an intense interest in the paper and in the countries I was privileged to cover as a resident correspondent. To have been present at the two most significant events in the second half of the twentieth century, the end of the communist system in the Soviet Union and the end of the apartheid system in South Africa, is something that does not easily fade from one's mind.

The paper is not what it was during my time there, and neither is Russia or South Africa. Things change, and the old ascetic John Edward Healy was right when, told by an Ascendancy lady that *The Irish Times* was not what it used to be, he replied, 'Madam, *The Irish Times* has never been what it used to be.'

If there are faults with today's *Irish Times* they are those of understaffing at the lower-paid levels, particularly in the sub-editing process. Minor grammatical, spelling and syntactical errors are consequently far more frequent than before; and it cannot be stressed too strongly that these minutiae can serve, in the context of a highly literate readership, to undermine the paper's credibility.

The decision to save a small amount of money by dropping the service from Agence France Presse (AFP) caused, in my view, a diminution of the paper's foreign coverage. It was Douglas Gageby who bought the AFP service in the first place as a balance against Reuters' concentration on what has become known as the 'Anglosphere'. I don't know who decided to drop AFP, but whoever it was could not have had the breadth of vision nor the journalistic acumen of Gageby, who was perhaps the paper's greatest editor. At the time of writing, the board of *The Irish Times* has decided to make a major investment in its editorial services. It is to be hoped that some of the money will be used to move away from the provincialism that Brady warned against in his valedictory speech.

When I left South Africa, the country was a beacon of hope for the entire continent. It still is, but the light from that beacon has begun to flicker. Thabo Mbeki is not Nelson Mandela. AIDS has ravaged the country and not enough has been done to counter it. There are signs of tensions within the ANC, but that may not be a bad thing. National liberation movements can become monoliths. They need internal splits that in turn can develop into genuine democratic opposition.

And then there was Russia, a country whose people and traditions I have learned to love. I covered Russia for *The Irish Times* for Yeltsin's entire presidency and for a great part of Putin's. I also served as an international observer for the Organisation for Security and Co-operation in Europe at the Duma and presidential elections.

Russia is returning to its position as a great country. Consequently, the opposition to its leadership has begun to grow more vociferous. If a new cold war is developing it has emanated from the West. Vladimir Putin is no Western-style liberal and has been excoriated by the political establishment, especially in the Anglo-Saxon confines of the United States and the UK.

I look back to the Yeltsin era as one of destruction. Boris Yeltsin was probably the right man to destroy what remained of the communist system. He was the wrong man to build something in its place. Vladimir Putin inherited a country that was in a shambles and – helped, admittedly, by rising energy prices – he has brought stability and a modicum of prosperity to Russia.

Yeltsin was lionised by Western leaders and Putin excoriated by them for his record on press freedom. Statistics show a different picture. From the time the Soviet Union came to an end at midnight on 31 December 1991 until the time of writing this book, forty-three journalists have been killed in Russia in the course of their duty. Of these, thirty-one died in seven years of Boris Nikolayevich Yeltsin's presidency and twelve over the same space of time under the presidency of Vladimir Vladimirovich Putin.

One of the journalists I knew well was Yuri Shchekochikhin, who lost his life in the Putin era. He was also a deputy in the Duma for the pro-Western Yabloko Party led by Grigory Yavlinsky, and we met frequently and shared a glass or two of his favourite Armenian brandy in his office in the parliament building. Yuri was the boss of the journalist Anna Politkovskaya, who was murdered later. He was getting too close to discovering corruption in a certain business empire and died a horrible death from poisoning.

My friend Robert Haupt, the ebullient Australian, has also passed on. His book, *Last Boat to Astrakhan*, was to be published by a leading US group and he was in New York for a meeting with his publishers when he was taken ill at lunch. He died within minutes, a glass of good red wine in his hand.

Lena Firsova, our sharp and satirical office manager, was paid off by *The Irish Times* and moved to *Newsday*, which later closed its bureau. She now works in the Russian Academy of Sciences, a place suitable for someone like her who speaks not only perfect English as well as her native Russian, but Hindi and Urdu. She was a graduate of both the Jawaharlal Nehru University in Delhi and Moscow State. Valeriy now drives for the US National Public Radio bureau in Moscow, but I know nothing of Olga's whereabouts.

For Boris and Masha and Yasha and the ex-*Baltimore Sun* Lena, and Nyusha and little Gleb, who must be big Gleb by now, I wish every happiness and good fortune in the new Russia. Each one of them is, I trust, far better off than they were in the old days.

In South Africa, Anna still cleans away for the masters and madams of Melville. Her husband John has died of AIDS. Peter still hacks away at the overgrown gardens, making the long journey to and from Sebokeng whenever he can. For them little has changed.

I was truly privileged to have been in Russia, South Africa and many other places. I have covered events in thirty-eight countries and some other territories that have never been officially recognised. I may have the only Irish passport that contains a visa from the unrecognised Republic of Abkhazia. If there are others, they are not many. I was there when Boris Yeltsin failed to get his passport stamped in Shannon.

Abkhazia was at that time a severely war-ravaged region that had broken away from Georgia. It was also exceptionally beautiful, with the foothills of the Caucasus mountains running down to the shores of the Black Sea. At night the howls of jackals wafted down from the hillsides.

The war had caused electricity to be cut off and running water was at a premium. The Black Sea became our bathroom, and our ingenious host, Yuri Avidzba, managed to improvise television reception by linking the TV set up to a series of car batteries. On the night before the Shannon debacle, Anatol Lieven, then of the London *Times*, and myself watched Yeltsin give an interview to tame Russian TV journalists before he boarded the plane at Seattle.

He was obviously drunk and kept repeating the phrase: '*Ya President Rossii. Ponimayesh?*' ('I am the President of Russia. Understand?') I looked at Anatol and Anatol looked at me. We both realised that something unusual could happen in Shannon on the following day. There were no phones working in Abkhazia and we knew our offices would be looking for us, so we hired a man to drive us to the Russian border. This guy, it turned out, had been notorious during the recent war for firing missiles at passenger aircraft that were coming into land at the airport in Sukhumi.

Back in Russia, I was able to get in touch with Dublin. I discovered that our suspicions about Yeltsin's condition were confirmed and that Boris had been unable to get off the plane.

Later, at a time when Ireland was plunged into political crisis over events that included paedophile priests, difficulties for the attorney general and an array of other events, the story made it to the main evening news bulletin on Russian TV. Next morning this was reported to me by Lena, who then asked me to give her the details of what was going on back in Ireland. I did so as best I could and my efforts elicited the following reply: 'Yes. I see. Our president was a very wise man to stay on the plane.'

Of my foreign postings, that of Russia was the one that affected me most in my outlook, both positively and negatively. I had been disappointed at the standard of living and personal freedom experienced by the people of Russia under the communist system and the wild variant of capitalism that had replaced it. I had been pleasantly surprised by the warmth and humour of the Russian people who befriended me. They were very far indeed from the picture painted of them by Western propagandists.

My coverage, particularly that from Russia, was criticised fiercely by both Eoghan Harris and the *Phoenix* editor, Paddy Prendeville, so I feel I must have been doing something right. There was, however, an unsolicited testimonial that I am particularly proud of. One morning in my post, I found a small book. It was an English-language adaptation of Ivan Turgenev's play *A Month in the Country*. The following message was inscribed on the title page: 'To Séamus Martin (in exile) – with admiration. Brian Friel.'

Dublin and Puisserguier, 2007

INDEX

M

Pugo, Boris 127, 139
Putin, Vladimir 243, 244, 306, 307
Pyke, Bobby 39, 40
Pyle, Fergus 282, 285

Q

Queen Victoria 290
Quinn, Brian 52
Quinn, Feargal 67

R

Rabbitte, Pat 189, 191, 192
Rachkovsky, Pyotr 172, 174, 175
Rama, Peter 254
Randolph, Eleanor 126, 140
Redmond, Bill 26, 38, 39, 42
Redmond, John 30
Reid, Don 272, 290, 292, 295, 301
Renwick, Sir Robin 91
Reynolds, Albert 235, 236
Rhodes, Cecil 100
Roche, Stephen 61
Rooney, Michael 52
Rossa, Jeremiah O'Donovan 172
Rudzate, Yelena 239
Russell, Tom 129
Rutskoy, Alexander 151, 179
Ryzhak, Boris 234

S

Sakharov, Andrei 166
Scanlan, John F. 173
Schmid, Regula 158
Schoon, Marius 208
Scott, Sir Charles 174
Shaw, Helen 225
Shchekochikhin, Yuri 307
Shevardnadze, Eduard 132, 196
Shine, Bill 54
Shishkin, Ambassador 173
Shushkevich, Stanislav 138, 139
Simpson, John 132
Sisulu, Walter 90, 91, 96, 98
Sisulu, Zwelakhe 91

Slattery, Fergus 94
Slovo, Joe 101
Smith, Colm 49, 74
Smurfit, Michael 57
Smuts, Jan 98
Smyllie, Bertie 288
Smyth, Gerry 279
Smyth, Paddy 99, 104, 139, 204
Sorokin, Grigory 239
Sparks, Greg 294
Spartakovich, Boris 155, 158, 237
Stalin, Joseph 152, 161, 179, 250, 252
Standing, Gordon 64
Staunton, Denis 195, 196
Streletsky, Colonel Valery 240
Sweeney, Paul 294
Sych, Valentin 239

T

Tarpishchev, Mr Shamil 240
Tatum, Paul 152, 239
Taylor, Cliff 268, 279, 298, 299
Thatcher, Margaret 90, 91
Thursfield, Peter 268
Traynor, Colm 25, 28
Traynor, Oscar 25
Treurnicht, Dr Andries 88, 89
Troy, Canon 20, 21
Tsiskirashvili, Dmitri 104
Tsvygun, Marina 183, 184, 185, 186, 187
Turgenev, Ivan 310
Tutu, Archbishop Desmond 96, 97, 98
Twomey, Moss 43

U

Unwin, Professor Stanley 263
Uranov, Gennady 83
Usov, Vladimir 131

V

Valentin, Fr 180, 181

By the same author:

Duggan's Destiny, a novel